BOOK XI IN THE RAIDING FORCES SERIES

RAIDING
ROMMEL

PHIL WARD

A RAIDING FORCES SERIES NOVEL

Published by Military Publishers LLC
Austin, Texas

www.philwardauthor.com

ISBN 10—1732766908
ISBN 13 — 978-1732766907

Distributed by Military Publishers LLC

For ordering information or special discounts for bulk purchases, contact

MILITARY PUBLISHERS LLC
3616 FAR WEST BLVD., SUITE 117, BOX 215 AUSTIN, TX 78731

DEDICATED TO
LT. COL. WILLIAM WYATT JR.

In 1942 while attending Southwest Texas Teachers College, William Wyatt Jr. volunteered for the United States Army Air Force. He received his commission as a 2nd Lieutenant and qualified to fly B-17 Flying Fortresses. After completing his training, Lt. Wyatt arrived in England where he was assigned to the 452nd Heavy Bomb Group stationed at Deopham Green in East Anglia.

After his first five combat missions, Lt. Wyatt was tapped for the critical job of lead pilot and flew an additional twenty-five combat missions leading the group to its targets and bringing them home.

One mission was a difficult long range three-way shuttle operation. The group flew from England to bomb Germany then continued on to land at an Allied Base located at Poltava, Russia. As usual, Lt. Wyatt was out front leading the way as the group Pathfinder. The return trip was Russia to Italy then back to England. For this mission the 452nd was awarded the Presidential Unit Citation.

After completing his first combat tour instead of going back to the States, having been promoted, Capt. Wyatt volunteered for the 55th Fighter Group Scouting Force & Reconnaissance. This unit was unusual because it flew both P-51 Mustangs and B-17 Flying Fortresses — unarmed photo reconnaissance. He flew a total of twenty-eight more combat missions with the 55th before returning home to San Marcos, Texas in 1945 then going to Texas A&M to complete his masters degree, retiring from the Air Force Reserves in the rank of Lieutenant Colonel in 1972.

Lt. Col. Wyatt was awarded the Distinguished Flying Cross w/oak leaf cluster (two awards), Air Medal w/silver oak leaf cluster and four bronze oak leaf clusters (nine awards), Bronze Star medal w/silver oak leaf cluster (five awards) and the Presidential Unit Citation. A true American hero.

His son William Wyatt III aka 'Wild Bill' was my fraternity brother and roommate in college after I returned from Vietnam. Enough said. That is classified.

RANDAL'S RULES FOR RAIDING

RULE 1:   The first rule is there ain't no rules.

RULE 2:   Keep it short and simple.

RULE 3:   It never hurts to cheat.

RULE 4:   Right man, right job.

RULE 5:   Plan missions backward (know how to get home).

RULE 6:   It's good to have a Plan B.

RULE 7:   Expect the unexpected.

RAIDING FORCES
ONGOING OPERATIONS

OPERATION GOLDEN FLEECE
"Pinch" operations to capture Nazi encoding / decoding equipment.
Cmdr. Fleming's project, aka OPERATION RED INDIAN.

OPERATION BOMBSHELL
Killing Luftwaffe pilots in places where they congregate.

OPERATION IRONCLAD
An amphibious assault by 5 Commando on the port of Diego Suarez.

OPERATION JUBILEE
Previously named OPERATION RUTTER, which was canceled. The
operation was resurrected and renamed JUBILEE.

OPERATION RED INDIAN
Cover name for OPERATION GOLDEN FLEECE.

OPERATION RUTTER
A frontal assault on an enemy port with the purpose of discovering how
difficult it would be to land ashore and capture a port city. Rutter was
intended to be a live-fire training exercise, a raid with a planned
withdrawal and no intention to stay. RUTTER was canceled. Then the
raid was revived as OPERATION JUBILEE.

OPERATION SOLID GOLD
Hunt down and kill Hauptmann Alfred Seebohm, master of signals
intelligence, Rommel's genius radio interceptor and his 621st Radio
Intercept Company.

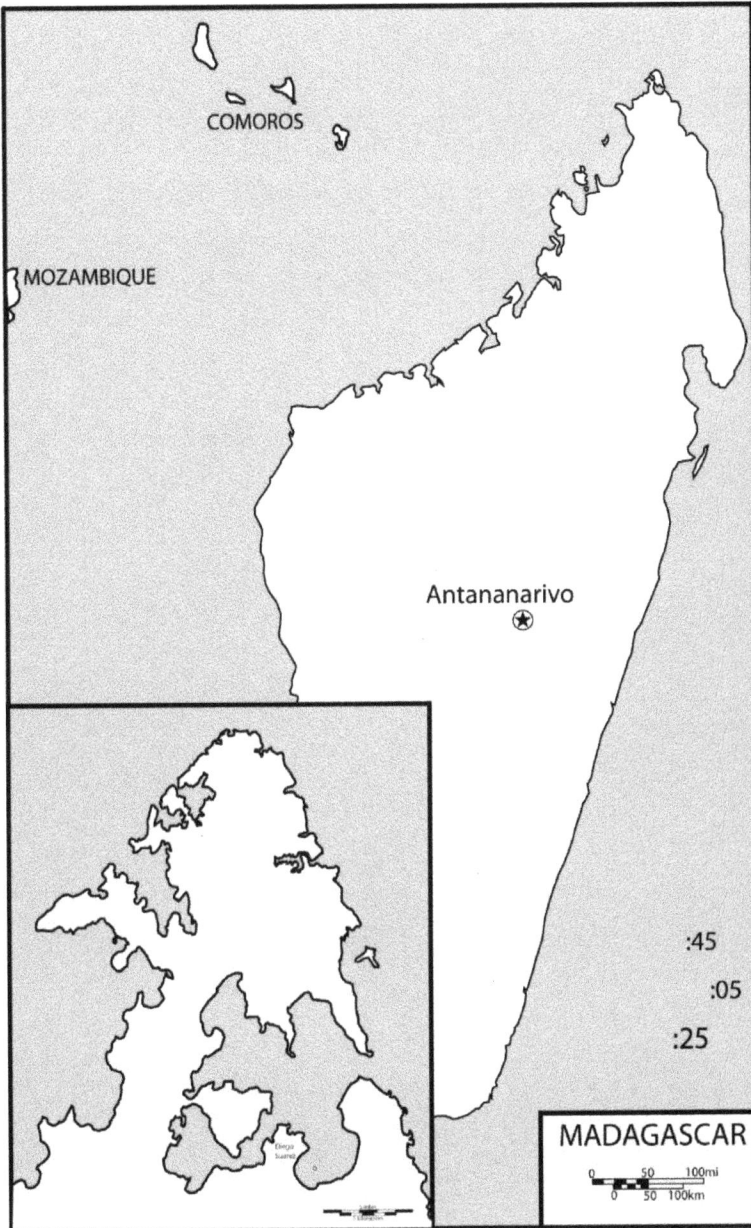

COMOROS

MOZAMBIQUE

Antananarivo
✪

:45

:05

:25

MADAGASCAR

0   50   100mi
0   50   100km

1
SNAFU

COLONEL JOHN RANDAL WAS SITTING IN THE EMPTY BAR
of the Continental Hotel on the north end of Colbert Street in Vichy
French Diego Suarez, Madagascar—the third-largest natural harbor in
the world. He was alone at a table with his back to the wall, sitting in a
huge bamboo chair with a clamshell fan back that stretched three feet
over the top of his head. The chairs were designed so that four of them
could be pulled together to form a discrete private booth.

It was that kind of place.

Col. Randal was reading a brochure he had picked up in the lobby
of the hotel when he checked in. Madagascar, aka the Red Island
because of its scarlet-colored dust, was the fourth-largest island on earth.
It was like a tiny continent surrounded by the Indian Ocean. Originally
settled by Asians, then the Bantus from East Africa, nowadays it was a
Vichy French colony run by expatriate French citizens.

The locals were called Malagasy.

Top Secret intelligence reports indicated that the Japanese were
eyeing the island for a submarine base. U.S. code breakers, having
cracked the Japanese diplomatic code called "Purple," had recently
learned Berlin was urging Tokyo to occupy Madagascar.

Hitler wanted Tojo to interrupt the British Eighth Army's sea lanes
prior to Rommel's next offensive. The Nazis hoped they could then
prevent British forces from receiving new tanks from the U.S. Then the

Desert Fox could drive the Allies out of Libya and Egypt, capture the Suez Canal, and knock England out of the war—information not in the pamphlet or known to Col. Randal.

Except for the part about Rommel trying to capture the Suez Canal—he knew all about that first-hand.

According to the guide, Madagascar was a mysterious place where it was difficult to separate fact from fiction. For example, at one time it might have been a pirate enclave that declared itself its own nation called Libertaria—or maybe not. Col. Randal thought a thing like that should not be so hard to pin down since it would have taken place only about a hundred years ago.

The island had 250 species of birds—44 percent of them only found on Madagascar.

It was home to the panther chameleon (the size of a housecat), the orange-red tomato frog, the giraffe-necked weevil—which had a long neck—and the satanic leaf-tailed gecko.

Ten of the island's mammals could not be found anywhere else in the world.

There was a three-foot-tall, three-toed bipedal humanoid creature with a bad attitude and long claws called the kalanoro. Only no one had ever actually killed, captured, or even photographed one because the animal's toes were backward so hunters went the wrong way when they tracked it.

And there was a tree that ate people.

And a beach not far from the hotel where the local French girls went topless—Col. Randal imagined they were as elusive as the kalanoro.

King was at the bar having a drink and talking to the bored bartender—tourism had taken a sharp decline since the start of the war. Captain "Geronimo" Joe McKoy, Waldo Treywick, and Acting Provisional Sub-Lieutenant Skipper Warthog Finley, DSO, OBE, RNPS, were off somewhere chartering a fishing boat.

Col. Randal and his party were hiding in plain sight. He was wearing an oversized Hawaiian shirt that concealed a pair of 1911 Colt .38 Supers, his High Standard Military Model D. 22 with silencer in a canvas chest holster, and his .9mm Browning P-35. He had on a faded pair of blue jeans and his old cowboy boots that were so soft they could be rolled up in a ball.

Col. Randal did not have any idea why he was in Diego Suarez. The United States was not at war with Vichy France. The British were not at war with them either, at least officially.

However, it had been deemed advisable that no one on the mission to Madagascar have a British passport. The Royal Navy *had* sunk the French fleet at Oran *and* invaded the French colonies of Lebanon and Syria.

The British Government was more than a little annoyed with the collaborationist Pétain regime because his Vichy Government had "invited" the Japanese to occupy the French colony of Vietnam.

Indochina gave the Japs a springboard to Malaya, which led to their being able to attack Singapore from the rear, inflicting the most embarrassing defeat on the British Empire in its storied history.

The U.S. was not exactly pleased with the Vichy government either. Part of the Japanese fleet that invaded the Philippines had staged in Cam Ranh Bay.

No one, including the French Colonial Army, wanted to see the Rising Sun flag flying over Madagascar. In Saigon, French officers were being required to salute Japanese privates—which was intended to be demeaning. However, it was difficult to predict what the local Vichy politicians might do.

Anything was possible.

Col. Randal had no knowledge of French plans or intentions regarding the Japanese.

What he did know was that tomorrow morning at sunrise 5 Commando was going to conduct an amphibious assault, storm ashore, and attack the port of Diego Suarez right about where he was sitting— OPERATION IRONCLAD.

Before that happened, Col. Randal had been ordered to "Meet an agent or agents known to you."

TWO FRENCH WOMEN DRIFTED INTO THE COLONIAL HOTEL'S bar in their swimsuits—wearing their tops. Diego Suarez had a relaxed dress code, being a beach town in a French colony. Swimwear was acceptable attire almost anywhere.

The women went to the bar and ordered drinks.

Captain "Geronimo" Joe McKoy came in with Waldo Treywick. They went to the bar and ordered drinks.

Rikke Runborg walked in wearing her swimsuit, which caused the droopy-eyed bartender to perk up. Ballet-dancer-fit, Rocky rippled over to Colonel John Randal's table against the wall and sat down in one of the large, clamshell-backed wicker chairs.

Rocky's arrival cleared up the question of who the "agent or agents known to you" would be. However, she was the last person he would have ever expected to be entrusted with a secret mission in a foreign land.

Rocky was a Nazi spy—or had been—and might even be the Russian agent Marina Lee, who stole the British battle plans and gave them to the Wehrmacht, resulting in the loss of Norway early in the war. Nowadays she was a double agent working for the Secret Intelligence Service, MI-6, out of Cairo. It was said that she was Field Marshal Erwin Rommel's most trusted spy. Somehow, Rocky had managed to convince the Desert Fox to leave Africa and fly to Italy to celebrate his birthday the day before OPERATION CRUSADER kicked off.

Some in MI-6 believed Rocky to be the single most valuable intelligence asset the Middle East Command possessed . . . which would make risking her on a hazardous mission in a backwater like Madagascar seem like a bad idea. On the other hand, there were those in Counterintelligence MI-5 who believed Rocky was a triple agent— meaning she was still working for the Germans.

Or possibly the Russians . . . or maybe the Germans *and* the Russians. And that made sending her on any mission even more problematic.

For all those reasons, Col. Randal would not have been more surprised if one of the bipedal, three-toed kalanoro had strolled in.

The bartender came over to take Rocky's drink order. King went to the jukebox, studied the menu of songs, selected several and dropped coins in the slot. Soon a wild, throbbing, big band jungle song—heavy on the drums—was blaring.

It was believed the hotel rooms might be bugged. In the event the bar was as well, no listening device ever invented was going to be able to record in a room with that noise booming.

Rocky pulled the other two chairs in close, leaving a small crack so Col. Randal could keep an eye on the door.

"Hello, John," she said, in her sexy Norwegian accent.

"Hello to you, Rocky," Col. Randal said. "Enjoying yourself at the beach?"

"I was by the pool on the roof," Rocky said, "to observe when you checked in."

That sounded like pretty good spycraft to Col. Randal—not that he knew much about the subject.

The bartender brought Rocky her drink. He acted like he wanted to hang around and join the conversation. She had that effect on men.

Hair the color of ice, big white teeth, and a fabulous tan, she tended to suck the oxygen out of a room. For the first time, Col. Randal noticed her eyes were the color of ice too.

He let Rocky go first. So she did.

"Percy Mather—a well-connected, highly-thought-of French businessman who has lived here for many years—is SOE's man in Madagascar," Rocky said. "Our mission is to bring him out before British Commandos come calling tomorrow morning. Or—it was.

"Unhappily, our assignment has turned into what you Americans call a SNAFU—Lady Jane taught me the expression. She thinks it is funny."

"I see," Col. Randal said, which meant he did not have a clue what she was talking about.

"SOE has chartered a sixty-foot dhow called the *Lindi*, equipped with a long-range radio and sonar. It has been charting the coastline in the invasion area. The crew has performed magnificently—when it comes to the mapping. They determined that an island is marked on the chart literally a mile and a half from where it is actually located, which could have caused the Royal Navy invasion fleet to run aground," Rocky said.

"That," Col. Randal said, "would not be good."

"For the preponderance of their duties, however, the *Lindi's* crew is incompetent, or cowards—possibly both," Rocky said.

"The dhow rendezvoused with Percy two nights ago on an isolated beach and brought him a bottle of knockout drops. SOE's orders were for him to throw a party tonight for all the senior military and political leadership in Diego Suarez and place the drops in the punch bowl. It was hoped everyone in attendance would wake up twelve hours later to find 5 Commando patrolling the streets," Rocky said.

"This is where the SNAFU occurred. The agent from the *Lindi* who delivered the knockout drops mentioned that the effect only lasted three minutes—enough time for a spy to get away in an emergency.

"Percy asked for a clarification since that information did not match the original plan for the drops to work for twelve hours. Another rendezvous was scheduled for the next night—last night. The *Lindi* failed to appear.

"Percy had no way to hand over the secret intelligence documents he had brought with him. He could not confirm how long the knockout drops would last. So after a long, fruitless wait, he cut the phone cable that ran along the coast road, knocking out all landline communications between Diego Suarez and the rest of the island, then returned to the Continental Hotel."

"Sounds like a good man," Col. Randal said.

"Regrettably," Rocky said, "when he arrived back here, Percy was arrested by the *Centre d'Information Gouvernemental*—the Vichy Colonial Secret Police—CIE. The CIE found all the notes and sketches he was carrying. He was turned over to the army who threw him in a prison cell and offered the services of a priest.

"Percy is scheduled to be put in front of a firing squad at dawn.

"Would you agree," Rocky said, "the situation has deteriorated into what you refer to as a FUBAR?"

COLONEL JOHN RANDAL LOOKED OUT THROUGH THE CRACK between the two empty chairs. Captain "Geronimo" Joe McKoy and

Waldo were dancing with the two French women over by the jukebox. Acting Provisional Sub-Lieutenant Skipper Warthog Finley was sitting at the end of the bar nursing a beer. He established eye contact with Col. Randal and made a slashing motion across his throat.

Not going to be any boat off the island.

"Now," Col. Randal thought, "we have a FUBAR."

AN UNSHAVEN MAN IN A RUMPLED WHITE TROPICAL SUIT came into the room, headed straight to the bar, ordered a drink, threw it down in one gulp and then ordered a refill.

Rocky saw him pass by the crack between the two chairs screening their table. She pushed one of them back to get a better look at the newcomer. The two locked eyes.

The man in the rumpled suit threw down the second drink, ordered a third, then strolled over to where Colonel John Randal and Rocky were sitting.

"John," Rocky said, "allow me to introduce you to Percy Mather."

Col. Randal said, "I thought you were getting shot in a few hours."

"That may still be on," SOE's man in Madagascar said. "The Vichy military commandant in Diego Suarez decided to play it safe—keep all his options open. I am out on 'house arrest' as long as I agree to stay confined to the Continental Hotel—the bartender is CIE, as are the desk clerks."

"Do the authorities know the Commandos are coming?" Col. Randal asked.

"Not as far as I am aware," Percy said. "Heard rumors something is up—no idea what."

"We will rescue you," Rocky said.

"Maybe not," Col. Randal said. "There's no boat available to take us off the island."

"Correct," Percy said. "The few fishing boats in Diego Suarez have been impounded by the navy to prevent the locals from using them for potential anti-Vichy resistance activities."

"We need to be away before morning," Rocky said. "Surely there is some craft available for the right price."

"I had a list of the ships operating out of Diego Suarez but it was confiscated. I believe I can recall it from memory," Percy said, "The converted liner *Bougainville,* packed with guns and welded-on armor plate, rated an auxiliary cruiser, the *D'Entrecasteaux*—an antisubmarine sloop and two submarines—the *Beveziers* and the *Le Heros.*"

"Any others?" Rocky asked.

"There is one small steamer," Percy said. "The SS *Wartenfels* arrived here in March after a mad dash from Portuguese East Africa where she had been interned since the beginning of the war."

Col. Randal clicked on, "A Nazi ship?"

"German flagged," Percy said. "There is speculation a Kriegsmarine wireless team is on board monitoring British merchant traffic in the Mozambique Channel. I have never been able to confirm the report."

"Give me a minute," Col. Randal said.

He stood up, walked over to the bar and stood next to Acting Provisional Sub-Lieutenant Skipper Warthog Finley—but ignoring him.

"Would you take the lady at my table another of whatever she is drinking," Col. Randal said to the bartender.

The man mixed the drink and rushed to deliver it to Rocky.

Col. Randal stood staring straight ahead at the mirror, not looking at his reflection but watching Captain "Geronimo" Joe McKoy and Waldo behind him, cutting the rug with the two French women. He was pretty sure that the wild improvised dance they were doing did not have a name.

Col. Randal said, "Ever hear of a ship out of Portuguese East Africa called the SS *Wartenfels?*"

"I have," Skipper Finley said, taking a sip of the beer he was drinking from the bottle. "German freighter. The Portuguese have the ship interned. Me and Wino moved her to a new berth for the port authorities one time before you showed up and ruined our reputations as honest, hard-working tugboat men."

"The *Wartenfels*," Col. Randal said, "is docked here in Diego Suarez."

"Colonel," Skipper Finley said, "that tramp steamer is our ticket outta here. Take down her crew, leave me a couple a' men alive to black-gang the engine room and I can sail us to meet the Royal Navy— or all the way back to Egypt if need be."

Col. Randal said, "Get your bags packed."

"I ain't had time to *un*pack."

Col. Randal turned to go, glanced at King, then over to the bartender, still at the table talking to Rocky.

The Merc stared back with no visible expression.

RIKKE RUNBORG LEFT FIRST, RETURNING TO THE POOL ON the roof. Colonel John Randal went up to his room. Percy Mather had another drink, then went to his room, put on his swimming trunks, and walked up to the pool to nap in the sun—he had not slept well in jail. Acting Provisional Sub-Lieutenant Skipper Warthog Finley finished his drink and wandered upstairs to the pool area where Percy pointed out the location of the SS *Wartenfels,* which was clearly visible from the roof of the hotel. Captain "Geronimo" Joe McKoy and Waldo Treywick hung out with the French women for an hour, then went to their rooms.

King stayed in the empty bar.

AT 2300 HOURS, COLONEL JOHN RANDAL REACHED THE pier where the SS *Wartenfels* was docked. He thought, incorrectly, he was the first one there.

Rocky arrived, no longer wearing her swimsuit but a dark blouse and a pair of black slacks tucked into suede rubber-soled half boots. The .32 Sauer Model 13 that Col. Randal had given her was in her purse. She moved as silently as a butterfly and was almost invisible in the dark. Clearly a professional.

The two decided to stroll down the dock to do a walk-by of the SS *Wartenfels.* No one else was in sight except a couple of men on the pier, night-fishing: Captain "Geronimo" Joe McKoy and Waldo.

It was a moonless night. The kind Commandos prefer to carry out their raids. They would be coming about three hours from now.

There were no lights on the wharf. Madagascar was not on blackout since the colony was not at war. It was just that no one had ever gotten around to installing lights.

"Evenin'" Capt. McKoy said when Col. Randal and Rocky walked by.

"Catching anything?" Col. Randal asked.

"Not a' nibble," Waldo said. It would probably have helped if they had put bait on their hooks. The SS *Wartenfels* was moored not more than ten feet away.

Tramp steamer was a good description. The ship was a rust bucket. A dim light was glowing in the wheelhouse on the bridge, and the sultry sound of *Lil' Marlene* was drifting out of what was most likely the radio shack. That would make at least two people standing watch on the upper deck. Percy Mather had said most nights the bulk of the crew was most often found in one of the local bars or bordellos.

The gangplank was unguarded. Long, boring duty interned in Portuguese East Africa for over two years and now berthed on the remote tip on the north end of Madagascar had lulled the German crew into a false sense of security.

That was good.

Col. Randal and Rocky continued on past to the end of the dock. They faked gazing out at the ocean like lovers for a while, then turned to go back. Acting Provisional Sub-Lieutenant Skipper Warthog Finley was standing on the jetty next to the SS *Wartenfels* talking to someone on board. He knew the crew from when his tugboat, the *King Kong,* had moved the ship to a new berth in Portuguese East Africa.

The two fishermen had called it a night. They were waiting when Col. Randal and Rocky walked ashore. King and Special Operations Executive (SOE) agent Percy Mather were there as well.

Percy said, "Quite the commotion at the Continental as we were surreptitiously effecting our departure out the back door. The relief shift found the bartender dead in the wine cellar. Man apparently slipped, fell down the stairs, and broke his neck."

"That's too bad," Col. Randal said.

Skipper Finley walked up. "Talked to the cook who'd come out on deck to smoke a cigarette. There's five men on board. The captain, who's drinking in his cabin, the radio operator, two men in the engine room to keep the steam up, and the cook—everyone else is out on the town.

Col. Randal said, "King, team up with Skipper Finley. You've got the ship's captain—lead out first. Captain McKoy, you and Mr. Treywick go below and seize the two sailors in the engine room, we want 'em alive to man their duty station.

"I'll take the radio operator.

"King, once the captain's secure, deal with the cook."

"Mr. Treywick, loan your silenced High Standard .22 to Percy. That Fritz Special 38/44 of yours won't be heard from the bowels of the ship if you have to use it. Try not to—we need the stokers in one piece.

"Percy, you and Rocky stand by ready at the gangway. Don't let anyone on or off the ship."

"Questions?" Col. Randal said. "Let's do this."

King and Skipper Finley started up the pier. Col. Randal was right behind them. Then came Capt. McKoy and Waldo. Rocky and Percy waited a few moments to give them a head start, then they strolled up the dock.

There was no one at the gangway when King and Skipper Finley stepped on board the SS *Wartenfels.* However, the cook, a chain smoker, came back out on deck to have another cigarette. King shot him three times with his silenced .22 High Standard Military Model D.

Skipper Finley led the way to the captain's cabin.

Right behind them came Col. Randal, who stepped over the body of the cook and followed the two up the stairs to the upper deck.

Capt. McKoy and Waldo came aboard and saw the dead cook lying in their path with a glowing cigarette still in his lips.

"They claim," Capt. McKoy said, "smokin' can be hazardous to your health."

Waldo said, "Killed *him.*"

They went below, pistols at the ready.

On the upper deck, Skipper Finley pointed to an open door. King stepped into the lead. He went in and found the ship's captain passed out drunk on his bunk. They tied him up, shut the door and went to the bridge to prepare the SS *Wartenfels* to get underway.

When King and Skipper Finley disappeared into the captain's cabin, Col. Randal moved on past and walked toward the open door where the music was coming from. Glenn Miller's "In the Mood," as popular in Berlin as in London or New York.

Col. Randal stepped into the radio room. There was a sailor sitting in a chair in front of a bank of radios. Next to the radios was a .9mm Luger P-08. While Col. Randal was trying to say *"hände hoch,"* the Nazi lunged for the pistol.

WHIIIIICH, WHIIIIICH.

The silenced .22 did not sound any louder than a match striking.

Col. Randal rolled the dead German out of the chair. Next to the Luger, he found what he was looking for—a wooden box with a typewriter device inside. He had no idea what the machine did exactly— only that Commander Ian Fleming of the Naval Intelligence Division (NID) would go to any length to get his hands on one.

Even that knowledge was more than Col. Randal was cleared to know.

Capt. McKoy and Waldo made their way down to the engine room. They slipped inside and found two sailors on duty. The Germans wisely surrendered.

"You boys must be married men," Capt. McKoy said as he indicated with the barrel of his Colt. 38 Super pistol for them to start shoveling coal.

"Made yourself a good decision. We're gonna get along real good."

The SS *Wartenfels* slipped the dock and made her way out of the harbor with Skipper Finley at the helm. It required some tricky navigation because the trip was a long, circuitous voyage around the north end of the island. Fortunately, Percy was a skilled yachtsman and knew his way into and out of Diego Suarez. He served as the pilot.

No one paid the slightest attention to the *Wartenfels.*

The ship was German-flagged and could come and go as she pleased. No sane French naval officer would dare to interfere with a Kriegsmarine vessel underway. Everyone in Diego Suarez knew there was a long-distance radio aboard. The story about her being a merchant steamer was a fig leaf—the SS *Wartenfels* was a spy ship.

Once they were out of the harbor and could feel the swell of the open seas, everyone started to breathe a little easier. As soon as he could be spared from the bridge, Percy went to the radio room and tuned to a frequency Col. Randal supplied. Then the Frenchman began to transmit the mission identifier, *Shortcake Harvester,* and the code word GOLDEN FLEECE that Col. Randal had given him.

An acknowledgement came back right away.

Percy transmitted a brief message explaining the *Shortcake Harvester* team was aboard a captured enemy ship en route to attempt to rendezvous with the Royal Navy.

The comeback was to report to the commander of Force H, Rear Admiral Edward Syfret, for instructions. It included the necessary radio frequency to make contact with the flagship of the Royal Navy's invasion fleet.

"Percy," Col. Randal said, "none of this ever happened."

2
YOU AIN'T SUPERMAN

COLONEL JOHN RANDAL WAS IN THE RAIDING FORCES' Headquarters (RFHQ) briefing room, sitting in the audience of officers and NCOs who had survived the four-week "Blood in the Sand" training that Captain Roy "Mad Dog" Reupart, MC; Sergeant Major Mike "March or Die" Mikkalis, DSM, MM; and the ex-Foreign Legion veterans of Blue Patrol had conducted for the men of the U.S. 575th Parachute Infantry Regiment, "Rangers." He was listening to Captain "Geronimo" Joe McKoy give a lecture on his view of war—a subject he knew quite a bit about, having served in at least six he admitted to.

Drop-dead gorgeous Major the Lady Jane Seaborn, LG, OBE, RM slipped in at the last minute and sat in the back row. The Rangers were her new pet project.

Capt. McKoy said, "Boys, you ain't Superman . . ."

The hard training and the selection process that went along with it had decimated the ranks of the 575th officers—over a 60 percent failure rate. Any of the washouts who desired could repeat selection when the Ranger Company training at Achnacarry's Commando Castle in Scotland completed the school, returned, and went to the desert for their "Blood in the Sand." Those electing not to had already been assigned to Middle East Headquarters staff.

Capt. McKoy said, "If you're short of everything except bad guys—you're in combat."

The Ranger NCOs had an equally high failure rate. They had been given the same second opportunity to pass selection as the officers—at least most of them been given the opportunity. Before shipping them out to Egypt, Airborne Command at Ft. Benning had loaded down the 575 with non-coms they wanted to get rid of.

There is no salvaging a bad NCO.

Capt. McKoy said, "If it's stupid but it works—it ain't stupid..."

Most of the Rangers below the rank of sergeant had made the cut on the first try. Even the ones who had been let out of the stockade or transferred in from other airborne regiments for being slackers or troublemakers. To be fair, the troops were not being graded on the same scale as the officers or NCOs, but their performance was a pleasant surprise to everyone in Raiding Forces.

Captain Billy Jack Jaxx, MC, was sitting next to Col. Randal. Speaking so low that only Col. Randal could hear him, he said, "I need Lieutenant Morgan assigned to the I&R platoon, sir. My plan is to organize two sections—one under Clay Hays and one under Dan . . ."

"Negative," Col. Randal said, not turning his head. "You can't have him."

Capt. McKoy said, "If the enemy is in range, so are you . . ."

"*Sir?*" Capt. Jaxx could not remember the last time the colonel had turned a request down flat.

"Dan led the 575th Regimental Recon Platoon and was on the Regiment's Rifle Team," Col. Randal said. "He's experienced commanding a jeep platoon and a long range shooter. Lt. Morgan's going to understudy Scout Patrol, then form his own, configured like Roy's—made up of mostly Rangers. Find someone else."

Capt. McKoy said, "Tracers work both ways . . ."

"In that case, sir," Capt. Jaxx said, "you have to give me first pick of the rest of the officers. I need the best of the best."

"You got it, Jack."

"To conclude," Capt. McKoy said, "keep in mind at all times, grenades with five-second fuses generally pop in three, the lowest bidder always gets the contract, there ain't no such thing as 'friendly' fire and if you're doin' somethin' that ain't workin'—try to do less of it.

"During this period of instruction we've covered . . ."

COLONEL JOHN RANDAL SPOKE BRIEFLY TO THE
assembled Ranger officers and NCOs. A large rectangular map of Egypt
and Libya was on a three-legged stand in front of his audience. He
wanted to give Raiding Forces' new leaders his view on the type of
operations they could expect to perform in the future and explain why
they would be carrying them out.

And, he wanted them to start feeling like they were part of the team,
having passed selection.

"Everything I am about to tell you is classified," Col. Randal said.
"This is a map of our Area of Operations. It consists of Western Egypt
and all of Libya. The narrow strip that runs along the Mediterranean
Coast from the Via Balbia to the Great Sand Sea is described as 'good
going,' meaning the ground is relatively firm. This is where all the heavy
fighting takes place—fifteen hundred miles long by fifty miles wide.

"What it means is the bad guys have long lines of communication,
starting in Italy across the Mediterranean to Tripoli, ending up at the
front down here around Tobruk. Once material reaches Tripoli via air or
sea, it has to be trucked forward. And, that makes Afrika Korps' long,
skinny supply lines vulnerable to high-speed, small-scale raiding—
which we specialize in.

"Raiding Forces' Desert Patrol primarily operates in the narrow
'good going' strip—only retreating into the Great Sand Sea to hide or
get away from pursuers. Our gun jeep patrols do short, intensive, two-
week operations that rely on hard intelligence that allows them to attack
soft targets. We operate primarily against the Via Balbia paralleling the
coast—the *only* hard-topped road in the entire AO.

"Raiding Forces' number one target is thin-skinned enemy wheeled
transport trucks, which are difficult for Afrika Korps to replace. Fewer
trucks means less food, fuel, ammunition etc., for Rommel's fighting
troops. Replacements for the trucks we destroy have to be shipped in
from Italy, across the Mediterranean. They take up shipping space that
could be bringing war materiel like tanks, artillery pieces, ammunition,
etc. to shoot at us, which is a good thing.

"Of equal strategic value is destroying Axis fuel storage facilities.
The enemy is always facing a fuel shortage. Keep in mind that long
supply line. The trucks carrying Rommel's supplies down the Via Balbia

burn up a huge amount of gas—some reports say as high as 40 percent of Afrika Korps' total allotment.

"We also attack isolated targets of little military value in order to draw off Afrika Korps' limited number of ground combat troops to guard them from future attacks that we'll never make—unless we do.

"We specialize in Economy of Force pinprick raids designed to degrade the opposition's troop strength by forcing Rommel to guard worthless targets. However, it's also as a form of psychological warfare intended to make the enemy believe Raiding Forces is hiding behind every sand dune. And maybe we are.

"From time to time Raiding Forces also performs TOP SECRET strategic missions to accomplish specific high-value tasks. You may or may not be involved with them. These missions are 'Need to Know'—not to be discussed with anyone—ever.

"What I want you small unit leaders to keep in mind at all times is that we operate on the principle of hitting and running, constantly on the move—living to fight another day. We don't stand and do battle. We don't defend. We don't take on suicide missions, and there are no acceptable losses," Col. Randal said.

"The men you command are valuable national assets. Don't ever take unnecessary risks with them. The Rangers are *my* people now, and in Raiding Forces we take care of our troops.

"Is that clear?"

"CLEAR, SIR!"

When he finished, the happy psychological warrior, Captain Hawthorne Merryweather, passed out an example of the Political Warfare Executive (PWE) material the officers and NCOs could expect to be leaving behind on operations. Printed on the cards in English, German, and Italian was:

IF EVERYTHING AROUND YOU IS
BLOWING UP—IT'S PROBABLY US.
SEE YOU SOON.
RAIDING FORCES.

COLONEL JOHN RANDAL AND RECENTLY PROMOTED
Lieutenant Colonel Sir Terry "Zorro" Stone, KBE, DSO, MC, were in
the small map/briefing area of the third-floor suite that Col. Randal
shared with Major the Lady Jane Seaborn.

Lt. Col. Stone appeared as if he were at death's door. The wound he
had received during CRUSADER had taken its toll. The Errol Flynn
look-alike, former Life Guards officer was struggling to recover from
his morning workout with Rikke Runborg and Lady Jane's Royal
Marines.

Zorro had yet to make it through the entire drill.

Col. Randal had decreed that Lt. Col. Stone could not go back on
full duty until he was able to complete one evolution of Rocky's daily
physical training routine, and he was sticking to that order.

"You don't look so great, stud," Col. Randal said. "Still having
trouble keeping up with the girls?"

"I am in mourning, actually," Lt. Col. Stone said. "The bloody
Green Mice, as the Regia Aeronautica is called now days, bombed
Mary's in Alexandria last night."

"Mary's?"

"Better known as the 'Officers Club,'" Lt. Col. Stone said. "Best
bordello in all Egypt—more's the pity. Oh, well."

"Hoping to take out the cream of Middle East Command's officer
corps, no doubt," Col. Randal said.

"The Rangers who have completed Special Warfare Training should
start arriving back here any time. The way I see the reorganization—you
command the Raiding Regiment, made up of the Lancelot Lancers
Yeomanry, Desert Patrol, and what we're going to call Ranger Force.
Plus you are also the Deputy Commander of Strategic Raiding Forces—
that was our deal."

Lt. Col. Stone said, "Looking forward to this, John."

"I'm giving you the Commando-qualified Rangers under Major
McCloud for the Raiding Regiment as soon as they get here."

"Now why would you do that?" Lt. Col. Stone asked. "Would they
not be best put to use in Sea Squadron?"

"Two reasons," Col. Randal said. "Number one, you are fit enough
now to evaluate them as they go through their 'Blood in the Sand.' You

and Major McCloud have your work cut out for you organizing Ranger Force into six patrols—my guess is we'll still be short of officers by the end of selection.

"I'm available to consult anytime."

"Definitely," Lt. Col. Stone said. "I know you relish organizing new units."

"Put experienced navigators in every patrol," Col. Randal ordered. "We're probably never going to have an all-British or all-American gun jeep patrol and that's fine with me. Don't let country of origin have any influence on you."

"Excellent," Lt. Col. Stone said. "The First Rule is 'There Ain't No Rules—Right Man, Right Job.'"

"Reason number two," Col. Randal said. "It may take a month or more to have all three of Sea Squadron's ships out of dry dock. The second group of Rangers to complete Commando School ought to be back by then. Some of them can be assigned to Major Corrigan's Sea Squadron."

"You have been giving this thought," Lt. Col. Stone said, as he was standing up to leave.

Col. Randal said, "Ever heard of a three-toed kalanoro?"

"Negative."

"Hunters can't track it because its toes are backward," Col. Randal. "When they try, they go the wrong way."

"A local Madagascar creature, I presume," Lt. Col. Stone said. "Interesting."

Col Randal said, "Reckon we might be able to do something like that with our jeep's tire treads?"

Lt. Col. Stone said, "You should try to stay away from exotic tropical islands, old stick."

COLONEL JOHN RANDAL AND MAJOR THE LADY JANE Seaborn were sitting behind a palm tree in the back of the Gezira Club having lunch. As usual, the place was packed. Lady Jane was entertaining Col. Randal with a story.

"In 1939, a Japanese military attaché—which, as you are aware—is a polite term for military spy, came up with an ingenious way to conduct a route reconnaissance of Syria, Palestine, and Egypt as a favor for Japan's friends and future allies, the Nazis. He mounted a motion picture camera on the dashboard of his car to film the roads and started his journey.

"When the attaché passed through Cairo," Lady Jane laughed, "R.J. managed to have the film switched—for a particularly vile Egyptian pornographic movie."

"Can't make this stuff up," Col. Randal said.

"John," Lady Jane asked, "I have been wondering. What prompted you to include Skipper Finley on the team you took to Madagascar? He had no training or experience to be a part of a clandestine mission."

"It's an island," Col. Randal said. "Raiding Forces' rules: 'Plan missions backward—know how to get home.' I figured if things went south we'd pirate a ship. *I* can't drive one."

"Rocky said you were *very* capable," Lady Jane said.

"So was she."

Changing subjects, Lady Jane said, "Did you realize the 575th Parachute Infantry Regiment has never had a distinctive unit insignia?"

"No," Col. Randal said. "They must've really been forgotten down there in the jungles of Panama."

"I shall work on that project later—let me show you what I designed as a cap badge and to replace the infantry crossed rifles the Five-Seven-Five's officers and men wear on their shirts and the lapels of their dress uniforms," Lady Jane said, as she reached for her bag and pulled out her sketch pad.

On the page was a drawing of gold crossed arrows.

"Oh, yeah," Col. Randal said. "Where did you get the idea?"

"Captain McKoy showed me the pair he wore on his campaign hat when he was Chief of Scouts during the Punitive Expedition in Mexico."

"Well," Col. Randal said. "I know the Rangers are going to like 'em—I do."

"With your approval," Lady Jane said, sounding pleased, "we can have the crossed arrows made locally."

"I think you hit a home run, Jane."

"Home run—is that good?"

Brigadier Raymond J. Maunsell, who liked to be called R.J., and James "Baldie" Taylor, walked in. The two men spotted them in the far back and made their way to the table. Col. Randal wondered if he detected a slight degree of tension between the intelligence officers and Lady Jane when they sat down.

Col. Randal said, "Jane was telling me about your switching the film on the Japanese military attaché."

"The things I do for England," R.J. said.

"A message from Admiral Godfrey, Chief of Naval Intelligence Division, arrived—commending you, Colonel, on turning the Madagascar mission into a RED INDIAN snatch."

What R.J. did not reveal, because he was the only person at the table cleared to know, was that the Enigma captured on the SS *Wartenfels* did not have the fourth rotor. Everyone in the "need to know" loop, from the President of the United States and the Prime Minister of the United Kingdom on down, was staying up nights praying to get their hands on that fourth rotor.

Nevertheless, the spy ship had been immediately returned to the dock where she had been captured. Then the Royal Navy sank the SS *Wartenfels* in her berth. Kriegsmarine spy ships had standing orders to scuttle rather than allow themselves to be boarded—the idea was to make it appear that was what had happened.

To complete the deception, the SS *Wartenfels* crew, who had been rounded up by 5 Commando in Diego Suarez before they had a chance to learn the ship had sailed, were paraded past the dock on their way into captivity. The German sailors could see the merchantman was sitting on the bottom, right where they had last seen her—the masts were sticking out of the water.

British Intelligence did not want the Nazis to suspect they had captured the encoding device—even without the coveted fourth rotor.

"Colonel," Jim said, "Dudley Clarke sends his compliments and requests your assistance with a deception operation."

Col. Randal said, "What's Dudley want done this time?"

Jim leaned in close and whispered the instructions.

Lady Jane gasped.

Col. Randal said, "Have you gone nuts, General?"

"It's a possibility."

"OK, tell Colonel Clarke no problem."

KING SAID, "SERGEANT MAJOR MIKKALIS, SIR."

"Send him in," Colonel John Randal said, studying the map in his third-floor suite. He was contemplating future operations. It was time to get what patrols they could back on operations as soon as possible.

Raiding Forces was going to have to phase in gun jeep patrols, starting with those ready now and gradually work up to full operational capacity down the road. That could take months.

Col. Randal had under his personal control his newly renamed Raider Patrol, Scout Patrol, Railroad Wrecking Crew II, and Lt. Jaxx's 575th Rangers I&R Platoon that was reorganizing into what Jack Cool was calling his Small Operations Group (SOG).

SOG even had a motto: Dirty Deeds Done Quick.

"You wanted to see me, Colonel?"

"We're not having this conversation, Sergeant Major," Col. Randal said. "I'm not issuing you an order. Is that clear?"

"Negative," said Sergeant Major Mike "March or Die" Mikkalis.

Ignoring him, Col. Randal said, "Give the Rangers a twenty-four-hour pass to Cairo starting tomorrow at sundown."

"Yes, sir."

"Every man will be assigned a jeep to drive to town," Col. Randal said. "Colonel Clarke is having the Rangers' new crossed-arrow insignia and U.S. 71st Airborne Division markings painted on the vehicles as we speak.

"As soon as the jeeps are painted, the Rangers' leave begins," Col. Randal said. "The idea is to give the impression the 71st Airborne has hit the town in a big way—people will see clearly-marked jeeps with the divisional markings on the bumpers flooding the city."

"There is no 71st Airborne Division, sir."

"Here's what I need you to do," Col. Randal said. "Tell the Rangers there's one final test before full acceptance into Raiding Forces—go into every low-life dive they can find and take on all comers.

"I want to hear reports of bar fights all over Cairo."

"Colonel," Sgt. Maj. Mikkalis said, "have you been drinking, sir?"

"The men will be arrested. However, they'll be taken to another location in Cairo and released," Col. Randal said.

"Immediately upon being turned loose, they're to repair to different bars and have at it again. No guns or knives—tell 'em try not to kill anybody."

"If you say so, sir," Sgt. Maj. Mikkalis said. "Maddest order of my military career—you *are* certain you are not having me on?"

"I'm going to be incommunicado from the moment the Rangers' leave begins," Col. Randal said. "No one is to know how to reach me."

"Where are you going to be, Colonel?"

"At the Mena House by the pool with Lady Jane," Col. Randal said. "Feel free to drop by for a drink.

"I wouldn't recommend going to Cairo."

COLONEL JOHN RANDAL WAS LYING OUT ON A LOUNGE chair by the private pool that went with the Mena House Hotel suite that Major the Lady Jane Seaborn reserved on a permanent basis. The Great Pyramid, only about a half-mile away, was in full view.

Lady Jane was on the lounge to his left, and Lieutenant Mandy Paige, OBE, RM, was on the lounge to the right—bookends in their matching black French-cut swimsuits. Rita and Lana were having their nails done by the hotel manicurist at a table near the deep end of the pool. The two Zar Cult priestesses would be dancing at the Kit-Kat Club tonight and needed to look their best.

They had a reputation to maintain.

Col. Randal was having a nice day.

Lt. Mandy was entertaining him with tales about the murky world of counterintelligence—R.J., Chief of Security Intelligence Middle East (SIME), was mentoring her in the dark arts. He had been sending his young Royal Marine protégée to every local course available on the subject.

"Counterintelligence is broken down into two categories," Lt. Mandy said. "Security and counterintelligence in one, and deception in the other. R.J. is in charge of security and counterintelligence, while Dudley Clarke handles deception at A-Force. The two work hand-in-glove."

"Security and counterintelligence are similar, but their methods vary. Think of SIME as one of your football teams—security and counterintelligence are separate components of the same club—like offense and defense.

"Security plays defense, setting up a perimeter to keep enemy agents from scoring by penetrating our most precious secrets.

"Counterintelligence, my specialty, is offense, meaning we go after the other team's players off the field to bribe, blackmail, or otherwise intimidate them to throw the game. In real life, with enemy agents we turn them into double agents working for our side, toss them in prison, or kill them.

"Like we used you to do with the belly dancer Hekmet Fahmey," Lt. Mandy said.

"All I . . ."

"So, John," Lt. Mandy asked, "which one would you say has the more sensational green eyes—Hekmet or Lady Jane?"

Col. Randal had phenomenal peripheral vision. Without needing to turn his head, he could see that Lady Jane was struggling not to smile while Lt. Mandy was wearing the expression of an innocent cherub.

He would have cheerfully put Raiding Forces' brand-new counterintelligence officer (a position that did not exist until she created it) in the rear take-down stranglehold and made her do the chicken if there had not been so many witnesses present.

King came out to the pool. "Here's the morning edition of the newspaper, Chief. Check out the headline.

AFTER NIGHT OF RIOTS U.S. 71
AIRBORNE DIVISION BANNED
FROM CAIRO CITY LIMITS.

"Brilliant," Lt. Mandy said, looking over Col. Randal's shoulder at the paper.

"There is no U.S. 71st Airborne Division, but A-Force wants Rommel to believe it exists. Dudley proved beyond a shadow of a doubt the 71st Airborne is real and disposed of it at the same time with a single headline.

"He really is the master of the game."

Col. Randal said, "I wonder how much trouble I'm in."

3
FAKE AMATEURS

COLONEL JOHN RANDAL WAS IN HIS SUITE DISCUSSING Raiding Forces' reorganization with Captain "Geronimo" Joe McKoy and Waldo Treywick. The three were studying a diagram of what Col. Randal and Lieutenant Colonel Sir Terry "Zorro" Stone had worked out at their last meeting.

"Looks real good on paper," Capt. McKoy said. "Where you gonna put my White Patrol?"

"You'll still be in Desert Patrol," Col. Randal said, "unless you want to switch to Ranger Force under Major McCloud—I've thought about that."

"Why not let White Patrol fall under your personal command along with Billy Jack, Roy, and Pyro Percy?" Capt. McKoy said

"I like it," Col. Randal said. "What that'll mean is you can be pretty much independent. Work with Mr. Zargo. Plan your own patrols, not limited to any one AO. Come and go as you please, unless I need you for a specific mission."

"That's what I'm talkin' about," Capt. McKoy said, sticking a thin cigar between his teeth. "You can use White as a' trainin' platform for the Ranger officers and NCOs. Between the two of us, we can evaluate our new junior leaders a' lot quicker."

Col. Randal said, "Good idea."

"Lady Jane on the horn, Chief," King called from his desk outside the door.

"Patch her through," Col. Randal said.

"John," Major the Lady Jane Seaborn asked, "have you ever heard of an M1941 Johnson Light Machine Gun?"

"Negative," Col. Randal said. "Never have."

He stuck his hand over the phone, "Captain, you know anything about a weapon called the M1941 Johnson LMG?"

"Not to my knowledge," Capt. McKoy said.

"Captain McKoy's never heard of 'em either," Col. Randal said.

"I am downstairs," Lady Jane said, "with three hundred of the machine guns loaded on trucks. Jimmy Roosevelt diverted them to us. They were part of a consignment for the Dutch Army in the East Indies, but the Japanese invaded before the weapons could be shipped."

"We'll be right down."

They headed downstairs, with King bringing up the rear. Capt. McKoy said, "I never heard a' the Johnson LMG, but I have heard a' Melvin Johnson. He's a' capt'n in the Marine Corps Reserve, a' lawyer who designs guns in his spare time.

"He developed the M1941 Johnson rifle to replace the M-1 Garand. Pretty good weapon; the Para-Marines adopted it, but the Corps turned it down for general issue because it had a' reciprocatin' barrel—can't mount a bayonet on it."

"What's a' reciprocatin' barrel?" Waldo asked.

"The recoil action has to be balanced for a' specific mass," Capt. McKoy said. "A bayonet on the barrel throws that off . . . and you know how U.S. Marines love their bayonets. So, except for limited special forces use, the Johnson was a' nonstarter."

"I didn't understand one word a' what you just said, Joe," Waldo said, "except for nonstarter."

"It's complicated," Capt. McKoy said. "Never heard Melvin invented a' light machine gun."

As they were going past the Operations Room, Col. Randal spotted Major Travis McCloud studying a clipboard.

"Have you ever heard of a M1941 Johnson Light Machine Gun?"

"Yes, sir," Maj. McCloud said. "The Machine Gun Committee evaluated them at the Infantry School while I was there."

"Come with us," Col. Randal said.

Lady Jane was outside. On her instructions, a driver had uncrated one of the light machine guns. The Buck Rogers-looking weapon was sitting on the ground on its detachable bipod sporting a long, thin barrel with a big, exotic triangle-shaped sight on the end. The magazine projected from the left side of the gun.

Maj. McCloud said, "A friend of mine was the officer-in-charge of the Machine Gun Committee. Since I was the OIC of the Airborne Tactics committee and needed to be kept in the loop about any new small arms that might be useful for parachute operations, he invited me to participate in the trials. The Johnson LMG is an excellent weapon, sir."

"Looks like more of a' automatic rifle," Capt. McKoy said, "than a' light machine gun."

"That's what the inventor told us," Maj. McCloud said. "The specs, if I remember correctly, are .30 caliber, 20-round single stack magazine fed, weighs thirteen pounds but you can knock off almost two pounds if you remove the bipod. It has an adjustable cyclic rate of three hundred to nine hundred rounds per minute."

"Lighter than the BAR," Col. Randal said.

Capt. McKoy picked it up and brought the Johnson Light Machine Gun (LMG) to his shoulder. "Take a little gettin' used to having the magazine stickin' out on the left side like it does, but this gun has a' pretty good feel to it."

"The army already had the BAR and the Browning M1919A1 belt-fed light machine gun or they would have adopted it," Maj. McCloud said. "The NCO instructors on the committee rated it high. Personally, I thought the Johnson was the best weapon of its class I ever fired."

"You done good, Lady Jane," Capt. McKoy said, handing the weapon to King. "We can put these to some real serious use."

The Merc said, "Beautiful."

Maj. McCloud said, "Johnson M1941s are easy to disassemble and reassemble for airborne operations. A lot better handling aboard an aircraft than a BAR or Browning M-1919 A-1."

Lady Jane asked, "You do not mind if there is no bayonet, do you, John?"

Col. Randal said, "No."

Captain Billy Jack Jaxx walked out of RFHQ to see what was going on. King handed him the LMG. Raising the Johnson to his shoulder, Jack Cool said, "Bad to the bone."

"I don't know if the .30 M1941 LMG will represent an increase in firepower over our .9mm Beretta M-38s up close and personal the way we usually do it," Capt. McKoy said. "But it'll definitely increase the power of our fire."

"We coulda' used us a' couple a' these," Waldo said, "huntin' bad cat in Abyssinia—thirty-aught-six, twenty rounds fast."

Col. Randal said, "Roger that."

Once again, Raiding Forces was adopting cast-off equipment no one else seemed to want . . . and they were glad to get it.

MAJOR THE LADY JANE SEABORN SAID, "CAPTAIN MCKOY, Waldo, and I are flying to Kenya this afternoon. The bank I have a relationship with in Nairobi has made arrangements for them to transfer their gold from the basement of the American Consulate and sell it to the Credit Suisse—a Swiss bank.

"Do you think you can survive by yourself for a few days?"

Colonel John Randal looked up from where he was cleaning his pistols, on newspapers spread over the coffee table in the living area of their suite. "International finance—I'm impressed."

Lady Jane laughed. "You know I do not have the first idea about banking."

"Well," Col. Randal said, "you knew about those gold coins having a numismatic value."

"Father was an avid coin collector," Lady Jane said. "When I was little, I helped him catalogue his collection."

"Have you figured out a way to sell the coins?" Col. Randal asked.

"My people are working on it," Lady Jane said. "Proving to be a difficult proposition—everyone will pay a premium for gold, but coin collecting is not in vogue due to the war."

As she was leaving with King, who was carrying her bags, Col. Randal said, "Have a nice trip."

Flanigan stuck his head in the door, "I shall be on the desk, sir."

"Keep the bill collectors away," Col. Randal said, "and the insurance salesmen."

The burly ex-policeman from RAF Habbaniya, who now served as Lady Jane's chauffer / bodyguard, said, "No one gets by me, Colonel."

Lieutenant Mandy Paige arrived in her blue jean cutoffs and peewee cowboy boots. "Lady Jane ordered me to keep you company while she is away. What would you like to do first, John?"

"Do?"

"How would you feel about us having lunch at the Gezira Club?"

"OK."

"Let me go change," Lt. Mandy said. "Lady Jane issued strict instructions to make sure you take the next few days off. You never had a chance to complete your rest and recreational leave.

"And, that is exactly what I intend to do."

COLONEL JOHN RANDAL AND LIEUTENANT MANDY PAIGE were sitting at a table behind a palm in the back of the Gezira Club. She was entertaining him with a story just like the ones Major the Lady Jane Seaborn always told. Lt. Mandy was fun to spend time with.

"Have you noticed the change in the 'gabardine swine'?" Lt. Mandy asked.

"Can't say I have."

"They started growing beards and wearing unpolished desert boots to acquire the salty desert look. Like they just came in off a long patrol," Lt. Mandy laughed. "We will not be able to call them 'gabardine swine' much longer."

"Yeah," Col. Randal said, looking around the room, "you're right."

Raiding Forces' personnel were required to trim their beards and wear neatly-pressed uniforms on pass. Not so the GHQ staff.

Lt. Mandy said, "The tall officer at the bar is Captain David Stirling, the commander of the Special Air Service."

"I know," Col. Randal said. "He's here nearly every time Jane and I come in."

"The SAS was under a cloud after most of their troops were killed or captured on their first mission. No one even reached the objective," Lt. Mandy said. "However, they redeemed themselves toward the end of OPERATION CRUSADER with a raid on Benghazi.

"Really?"

"The raid did not do much actual damage," Lt. Mandy said. "But the Short Range Patrol lads at GHQ—formerly known as 'gabardine swine' and now masquerading as veteran desert operators—were thrilled to have anything they could point to and call a success.

"Now the SAS are the darlings of the Operations Staff."

Col. Randal said. "The SAS's commander is at the bar here a lot."

"Stirling's troops are roughing it in tents in the desert training under Jock Lewes," Lt. Mandy said. "David stays in Cairo. The men imagine he's in intense discussions at GHQ planning their next mission.

"Actually, he spends most of his time partying at the flat shared by his brother, Bill, and Peter Fleming—Ian's brother. I was there once. They keep a pet donkey."

"In the apartment?"

"David was in the kitchen looking at maps, hoping to dream up a mission to propose to Operations at GHQ, while a mad drinking party was taking place in the living room with Peter, Bill, their dates, and the donkey—unbelievable.

"No idea of the meaning of the word security."

"I understand they've had success raiding airfields," Col. Randal said.

"True," Lt. Mandy said. "The Long Range Desert Group provides a taxi service to transport them to their objectives—SAS is not able to operate on their own. Once they reach the Objective Rally Point, the SAS carries out an attack on the targeted airfield. Then the LRDG brings them home.

"The SAS are amateurs by their own admission. An attitude of non-professionalism is pervasive in a lot of regiments. It's a contrived amateurism.

"I think it is a form of showing off."

"I see," Col. Randal said. Which meant he did not.

Lt. Mandy said, "Jim told me about an officer selected by SOE to parachute onto Crete and operate behind the German lines.

"He needed to complete parachute school first but could not be bothered with having to endure long days of boring training in the hot sun. Not to worry, he sent his batman to take the course and had him explain what he had learned in his room at Shepard's Hotel at the end of each day."

Col. Randal said, "The SAS don't seem to give up."

"Suffer horrible casualties," Lt. Mandy said.

"So do we."

"Only because Raiding Forces was misused in CRUSADER," Lt. Mandy said. "Not because we effect a fake brave veneer of intentional amateurism when going out to do battle.

"We're professionals."

James "Baldie" Taylor appeared at their table, "Mandy, would you go powder your nose?"

"In the movies, when some gangster says that to a gun moll," Lt. Mandy said, "he always gives her money."

Jim said, "How much do you want?"

"Just joking."

As soon as Lt. Mandy departed, Jim sat down at the table. Col. Randal clicked on. He was not sure why.

"Two things," Jim said. "I am not authorized to tell you either of them."

Col. Randal took out a cigarette and lit it with his battered U.S. 26th Cavalry Regiment Zippo.

"First," Jim said, "Dudley wants you to know that sending the Rangers into Cairo to break up the place worked spectacularly—better than hoped for."

"They've been banned from Cairo," Col. Randal said.

"No," Jim said. "The *71ˢᵗ Airborne Division* has been banned from Cairo. Since there is no 71ˢᵗ Airborne Division—no harm, no foul. The part I am not supposed to tell you is German intelligence now is routinely overestimating Allied troop strength in the Middle East by thirty percent.

"Good," Col. Randal said. "Has to work to our advantage someday."

"It will," Jim said.

"The second subject is more sensitive and personally painful to discuss. I am only talking to you about it because of our close relationship. I could find myself in serious trouble for this—imprisoned in the Tower of London-type trouble."

"General," Col. Randal said, "you have my word that anything you say will never leave this table."

Jim said, "The hunt for the Axis spy with access to Middle East Headquarters has reached a white-hot fever pitch. Field Marshal Auchinleck is convinced all of his failures can be blamed on the mole.

"Y-Service has intercepted radio messages that corroborate Rommel calls the mole his 'Good Source.'

"No stone is being left unturned to ferret out the spy. To that end, an operative from MI-5 out of the London office was dispatched to the Shetlands to interview Commander Mallory Seaborn. The man is marooned on a windblown, treeless, semi-arctic island you can see completely across in every direction.

"Commander Seaborn commands a Royal Navy depot containing materiel that no one seems to have any need for. There is not a woman in three hundred miles.

"On the condition MI-5 can have him transferred to a safe rear echelon staff job at the Admiralty, Commander Seaborn indicated he would sign a statement that his wife is a card-carrying Fascist working for the Italian Military Intelligence Service, SIM.

"Claims Lady Jane's connection to the Blackshirts started before the war, when she was politically active in the Cliveden Set hosted by her socialite girlfriend, Lady Astor."

"Is this a joke?"

"Negative," Jim said. "Dead serious."

When Lt. Mandy returned to the table, Jim was gone.

She said, "John, you look like you have seen a ghost."

4
SOLID GOLD

"'*HARD* INTELLIGENCE,'" LIEUTENANT MANDY PAIGE SAID, "Means 'eyes on.'"

She and Colonel John Randal were sunning by the private pool in RFHQ's third-floor suite. Lt. Mandy was taking her assignment seriously, making sure Col. Randal was getting his R&R as ordered by Major the Lady Jane Seaborn.

The Raiding Forces' self-appointed counterintelligence officer was expounding on the finer points of evaluating intelligence reports.

"*Confirmed* report is when two or more informants have the same information that tallies.

"*Reliable* report is information from a single informant who has been subjected to a lengthy interview.

"*Rumors* are to be investigated whenever possible."

"You need to talk to Jim," Col. Randal said. "He used to be in charge of spreading rumors in the Gold Coast."

"Know what Jim told me?" Lt. Mandy said. "Most intelligence officers learn their trade by reading spy novels."

King stuck his head out the sliding doors, "Major Beauchamp, Chief."

"Send him out."

Major Everard Beauchamp walked out to the pool and took a chair by Col. Randal's lounge. He glanced at Lt. Mandy, who was stretched out on her lounge in a white French-cut swimsuit, wondering if she was related to Lady Jane.

Col. Randal said, "Now that you've completed what the Rangers are calling 'Blood in the Sand' and have had time to think about it—where do you see yourself fitting into Raiding Forces, Everard?"

According to Captain Roy "Mad Dog" Reupart and Sergeant Major Mike "March or Die" Mikkalis, the Louisiana National Guard officer had acquitted himself well during the training.

"It seems, suh," Maj. Beauchamp said, "you've disbanded the 575th PIR. To be perfectly candid, Colonel, I'm not sure."

"At this point and time, you are not cleared to know about the goal of certain government agencies that do not officially exist," Col. Randal said, "which is to have a combined U.S./British Special Operations unit on call to carry out national-level strategic missions.

"A standard parachute infantry battalion is of little use for those types of operations in Middle East Command. Airborne rifle companies don't fit into our TO&E. Using the Five-Seven-Five's paratroopers to expand Raiding Forces' troop strength—that's of high value."

"Yes, suh."

"Our basic element is the patrol. The most important and respected position in Raiding Forces is patrol leader," Col. Randal said. "I lead a patrol.

"You need to spend at least six months commanding a patrol, Everard. Then we'll take another look at how we can best use your talents."

"I'd like that, Colonel," Maj. Beauchamp said. "I was afraid you would try to make me a staff officer pushing paper here at RFHQ."

"We don't do that in Raiding Forces," Col. Randal said, "except for technicians like our Maintenance Chief, Mr. Rawlings, and his crew of mechanics. We don't have men in this outfit who don't take active part in combat operations—everyone fights.

"Lady Jane's Royal Marines perform all staff noncombat functions."

Lt. Mandy said, "And the Marines go on missions whenever we can get away with it."

"True," Col. Randal said. "I can't stop 'em."

"It strikes me, suh," Maj. Beauchamp said, "that Raiding Forces is a happy outfit. Everyone seems committed to winning the war."

"We work hard and play hard," Col. Randal said.

"Hook up with Colonel Stone. He'll help you start organizing your patrol. Then get back to me. I take a personal interest in the composition of our patrols.

"Look forward to it, Colonel."

Shortly after Maj. Beauchamp departed, Brandy Seaborn arrived in her swimsuit.

She, too, had instructions from Lady Jane to keep Col. Randal from doing anything strenuous until her return from Nairobi.

Unfortunately, Brandy was not going to be able to carry out those orders. She stretched out on a lounge next to Col. Randal and said only two words: "SOLID GOLD."

Col. Randal picked up the phone on the table and dialed King's number at his duty desk. "Find Billy Jack and have him report here as soon as possible—if not sooner."

As she was oiling one of her perfect, solid gold legs (the inspiration for the codename 'SOLID GOLD'), Brandy explained. "Field Marshal Auchinleck is monitoring our search for the 621st Radio Intercept Company. The Auk told me the only thing as important to him as discovering the enemy mole in GHQ is neutralizing Rommel's Merlin— Captain Albert Seebohm.

"Mr. Zargo is working full-time tracking the Nazi. He has a tentative location where Seebohm may turn up—not confirmed, but worthy of sending a team to investigate. Intelligence indicates he is scheduled to take a few days' leave at a small resort on the Mediterranean coast.

"You need to go there and kill him."

"How am I supposed to know what Seebohm looks like?"

"We have photos," Brandy said, reaching into her bag. "These 8x10s should prove helpful."

The phone rang.

"Colonel Randal."

"Jack Cool is here, Chief."

"You two come on out."

Captain Billy Jack Jaxx and King pulled up chairs.

Brandy started at the top and ran through her SOLID GOLD briefing again to include the coordinates of the objective.

"Parker is working on pinning down the exact date Seebohm will arrive at the resort. Once we have that last piece of the puzzle—you go."

Col. Randal believed a good order to his subordinate commanders should be "short and simple" as spelled out in Raiding Forces' Rules for Raiding. He liked orders that were open-ended enough to allow his officers to modify the directive to meet an individual situation and leave them free to do the job—under supervision. He did not micromanage his patrol or team leaders, but he did pay close attention to the tactics they chose for any given mission.

Col. Randal said, "Jack, you and King plan the operation.

"Get back to me with your thoughts in one hour.

"Let's see what you two studs can come up with—work a few of your SOG people into the mission, Jack."

"Will you be leading the team, sir?" Capt. Jaxx asked.

"What do you think?"

It was not really a question.

Lt. Mandy said, "Jane will be mad as hell."

VICE ADMIRAL SIR RANDOLPH "RAZOR" RANSOM, VC, KCB, DSO, OBE, DSC, Brandy's father, walked out to the pool unannounced. Flanigan, replacing King on the duty desk, had not even considered asking the admiral to wait while he was announced.

The Razor had three extraordinarily good-looking girls in Royal Navy uniform in tow. WRENS—Women's Royal Navy Service. Col. Randal was not sure what the 'E' stood for.

The female sailors were all sub-lieutenants. They wore the same rank insignia as their male counterparts except theirs were blue instead of gold.

VAdm. Ransom said, "Sub-Lieutenants Pippa Duncan-Sackville, Bentley St. Ledger and last but not least, Tabitha Walpole. Ladies, I would like to introduce you to Colonel Randal—your new commanding officer.

Col. Randal had not been expecting this today. The WRENS must have arrived in Egypt from England at approximately the same time VAdm. Ransom returned from Madagascar with recently promoted Captain Butch "Headhunter" Hoolihan.

He said, "Nice to meet you."

"The nearly naked blonde you will recognize as my daughter," VAdm. Ransom said. "The brunette is Lieutenant Mandy Paige, also known as the 'Heroine of Habbaniya.'

"As you can see, Col. Randal enjoys the company of beautiful women in his leisure time when he is not off slitting throats, so you ladies should fit right in."

Brandy said "Hello, girls." She knew all of them—had known all of them since they were born.

The WRENS said, "Hi, Brandy."

VAdm. Ransom said, "These young naval officers shall be manning my Director of Operations Division, Irregular office, here at RFHQ. All three have MOST SECRET—or TOP SECRET as we call it now— clearance. In practice, my WRENS will fall under the chain of command of Lady Jane's Royal Marine detachment.

"Lady Jane is away at the moment," Col. Randal said. "She knocked out a wall in the operations room to make a space for you to set up shop, Admiral. Check it out."

"Saw that," VAdm. Ransom said. "Outstanding—quite thoughtful of her, Colonel. I was expecting to be off in a closet somewhere."

"Mandy will help get you settled in your quarters," Col. Randal said to the WRENS.

"This place is like a hotel—there are plenty of bedrooms. Belongs to a member of King Farouk's family. Legend has it the King used to stage orgies here—at least that's what Lady Jane told me.

"Welcome to Raiding Forces."

"Thank you, Colonel," the WRENS chorused. The girls were having a difficult time trying not to stare at the scars on Col. Randal's chest where he had been mauled by a lion. They barely even noticed the two bullet holes.

"Pay no attention to those scratches," Lt. Mandy said. "A souvenir John picked up as a result of a one-night stand with one of the dancers at the Kit-Kat Club."

Whatever the WRENS had imagined their first duty station was going to be like, this was not it.

"Relax, girls," Mandy said as she escorted the WRENS to their rooms, "We have not had one single orgy since Raiding Forces moved in here."

S/Lt. St. Ledger said, "What a letdown."

Lt. Mandy said, "We are going to like you, Bentley."

After the WRENS left, Col. Randal said, "Raiding Forces has been alerted for a SOLID GOLD mission, Admiral. Brandy briefed it just before you arrived. We're standing by for an intelligence update and a preliminary assessment on how to proceed. Can you check on the status of the *King Duck*?

"My guess is Duck Patrol has a raid in its future."

VAdm. Ransom said, "I shall look in on the *King Duck* straightaway." He understood the urgency of SOLID GOLD missions, if not the origin of the codename identifier.

Precisely what VAdm. Ransom knew was that if Afrika Korps drove east, took out the fortress at Tobruk, marched on Alexandria and Cairo and captured the Suez Canal, England could be knocked out of the war— it could happen. The 621st Signals Company had demonstrated its ability to provide the signals intelligence Rommel needed to accomplish exactly that.

If Acting Provisional Sub-Lieutenant Skipper Warthog Finley's landing craft tank (LCT) was not ready to put to sea, she would be. It did not pay to stand in the Razor's way when he required a thing done.

"Thanks, sir," Col. Randal said, "I'll rest easy on the *King Duck.*"

VAdm. Ransom did not say so, but what he was *really* eager to do was assist Col. Randal with a GOLDEN FLEECE / RED INDIAN mission as soon as a suitable target turned up. All available resources of all the combined Allied intelligence services worldwide were working furiously to identify one. When they did, Raiding Forces was going to need to strike like lightning.

The Razor was 100 percent committed to doing his part to ensure Sea Squadron's components were ship-shape and ready to shove off on a moment's notice.

He had recently been selected to be the Royal Navy's representative on the Inter-Services Security Board (ISSB). It was an appointment orchestrated by Colonel Stewart Menzies, "C," Chief of the British Secret Intelligence Service, MI-6.

"C's" technique for boards was to cheat by stacking the deck.

He always had two votes in his pocket. On the ISSB he had three. MI-6 had a member, which was supposed to be SIS's only vote. Unknown to anyone, the army member was an MI-6 operative—vote number two, and the navy member, VAdm. Ransom—a recent inductee into the Secret Intelligence Service, was the third vote.

Col. Menzies played to win.

In his capacity as an ISSB member, the Razor was privy to all secret intelligence having to do with the military. He knew that the Kriegsmarine had recently implemented a fourth rotor on its Enigma encoding machine. That development had resulted in a skyrocketing number of Allied ships being sunk in the Atlantic.

VAdm. Ransom also knew the German Navy did not have enough of the new rotors to use with their U-boat fleet operating in other oceans. But it was only a matter of time. These were dark days for the U.K. and the U.S. merchant fleet.

The hard truth was that now, with Russia in the war, the Nazis could not win a total victory, but England might be forced to capitulate— starved into submission. Which would result in a negotiated peace.

Col. Menzies and Director of Naval Intelligence Vice Admiral John Godfrey—in full knowledge of the Admiral of the Fleet and the Prime Minister—had made it clear that VAdm. Ransom's top priority as Director of Operations Division (Irregular) was to assist Raiding Forces in its efforts to carry out a successful capture of a four-rotor Enigma Machine—without the Germans ever knowing.

The "without the Germans ever knowing" prerequisite was going to require a great deal of finesse to carry off.

Since VAdm. Ransom's daughter, Brandy, and grandson, Randy, were members of Raiding Forces and he had long considered Col.

Randal a virtual member of the family, the Razor was highly motivated to assist the Raiders in any way possible.

When VAdm. Ransom departed, Col. Randal said, "Your father has an eye for good-looking women. His WRENS look like showgirls."

Brandy laughed, "John, those are the daughters of the cream of the British aristocracy. The WRENS are an elite service. To apply, a girl must provide an 8x10 glossy headshot and three letters of recommendation.

"Only the ones who look like high-fashion models are accepted."

"Are you kidding? Can the navy do that?"

"Absolutely," Brandy said. "Jane wrote a letter of recommendation for each girl. So did Parker and I. Then we became concerned about the possibility that senior officers in the navy might take advantage of the WRENS under their command."

"No one's taking advantage of any women on my watch," Col. Randal said.

"Everybody knows that," Brandy laughed. "Why do you think those particular girls were assigned to Raiding Forces?

"The only person who gets taken advantage of around here is *you*, handsome."

Col. Randal picked up the phone and dialed the Operations Room, "Stephanie, is Pam down there?"

"Yes, sir."

"Put her on the line.

"Hi, John."

"Pam, can you have someone fly Lt. Hays and Frank Polanski back from Oasis X today?"

"Yes, sir."

Col. Randal said, "Billy Jack and King are working up a SOLID GOLD mission. Make yourself available."

"We were studying the target when you phoned," the Vargas Girl look-alike Royal Marine said.

"Great," Col. Randal said. "Don't say why I called—wouldn't want Jack to think I was looking over his shoulder. Say I was inviting you to lunch."

"*Are* you inviting me, John?"

Col. Randal said, "Would you like to have lunch, Pam?"

"Love to."

THE PHONE RANG. FLANIGAN WAS ON THE LINE, "CAPTAIN Hoolihan to see you, sir."

"Send him out."

Captain Butch "Headhunter" Hoolihan came out to the pool.

He was recently returned from Madagascar with Vice Admiral Sir Randolph "Razor" Ransom.

The Japanese had sent two midget submarine-carrying submarines, the I-10 and I-20, to attack the Royal Navy fleet conducting the invasion. The subs discharged their cargo of two midget submarines. One of the midgets sank, but the other, M-20b, successfully torpedoed the HMS *Ramillies*—a Revenge-class battleship.

Although the *Ramillies* did not sink, the attack caused a certain amount of angst and gnashing of teeth in the upper echelon of the Royal Navy. The navy had been suffering excessive losses lately and the idea of midget subs was a brand-new headache.

The Japanese crew of the M-20b beached their craft at a place called Nosy Tanikely and moved over land to a prearranged pickup point.

Capt. Hoolihan had landed with a small party of Royal Marines, followed the M-20b's crew, and killed them in a savage jungle firefight.

All in a day's work for the Headhunter.

Capt. Hoolihan said, "I ran into Mandy and the new WRENS, sir.

"She said it might be a good idea to come see you."

"I was going to reach out for you later, Butch," Colonel John Randal said. "We have a SOLID GOLD mission in the initial planning stage.

Duck Patrol, minus Frank's gun DUKW, which is currently parked at Oasis X, will most likely have a place in the operation.

"You want to take on one last mission before you ship out to Achnacarry?"

"Roger that, sir."

"Admiral Ransom is checking on the *King Duck*," Col. Randal said.

"It might be a good idea to recall your people from leave and put 'em on Stand By Alert."

"Yes, sir."

"Frank Polanski will be flying in from X later today," Col. Randal said. "You two get with Chief Rawlings to see about beefing up the firepower on the four gun jeeps you have available. We may have need of something a little heavier than the .303 Vickers Ks."

"Will 20mms suffice, sir?"

"Probably," Col. Randal said. "You'll be flying out to Scotland the minute we complete this mission, Butch. You're overdue to begin your tour as an instructor at the Special Warfare Training Center."

Which meant Col. Randal had to find a replacement leader for Duck Patrol and he had no idea who that might be. To date, Raiding Forces had suffered over one third of its officers KIA. He did not have a pool of qualified patrol leaders to draw from.

After the Headhunter left, Col. Randal dialed the Operations Room. "Stephanie, recall Guns from his leave. Have him report to Capt. Hoolihan."

"Yes, sir."

"I thought you were going to refrain from interfering with Billy Jack's planning," Brandy laughed. "You already know the concept of the operation Jack Cool is going to develop, don't you, John?

"I do."

COLONEL JOHN RANDAL AND LIEUTENANT PAMALA Plum-Martin, DSO, OBE, DFC, RM, were sitting behind a palm in the back of the Gezira Club restaurant. As usual, the place was packed, but the two were not paying attention to the crowd. They had served together for a long time and enjoyed each other's company—a relationship based on trust and mutual respect.

There were more than a few unhappy pilots in the room when they realized the snow-blonde Vargas Girl look-alike Royal Marine was having lunch with her boss.

Lt. Plum-Martin said, "Ronnie has requested to continue on as the RAF's liaison to Raiding Forces."

"Really," Col. Randal said. "Thought Flash Bang would be out of here the minute he was cleared for flight duty."

Lt. Plum-Martin said, "CRUSADER convinced Ronnie of the need for better inter-service cooperation between the RAF and the army ground forces."

"The Wing Commander's right about that," Col. Randal said.

"His boss, the Air Vice Marshal, has reluctantly agreed to allow him to stay on, with your permission, to run an experiment Ronnie put forward," Lt. Plum-Martin said.

"What kind of experiment?"

"Ronnie wants to attach an RAF jeep with a long-distance radio— manned by troops seconded from the RAF armored car squadrons—to each of the patrols. The RAF will keep a flight of four A-20 Havocs stationed at Oasis X—provided we supply the pilots.

"When a patrol requests air support, the A-20s will fly the mission. If the concept works, then the RAF will consider expanding the idea down to the battalion level in Eighth Army."

"Very good, Pam," Col. Randal said. "Close air support, additional long distance radios, and desert-qualified men to man the RAF jeeps."

"Done, done, and done," Lt. Plum-Martin said. "Clive Adair contacted his higher at Phantom HQ anticipating your approval of Ronnie's plan. A new Phantom troop is being flown out to Egypt to provide the radios and operators.

"And, Ronnie has a bribe for Raiding Forces in the event you were reluctant to carry out his test pilot program."

"A bribe?"

"Squadron Leader Johnny Page and his No. 1 Armored Car Company RAF from Habbaniya—assigned to Raiding Forces."

"You're kidding?"

"Johnny and company are en route from RAF Habbaniya to arrive tomorrow, minus their old Rolls Royce Silver Cloud armored cars," Lt. Plum-Martin said.

"We are only getting the armored car crew personnel tomorrow— not the fitters, etc. They are traveling overland with their Morris maintenance tenders. Chief Rawlston actually broke out in a smile when he heard the news about the mechanics."

"Outstanding," Col. Randal said. "We need to have lunch together more often."

S/Ldr. Page had served with Strike Force during the siege at RAF Habbaniya. No. 1 Armored Car troops had two years' worth of experience in the desert on patrol—they were old hands. A perfect fit for Raiding Forces.

"Right *Men,* Right Job." Lt. Plum-Martin flashed a dazzling smile as she paraphrased Raiding Forces' Rules for Raiding.

"Remember the poor old tanks, Walrus and Seal—they shall not be making the trip. Back on duty guarding the front gate for those two."

"I'm impressed," Col. Randal said. "All the pieces together in one neat package.

"So, Pam—why am I the last to know?"

"Wanted to surprise you, love."

Col. Randal said, "Mission accomplished."

5
THREE KNOCKS

MAJOR THE LADY JANE SEABORN WAS HOSTING A reception for the officers of the U.S. 575th Parachute Infantry Regiment (PIR) at Field Marshal Claude Auchinleck's residence—at least for the officers who had survived the "Blood in the Sand" training. Eleven officers, all highly-trained U.S. Army paratroopers, had entered with the first class. Five had been selected to continue on with Raiding Forces.

It was hoped that Raiding Forces would have at least twelve or thirteen new officers qualified by the time the three battalion companies had rotated through the training. That was the minimum number needed to fill all the new slots created by the reorganization following the infusion of U.S. troops from the 575th PIR.

Major Everard Beauchamp, Captain Earl Longstreet, Lieutenant Eddy Ryder, Lieutenant Tom Green, and Lieutenant Clint Hays were present, sipping cocktails while waiting to meet the field marshal.

Captain Duke Slater, while never assigned to the 575th PIR, was also present. Lady Jane had included him on the list since he was the only officer in the last American Volunteer Group (AVG) that would be arriving in Egypt.

Lady Jane had also invited the three WRENS, Sub-Lieutenants Pippa Duncan-Sackville, Bentley St. Ledger and Tabitha Walpole. She wanted them to feel a part of Raiding Forces right from the start, and their presence made the event more social.

While waiting for FM Auchinleck to appear, the new Raiding Forces' officers were making the best of the opportunity to chat up the WRENS. Colonel John Randal and Lady Jane were alone in a corner of the room. This was the first time they had seen each other since she had returned from Kenya with Captain "Geronimo" Joe McKoy and Waldo Treywick.

"Any problems moving the gold?" Col. Randal asked.

"No, it went like a campy spy movie." Lady Jane giggled. "Captain McKoy and Waldo appeared—unexpected and unannounced—at the American Consulate around midnight. There was a sleepy U.S. Marine corporal on duty, but otherwise the place was deserted.

"Captain McKoy showed his U.S. Marshal's badge. Waldo produced his CIC credentials and announced, 'We are not here.'

"The corporal was ordered to go into one of the interior offices, close the door, stay there and not come out until he heard three knocks."

"Three knocks?" Col. Randal said, "That's good."

"Then, a moving crew from the bank came inside and went straight to the basement," Lady Jane said. "They exchanged empty wooden crates for the ones filled with the gold bars Captain McKoy and Waldo spirited out of Abyssinia, re-covered the boxes under the tarp, muscled the crates of gold upstairs, loaded them on a moving van, and drove to the bank."

"The bank president, a chemist to inspect the gold, and my solicitor were waiting in the empty lobby with me. That part of the transaction went smooth as silk—exactly as King outlined—signed, sealed and delivered.

"Most likely," Lady Jane said, "no one will bother to peek under the tarp in the U.S. Consulate's basement for the next fifty years—if ever."

"No more gold bars," Col. Randal said. "Money safely wired to the United States. Captain McKoy and Waldo are millionaires—good job, Jane."

"The coins are proving to be more challenging," Lady Jane said. "We still have to work that out."

"Why not stash 'em in the Swiss bank's safety deposit boxes?" Col. Randal asked.

"Because if the Germans ever invade Switzerland they would nationalize the banks."

Col. Randal said, "There's no place safe these days."

"Agreed," Lady Jane said, "1942 is the most horrible year of the war by far and it seems to be getting worse every day."

Changing the subject, Col. Randal asked, "Any chance you can see your way to promote Pam?"

Lady Jane laughed. "She must have really charmed you during your cozy lunch at the Gezira."

"Roger that," Col. Randal said. "Pam convinced Wing Commander Gordon to have No. 1 Armored Car Company from RAF Habbaniya assigned to Raiding Forces. That's going to solve a lot of my problems—plus we get Squadron Leader Johnny Page, a real stud."

"Pam's promotion was confirmed before we left for Kenya," Lady Jane said. "I have only been waiting for the right moment to surprise her."

"Have I ever been ahead of you on anything?" Col. Randal asked.

Lady Jane said, "You are not supposed to be, John."

"Right," Col. Randal said. "What was I thinking?"

FM Auchinleck entered with two Free French officers, Major General Philippe Francois Marie Leclerc de Hauteclocque, who operated under the *nom de guerre* Leclerc, and his military aide, a tall, elegant Foreign Legion lieutenant sporting the thousand-yard stare of a veteran who has experienced long, intense periods of close combat: Lt. Preston Butterfield III.

FM Auchinleck made the introductions. "Col. Randal is the commander of Raiding Forces. He is currently working on the SOLID GOLD project you received a private briefing about."

Maj. Gen. Leclerc said, "Your reputation has preceded you, Colonel."

Having fought Vichy French on at least three occasions, Col. Randal wondered if that was a good thing.

FM Auchinleck's aide tapped a crystal glass with a knife—the signal to come to attention at military cocktail parties. Lt. Butterfield produced a small leather case for his general. Maj. Gen. Leclerc took out the *Légion d'Honneur,* pinned it to Col. Randal's blouse, then kissed him on both cheeks.

"By official decree—a Hero of France," Maj. Gen. Leclerc informed Col. Randal, who had not seen this coming. Not the medal. Not the kisses.

The attendees at the party clapped politely.

Lady Jane gave him a kiss he liked better.

Maj. Gen. Leclerc said, "I understand, Colonel, you are in need of a French-speaking officer for your patrol made up of mostly Free French Foreign Legion personnel."

"I am, sir."

"Allow me to offer you the services of my *aide-de-camp,* Lieutenant Butterfield."

"After joining the Legion at the outbreak of the war, he served with distinction in France with the 97th Foreign Legion Divisional Reconnaissance Group—GERD 97, an armored cavalry unit famous for its ferocious fighting withdrawal to Dunkirk. Evacuated to England, Lt. Butterfield volunteered to come out to Equatorial Africa," Maj. Gen. Leclerc said.

"Now, with the U.S. in the war, Lieutenant Butterfield has expressed a desire to serve under his own flag."

Col. Randal said, "Willing to jump out of airplanes, Lieutenant?"

"Willing—or will I, sir?"

Col. Randal said, "He'll do fine, General."

CAPTAIN "GERONIMO" JOE MCKOY HAD THE FIVE-SEVEN-Five NCOs who had successfully completed the "Blood in the Sand" gathered out front of RFHQ when Colonel John Randal and Major the Lady Jane Seaborn returned.

Lady Jane went inside, but Col. Randal walked up to the edge of the group to listen in.

"Boys," Capt. McKoy said, "this here is the Colt Monitor—a' factory production BAR with the kind a' modifications preferred by John Dillinger, Pretty Boy Floyd, Machine Gun Kelly, Bonnie and

Clyde and a' bunch a' other nefarious outlaws. They used to take the BARs they stole from National Guard Armories to Hyman Lehman, the master gunsmith out a' San Antonio, Texas, to get these modifications.

"Now I know Hyman. He works on some a' my guns. Says he never realized all them deceased people I just mentioned was outlaws—claimed everyone used aliases. You can believe that story if you want to, but I don't.

"The criminals wanted cut-down BARs to shoot out a' speedin' automobiles. J. Edgar Hoover saw some a' the ones Texas Ranger Frank Hammer and I captured from a' certain couple a'dead bank robbers, and he wanted 'em for his G-men to shoot out a' *their* cars while chasin' the bad guys.

"So Colt came up with the R-80 Automatic Machine Rifle—which they called the 'Monitor'. It weighs sixteen pounds unloaded, has a' cut-down eighteen-inch barrel, a' special oversized Cutts Compensator, shortened hand guard and stock with no bipod.

"The black market price for one a' these Colt Monitors was five thousand dollars, which was four years' salary for your average workin' man durin' the Great Depression.

"Colt gave me this 'un for my efforts deprecatin' the bank robbin' population of the criminal underworld," Capt. McKoy said. "Lest we forget, Frank Hammer and I provided 'em the model they used for the Monitor in the first place.

"You boys already know you're gonna be issued Johnson Light Machine Guns. So, what I'm proposin' today is that while y'all are gettin' used to the new Johnny Guns, we take all the Five-Seventy-Fifth's BARs up to the U.S. 27 Ordnance Company at Heliopolis and have 'em modified to R-80 Monitor standards.

"What say you, boys?"

There was a rumble of enthusiasm from his audience. The NCOs knew weapons. They liked what they saw—a lot of firepower in a small package. It was becoming clear that Raiding Forces paid attention to detail, provided their personnel with the best equipment possible—and let them carry the weapon of their choice.

A big deal to fighting men.

"Maybe," Capt. McKoy said, "I can work us out a' plan with the colonel to truck all you NCOs up to the 27th Ordnance Company. What they're a' doin' in Egypt is a' mystery. Since there ain't no U.S. combat outfits to give 'em any business, they work on repairin' busted British and captured Axis weapons.

"You men can take a' gander at all the exotic weapons, particularly handguns, they've got in stock. Pick yourself out one or two—we'll work out a deal with the 27th to let you have 'em.

"John?"

"Set it up," Col. Randal said. "I'll go with you. We've got plenty of jeeps."

COLONEL JOHN RANDAL AND LIEUTENANT COLONEL SIR Terry "Zorro" Stone were in the third-floor suite, studying the Raiding Forces' table of organization and equipment (TO&E). It was a work in progress. As it stood now, Raiding Regiment included Desert Patrol, Ranger Force, and Lounge Lizard Patrol (made up of the men from the Lancelot Lancer Yeomanry Regiment), plus attached Phantom operators.

The arrival of Johnny Page and his No. 1 Armored Car Company was going to provide four new officers and fifty-odd troops with desert patrol experience. He and Lt. Col. Stone had served together after the siege was lifted at RAF Habbaniya; his armored cars had been attached to Kingcol when it attacked into Baghdad, and they enjoyed an excellent working relationship.

The three Royal Air Force (RAF) platoon leaders were a prize. There were not enough veteran patrol leaders to fill all of Lt. Col. Stone's new Raiding Regiment patrol leader slots. The idea of sending green Ranger officers out into the desert to lead patrols seemed suicidal—though they were going to have to lead one sooner or later.

Each of the No. 1 Armored Car Company lieutenants would be able to step in to take command of a patrol from day one.

In addition, each of the three RAF armored car platoons had a highly qualified navigator—a military specialty in short supply in Raiding

Forces. There were not enough navigators to go around, and that was a serious problem.

Col. Randal could give field commissions to worthy NCOs, create officers and make them patrol leaders. But there was no way to wave a magic wand and produce a navigator.

He said, "I nearly forgot—we have a new Foreign Legion officer. An American named Preston Butterfield III. Comes highly recommended. He can take command of Blue Patrol once it completes its duties training the Rangers. I'll have him report to you as soon as he arrives."

"Excellent," Lt. Col. Stone said. "By the way, only two platoons of Rangers returned from Special Warfare Training Center. What happened?"

Col. Randal said, "One platoon was retained at Seaborn House. We need an experienced officer to command it. Where are we going to find one? Has to be an Achnacarry graduate."

"Butch?" Maj. Stone said.

"He's the best-qualified," Col. Randal said. "But I'm not about to let him remain in England after he completes his tour as an instructor."

"Dick Courtney has gone through Achnacarry," Maj. Stone said.

Lieutenant Dick Courtney was a Gold Coast policeman recruited by Col. Randal when Raiding Forces was marshaling for OPERATION LOUNGE LIZARD, the cutting-out operation on the Portuguese island of Rio Bonita.

"Dick was an excellent Mule Raiding Battalion troop commander with Force N in Abyssinia," Col. Randal said. "He's doing an outstanding job as a patrol leader now.

"Been in Africa almost all his life. He needs to serve out here."

"Roy Kidd?"

"Not about to give up my most successful truck killer."

"Mad Dog is qualified."

"We need him to conduct training from time to time— irreplaceable," Col. Randal said.

"Lionel Chatterhorn?"

"Not a chance. He's living the dream. Always wanted to be a desert explorer—likes raiding even better."

"Well, old stick," Lt. Col. Stone said, "finding the right man does appear to be a problem.

"How about Cord Granger . . ."

Col. Randal said, "Talk to Lieutenant Courtney. See if he has an interest in being assigned to Seaborn House—a promotion goes with it. Tell Dick to come see me if he is."

"Lt. Col. Stone said, "I shall hate to lose him."

"Don't forget, Terry," Col. Randal said, "you have a requirement to assign an RAF radio jeep to every patrol to coordinate close air support as part of Wing Commander Gordon's experiment. That means you can cut one gun jeep from each patrol. I want to keep patrol size uniform at six jeeps per."

"Works for me," Lt. Col. Stone said. "Gives me a pool of experienced operators to plug in where needed. Spread talent around. I like it.

"Get back to you with a plan as soon as I develop one, John."

COLONEL JOHN RANDAL WAS IN THE LIVING AREA OF THE suite cleaning his pistols on the coffee table. He had spread out newspapers to protect the mahogany.

Flanigan announced, "Three navy sub-lieutenants to see you, Colonel."

"Send 'em in."

The WRENS came in and sat on the floor in a semicircle around the coffee table. They appeared to be on a mission, which Col. Randal did not fail to note. The girls were in high spirits.

Sub-Lieutenant Bentley St. Ledger said, "Colonel . . ."

"Whoa," Col. Randal said, "we have an understanding among the officers in Raiding Forces. When we're alone, you get to call me by my first name—like cavalry regiments. Not everybody does it, but I like it when they do."

"OK—John," S/Lt. St. Ledger said. "We have a request."

"What might that be, Bentley?"

"Our hope is to be full-fledged members of the Raiding Forces' team."

"I see," Col. Randal said, which meant he did not have a clue what the WRENS were up to. Long experience with Lieutenant Mandy Paige had taught him to be cautious when dealing with smart, high-spirited girls.

Sub-Lieutenant Tabitha Walpole said, "We would like to be parachute-qualified like Lady Jane's Royal Marines."

"Oh," Col. Randal said. "Great."

"You mean we can?" asked Sub-Lieutenant Pippa Duncan–Sackville in disbelief.

These girls were from the Six Hundred—the powerful families who controlled England. They had spent their entire lives cloistered in upper-class British society, being told "no" to virtually any new idea—conforming, keeping up appearances, and maintaining the status quo being the ironclad rule.

"Sure," Col. Randal said. "Just don't expect to be jumping out of airplanes in the dark of night with a dagger in your teeth on a secret mission any time soon."

The girls laughed. Their enthusiasm was infectious. This was the first time in their lives they were out in the world on their own. They had been to school in Switzerland, but it had been regimented, sheltered, and rigorously chaperoned. They clearly wanted to make a go of it.

Col. Randal could respect that.

S/Lt. St. Ledger said, "Mandy told us parachuting was better than sex."

"That's a little more detail," Col. Randal said, "than I care to comment on, Bentley."

"Brandy and Legs Parker, sir," Flanigan called from the door.

"Send 'em in."

Team Sundance, as the two were known for the SOLID GOLD assignment, walked in. Col. Randal clicked on the minute he saw them. The women were not on a social call.

He noted they did not ask the three WRENS to leave the room. Captain Penelope "Legs" Honeycutt-Parker, OBE, GM, RM, said, "We have a Y-Service radio intercept confirming Seebohm will be at the target, arriving this afternoon to spend two days' leave."

Brandy said, "Mr. Zargo has not been able to place an operative on site in time to get an eyes on verification of the Nazi's arrival."

"Flanigan," Col. Randal called to the ex-policeman at the desk outside the suite, "get Billy Jack and King up here—now."

"Sir!"

As they waited, Col. Randal said, "Ladies, what we're discussing is a SOLID GOLD mission, classified TOP SECRET. Everything you hear is 'Need to Know' and you will not discuss it with anyone—clear?"

The WRENS said, "Clear!"

The girls were more than a little taken aback and excited by the sudden turn of events. Raiding Forces was a place where anything could happen at any time—and did.

They were in the war now.

Brandy said, "Since this mission will involve Sea Squadron, it falls under the Director of Operations Division, Irregular—your first mission to plot, lieutenants."

They heard boots thundering up the stairs, and Captain Billy Jack Jaxx and King burst into the room.

Col. Randal said, "The SOLID GOLD is a go for tonight—lay it out for Brandy and Parker."

Everyone moved to the suite's small briefing area with a wall map of the entire Mediterranean coastline.

The WRENS had not met Capt. Jaxx. They were intrigued. Jack Cool had never met the WRENS. They reminded him of the Tri-Delts at the University of Texas—which could spell trouble.

"The target is a small, secluded resort hotel reserved for German VIPs located on a spit jutting out into the Mediterranean," Capt. Jaxx said, tapping the map with the tip of his Fairbairn knife. "About here.

"You can see it's not on the Via Balbia's right-of-way—perfect for what we have in mind. The hotel is situated about a mile down a gated, private drive from the main highway. We won't find any enemy convoys laagered in the immediate vicinity when we arrive under cover of darkness.

"The plan is for the *King Duck* to transport Duck Patrol to within three miles of a beach located one half-mile west of the resort. The DUKWs will be launched, make their way to shore, move inland to the objective and engage it with its organic weapons.

"On command, Lieutenant Plum-Martin and Wing Commander Gordon will roll in, drop four 250-pound bombs on the target, then strafe it with the combined eight 20mm machine guns of their A-20s."

"Nothing should make it out alive—questions?"

"What are Duck Patrol's organic weapons?" Brandy asked.

"Frank is having Chief Rawlston mount a 37mm COW on one DUKW. The other three will each have a pair of 20mm Oerlikons in addition to a pair of Browning .50 caliber machine guns," Capt. Jaxx said.

"We'll be packing lot of heavy firepower and it's going to be up close and personal when we engage, Brandy—point-blank."

"What is to prevent the Nazis from escaping out the far side?" Capt. Parker asked.

"Colonel Randal, King, Lieutenant Hays, and yours truly will be there, armed to the teeth, hoping they try."

Jack Cool.

"Nicely done, Captain," Brandy said. "Not a perfect plan. I would prefer someone put eyes on Seebohm. But it sounds like the best we could hope for under the circumstances.

Capt. Parker said, "Sounds deadly."

Col. Randal said, "Make it happen."

STRAPHANGERS HOPING TO GO ON THE SOLID GOLD mission started to turn up almost from the minute Team Sundance, the WRENS, Captain Billy Jack Jaxx and King left the suite.

Captain "Geronimo" Joe McKoy and Waldo Treywick, flush with success after successfully extracting their gold bars from the basement of the U.S. Consulate in Kenya, rolled in to Colonel John Randal's suite on the third floor.

Capt. McKoy said, "We heard Duck Patrol is about to sail on a' mission you're headin' up tonight. Me 'n Waldo wanna' tag along, John."

Col. Randal said, "Go see Jack."

James "Baldie" Taylor arrived not long after.

Jim said, "Count me in for the SOLID GOLD."

Col. Randal said, "Go see Jack."

Lieutenant Mandy Paige came in wearing her blue jean cut-offs and peewee cowboy boots.

Lt. Mandy said, "I want to go."

Col. Randal said. "No."

Vice Admiral Sir Randolph "Razor" Ransom appeared.

The Razor said, "Do you mind if I observe tonight?"

"Sir," Col. Randal said, "you are way too senior for me to allow to land behind enemy lines—Director of Operations, Irregular."

VAdm. Ransom said, "Knew there would be a downside to the position."

"Jack Cool on the horn," Flanigan announced from his desk outside the suite.

"Sir," Capt. Jaxx said, "Duck Patrol only has four DUKWs slated to go ashore tonight. If any more people show up requesting permission to accompany the raid, I'll have to add two or three more to accommodate 'em."

"Four's the magic number, Jack. Keep it small," Col. Randal said. "But I've been thinking—why not bring my Raider Patrol 81mm mortar crew along?"

"Not you too, Colonel?"

"Couldn't help myself, Jack."

"Good idea, sir," Capt. Jaxx said. "I should have thought of the mortars myself."

Drop-dead gorgeous Major the Lady Jane Seaborn returned from wherever she had been all morning.

"Hell, no," Col. Randal said, "you can't go."

"What are you talking about, John?"

6
STRIKE FROM THE SEA

THE *KING DUCK* HAD STEAM UP AND WAS READY TO SET sail two hours before sunset. When Colonel John Randal and Major the Lady Jane Seaborn arrived at the dock, a crowd had assembled. There was a drumbeat of excitement in the air.

DUKWs were being hoisted aboard. Captain Billy Jack Jaxx and King were supervising the preparation of the manifest of the personnel involved in the raid. Two Royal Marines were typing up the manifest as people arrived.

A mixed bag of military professionals from different branches of the service and different elements in Raiding Forces were participating in the raid. A lot of straphangers would be along for the ride, but most of the military tourists would not disembark the *King Duck* when Duck Patrol launched.

To the uninitiated, the scene appeared to be absolute chaos. In fact, it was quite orderly. Capt. Jaxx had things well in hand.

James "Baldie" Taylor was there. The MI-6/SOE Chief of Special Operations Middle East Command had managed to talk Jack Cool into letting him man one of the Browning .50 calibers on Col. Randal's command DUKW.

Brandy Seaborn and Captain Penelope "Legs" Honeycutt-Parker were already on board the LCT. It was their mission. They were going to see it through to the end.

Brigadier Raymond J. Maunsell, the chief of SIME, who liked to be called R.J., was waiting to board. He would not be going ashore. However, R.J. was not about to miss this raid.

Captain "Geronimo" Joe McKoy and Waldo were smoking cigars and watching the loading. Capt. McKoy was going to be manning a Browning .50 caliber gun on Col. Randal's command vehicle.

Waldo would also be taking a gun—there were three .50 cals mounted on each DUKW, two in back, and one on the passenger side of the front seat.

Guns, the ace Royal Naval Patrol Service gunner who had volunteered for Desert Patrol to get away from sea duty—having been torpedoed several times and not caring for the experience—was on hand to man Col. Randal's twin 20mm Oerlikon.

Squadron Leader Johnny Page, the CO of No.1 Armored Car Company, had just arrived from RAF Habbaniya and been invited to go along. He was looking forward to his first Commando raid.

Wing Commander Ronald Gordon and recently-promoted Captain Pamala-Plum Martin were on the dock to see the Raiders off. They would be flying the mission later in the evening covering Duck Patrol's withdrawal in a pair of A-20 Havocs, each armed with four 20mm cannons and two 250-pound bombs.

Capt. Plum-Martin said, "Jane told me to thank you for my promotion, John."

"Not true," Col. Randal said. "She had your orders cut before I ever mentioned the idea to her."

The Vargas Girl look-alike Royal Marine said, "It's the thought that counts, love."

Vice Admiral Sir Randolph "Razor" Ransom drove up with his three WRENS—Sub-Lieutenants Tabitha Walpole, Pippa Duncan-Sackville and Bentley St. Ledger. The girls were wearing battle dress uniform (BDU), including Colt .38 Supers in flap holsters on their web belts— Lady Jane had issued the sidearms. The three looked very buttoned-down and proper in tailored BDUs and billed caps pulled down to make a straight line over their eyes, as specified by navy regulations.

The girls had not expected to go on a Commando raid the first night they reported in—welcome to Raiding Forces. When Col. Randal saw the WRENS starting to board the *King Duck,* he said, "What . . ."

"Relax, John," Lady Jane said. "Surely you do not believe observing tonight's operation from the deck of Warthog Finley's LCT is remotely as dangerous as what the girls faced nightly during the Blitz in London."

Col. Randal knew Great Britain had more women in uniform than any country in the world except Russia. And he knew things had been tough during the heavy bombing of London. Still, he did not much care for the idea of the WRENS going in harm's way.

Frank Polanski was inspecting the Coventry Ordnance Works (COW) 37 mm cannon mounted on what would be the gun DUKW tonight. The ex-Marine and former mercenary was a heavy weapons man. Lieutenant Clint Hays had flown in with him.

Lt. Hays reported to Capt. Jaxx, who introduced him to Captain Butch "Headhunter" Hoolihan, the Blue Patrol Leader, who immediately assigned him to man one of the Browning .50s on Jack Cool's DUKW. The Ranger lieutenant had thrown himself into the process of becoming a member of Raiding Forces. His performance was quickly earning him the respect of the Raiders. He did not know it yet, but Hays was slated to be assigned to the "Dirty Deeds Done Quick" small operations group (SOG).

Capt. Jaxx needed one more officer for his SOG. He had his eye on Lieutenant Eddy Ryder of the 575th PIR. The lieutenant had been invited to come along to man one of the other .50 cal. Brownings on Jack Cool's DUKW. Lt. Ryder did not realize it, but the SOLID GOLD mission was the Raiding Forces' equivalent of a job interview.

Sergeant Rex Blackburn, Raider Patrol's 81mm mortar expert, walked up to Col. Randal. "I'm loading twenty-five HE rounds, sir. If that does not produce the desired effect, nothing will, Colonel."

Col. Randal said. "On my command, Sergeant, bring it fast."

"On time, on target, sir!"

Foreign Legion Lieutenant Preston Butterfield III appeared and was sent on board the LCT straightaway.

Lieutenant Mandy Paige arrived. She was piqued at Col. Randal for turning her down when she initially requested to come along. "R.J. invited me to observe with *him*."

"I didn't realize the *King Duck* had turned into a party boat," Col. Randal said.

He knew it was a waste of time to try to keep Lt. Mandy out of anything she wanted to be involved in. So, he did not even try.

"Jane," Col. Randal said, "call RFHQ and order all the Ranger officers to report to the dock. They might as well join this circus too."

The U.S. Attaché to Middle East Command, Colonel Bonner Fellers, arrived. He had heard that troops from the 575th Parachute Infantry Regiment were going to take part in an operation.

"Mind if I come along as an observer?" Col. Fellers asked.

"Negative. This is a TOP SECRET mission," Col. Randal said. "You don't possess the Need to Know."

"I have a TOP SECRET clearance," Col. Fellers protested.

Col. Randal said, "Can't have a detailed report on Raiding Forces' methods and tactics sent back to the War Department. Who knows who would have access to it?"

He knew Col. Fellers was the War Department's most important conduit, providing perspective on operations in Egypt and Libya. What Col. Randal did not know was that the colonel routinely reported British generals were bad, their equipment inferior and that FM Auchinleck was likely to lose the war in Africa—he simply did not want a report on one of Raiding Forces' classified operations floating around.

"Understood," Col. Fellers said. "I'm just trying to do my job."

"I hear you're good at it," Col. Randal said. "No hard feelings?"

Col. Fellers said, "Negative. I understand. Good luck tonight. You're playing for big stakes."

Field Marshal Claude Auchinleck's staff car drove on to the dock. There were none of the usual flags flying or motorcycle outriders escorting him. He did not want to advertise a strategic mission about to get underway.

The field marshal stayed in the car. The success of this mission was of high importance to him. He did not want to interfere.

Col. Randal walked over and reported.

"I came to see your SOLID GOLD off for my own personal satisfaction," FM Auchinleck said, from the back seat of the staff car. "One cannot overemphasize the significance of eliminating Seebohm tonight."

"Understood, sir."

"Godspeed, Colonel."

"We'll do our best, sir."

COLONEL JOHN RANDAL BRIEFED THE MISSION ONE LAST time as soon as the *KING DUCK* slipped its dock and made way. Duck Patrol and all attachments who would be landing ashore made up the front row. They all sat cross-legged on the deck in front of a large map on a tripod. The rest of the audience, everyone on the LCT not performing some duty, gathered around, hung over rails or stood in the backs of the DUKWs to watch.

Col. Randal flipped the canvas cover over the back of the map, revealing a simple schematic of the objective that showed the point of land jutting out into the Mediterranean, the hotel, and the beach Duck Patrol was scheduled to land on. Armed with a four foot-long pointer with a red-painted tip, he walked Duck Patrol through the details of the operation from beginning to end.

He started with a brief Mission Statement designed to tell everyone *what* they were going to do. Col. Randal said, "The Nazis have a VIP resort where certain high-value German officers take short leaves with their girlfriends to relax at the beach. It is located on this point, one mile off the Via Balbia. Our mission is to land Duck Patrol ashore, destroy the hotel, and kill everyone inside."

Next was the Concept of the Operation, designed to explain *how* they were going to accomplish the mission. Col. Randal said, "*King Duck* will sail to within three miles of the target. Captain Hoolihan's Duck Patrol will disembark, land ashore, drop off an 81mm mortar team under Sergeant Blackburn on the beach, and make an approach-march to the grounds of the hotel. There, they will take up a firing position and, on my signal, take it under fire with all organic weapons on the DUKWs.

As Duck Patrol is moving into position, a small party consisting of Captain Jaxx, Lieutenant Hays, King, and myself will exit the DUKWs, work our way on foot to the rear of the hotel and set up an ambush, making sure to stay out of the line of fire. We will be prepared to engage anyone attempting to exit out the far side of the building.

"Once the ambush team is in place, I will put up a single green flare to signal Captain Hoolihan to initiate the attack. When Duck Patrol has exhausted its ammunition, the Headhunter will fire two red flares to signal my team to return, board the DUKWs and exfiltrate back to the beach, pick up the 81mm mortar crew, then motor back to the *King Duck.*

"Upon linking back up with the DUKWs, I will fire three red flares as we begin our withdrawal. They are the signal for the 81mm mortar team to fire for effect on the hotel—twenty-five rounds HE quick.

"When Duck Patrol arrives back on the beach, it will pick up Sergeant Blackburn's mortar crew; the DUKWs will take to the sea and return to the *King Duck.*

"At that point, I will fire red over green flares as a signal to Wing Commander Gordon and Captain Plum-Martin, who will be on station overhead in a pair of A-20 Havocs, to signal they are cleared to make their attack run on the hotel.

"Once Duck Patrol is back on board the *King Duck,* Skipper Finley will make a high-speed dash back to the cover of the RAF air umbrella outside of Alexandria before sunrise.

"What are your questions?"

No one had any questions.

Col. Randal had not mentioned Hauptmann Alfred Seebohm. Anyone who had a Need to Know about the real target of the raid already knew. That part of the mission was classified. Even to most of the men going on the raid.

The briefing was a "frag," or fragment of an order, short and simple in keeping with Raiding Forces' Rules for Raiding. Duck Patrol had already been given a Warning Order and a Patrol Order. It was redundant. Col. Randal's briefing was only to double triple check to make sure there were no late-breaking questions or misunderstandings.

Every man and woman knew their assignment. They knew what every other person's job was. In the event of casualties, Duck Patrol would be able to task-reorganize on the move under fire and continue the mission.

The raid was on.

THE NIGHT BECAME COLD AT SEA WHEN THE SUN WENT down. Colonel John Randal was sitting behind the wheel of his command DUKW, number one in the line of four that would disembark down the ramp when the *King Duck* arrived on station three miles off the target beach. He was not going to drive it—Captain Butch "Headhunter" Hoolihan would be driving when the two-and-a-half-ton truck rolled into the sea.

Captain "Geronimo" Joe McKoy was sitting on the passenger's side. Waldo Treywick and Guns were on the bench seat behind them. Lieutenant Mandy Paige appeared at the driver's side of the DUKW, crawled in over Col. Randal and curled up on the bench seat against his shoulder to keep warm.

She was considering forgiving him for turning down her initial request to come along tonight.

"Where's Billy Jack?" Col. Randal said. "I thought you'd be hanging out with him."

Lt. Mandy said, "Jack Cool is acting in the capacity of self-appointed unofficial escort officer for the WRENS at the moment."

Capt. McKoy said, "Smokin' lamp's lit, Guns. Why don't you go find someplace and light up one a' Waldo's cigars."

After the Royal Navy Patrol Service ace gunner had departed, Capt. McKoy said, "You shoulda' come along on the Kenya trip, John."

"I heard it went down as planned."

Waldo said, "What a' hoot. Them fake CIC credentials you had made for me really done the trick, Colonel. And Joe, well, he told the duty Marine to go in an office with no windows and not come out until he got the signal.

"Joe disconnected the phone and brought it out a' the office. Then he went out to the truck and got the man a' case a' South African Tusker beer to keep him occupied."

Capt. McKoy said, "Nobody likes beer better 'n a' United States Marine."

Col. Randal said, "Nice touch, Captain."

"King gave us good advice," Capt. McKoy said. "And Lady Jane's man made the rest a' the deal real easy. Sure got me 'n Waldo outta' a' genuine pickle about U.S. citizens not bein' able to own gold.

"I'd been plenty concerned about crackin' that nut."

"How does it feel being millionaires?" Lt. Mandy asked.

"It don't feel like nothin'," Waldo said, " 'cept you can buy better cigars."

Col. Randal took off his bomber jacket with the fur collar and draped it over Lt. Mandy. He pulled on his sand green parachute smock, which he intended to wear ashore. It had big pockets full of grenades, flare rounds and other toys that might come in handy later.

"Hmmmmm! What a fabulous leather jacket, John," Lt. Mandy said. "Where did you find this? I want one."

"A one-eyed bandit chief named Gubbo Rekash gave it to me in Abyssinia. Captured from an Italian pilot," Col. Randal said. "Probably your old boyfriend."

"I never dated an Italian pilot," Lt. Mandy laughed. "That was a joke. What does Gubbo Rekash mean?"

"Cheap Bribe . . ."

KAAAAWHAAAGA! KAAAAWHAAAGA! KAAAAWHAAAGA!

A loudspeaker blared, "*NOW HEAR THIS. NOW HEAR THIS. ALL HANDS, MAN YOUR ACTION STATIONS! COLONEL RANDAL, REPORT TO THE BRIDGE!*"

Jumping out of the jeep and running up the stairs of the ladder to the bridge, Col. Randal had no idea what was happening. It could be anything. Sailors were racing to their action stations as if their hair was on fire.

When he arrived, Acting Provisional Sub-Lieutenant Skipper Warthog Finley was standing with a group consisting of Vice Admiral Sir Randolph "Razor" Ransom, James "Baldie" Taylor, Brigadier

Raymond J. Maunsell, Captain Penelope "Legs" Honeycutt-Parker, and Brandy Seaborn.

"Two US. Navy destroyer escorts (DEs) screening our mission were pinging and scored a solid contact, Colonel," Skipper Finley said. "We got us an enemy submarine dead ahead. Request permission to attack— ain't any time to waste—we should have already been doing it. The navy ain't going to be able to get there in time."

Col. Randal was the raid commander, but he was not the mission commander –Brandy was. She and Capt. Parker were running SOLID GOLD. It was not his call. However, it was not necessary for anyone who was not already aware of it to know the command structure.

Brandy said, "So, what are you requesting, Skipper?"

"I want to make an attack run," Skipper Finley said. "I need permission to break off and attack that sub, and I need it fast."

"How much time is this going to cost us?" Col. Randal asked.

"Only have enough depth charges for one pattern," Skipper Finley said. "Give me a half hour—maybe less."

Col. Randal ran through the mission in his head. They had to reach the SOLID GOLD target, carry out the raid, re-embark and sail back to the RAF air cover outside Alexandria before sunrise.

Since the *King Duck* was signaling checkpoints to Wing Commander Ronnie Gordon and Captain Pamala Plum-Martin as they crossed, a delay would not affect them. The pilots could adjust the time they took off.

VAdm. Ransom was clearly chomping at the bit to take charge—as was his right as the Director of Operations (Irregular). The *King Duck* was a Royal Navy Patrol Service ship which fell under his command. However, to his credit, the Razor restrained himself.

Jim and R.J. were not showing any expression. They were interested spectators to the high drama unfolding.

Col. Randal glanced at Brandy. She winked.

"Let's do it," Col. Randal said. "Kill your sub, Skipper Finley."

The entire decision-making process had lasted less than thirty seconds, but it seemed like a lot longer.

Skipper Finley did not waste a second. He started barking commands. The *King Duck* swung on to a new heading. It was racing as fast as an ungainly LCT can go, straight toward the location where the destroyer escorts' ASDIC sonar had made contact.

"NOW HEAR THIS. THIS IS THE CAPTAIN SPEAKING. WE HAVE ESTABLISHED CONTACT WITH AN ENEMY SUBMARINE AND ARE MAKING AN ATTACK."

The crowd on the bridge was gathered around the outside of the tiny radio shack while Skipper Finley leaned inside to discuss developments with his operator. He gave a running commentary of developments to the observers.

"DEs always ping any time they put to sea. They got a hit dead ahead. I have notified them the *King Duck* is a special-purpose vessel with six depth charges. The two DEs will vector us to the target. Now what we do is we run straight at it and lay down our pattern."

VAdm. Ransom explained, "Normally when a ship is pinging, when it gets within three hundred yards of the submarine, it loses contact and has to guesstimate distance to the sub. In our case, the two DE's are going to vector us to the target and when we reach the intersection of the two azimuths they provide, Skipper Finley will drop his depth charges.

The moon was out, and the night was cold. A shiver of anticipation ran through the people on the bridge. Fighting submarines was not something they did every day.

And, everyone was aware that the sub might fight back with deck guns and torpedoes.

Brandy was leaning against Col. Randal. She whispered, "Did I make the right call?"

"Roger."

"Father was about to have a cardiac arrest," Brandy giggled. "He wanted to go after the sub so badly."

"I saw that."

"Estimated depth," Skipper Finley announced, "three hundred feet."

"STAND BY TO LAUNCH DEPTH CHARGES," he shouted to the crew standing by the improvised rack on the stern of the LCT.

VAdm. Ransom took out a stopwatch, "At three hundred feet, it will take approximately twenty-eight seconds for the depth charges to reach their depth."

"EXECUTE, EXECUTE, EXECUTE!" Skipper Finley commanded.

The sailors on the stern released the depth charges, and the big cans began rolling into the sea. Everyone on board the *King Duck* rushed to the nearest rail and leaned over to see the results.

Nothing happened.

VAdm. Ransom stared at his stopwatch. He started counting down at ten seconds. "Ten, nine, eight . . ."

Off the stern, the depth charges started going off. There were six of them—muffled explosions going off like a string of dominoes. Geysers shot twenty feet into the air, and the surface of the Mediterranean roiled white foam circles in the moonlight.

Skipper Finley's radio operator was on the radio reporting the contact and requesting support from any Allied warship in the area. The two DE's were racing to close up on the submarine.

VAdm. Ransom and Skipper Finley were studying the area where the depth charges had been dropped through night glasses. Nothing but dead fish appeared on the surface.

Then a gasp went up from the crowd on the bridge as the nose of a submarine rose out of the water. Every person on the *King Duck* who could man a weapon immediately engaged. Some were even firing their handguns at the sub.

Skipper Finley had packed on as many antiaircraft machine guns aboard the *King Duck* as he could scrounge, making his LCT a virtual flak ship. An impressive amount of firepower was being directed at the submarine porpoising in their wake. Duck Patrol members were lining the rail firing their individual weapons—M-1941 Johnson LMGs— getting their first introduction to combat.

A blizzard of fire was vectored toward the enemy craft.

"Italian—Regia Marina," VAdm. Ransom said. "Platino-class."

Then the submarine slowly rolled over and disappeared beneath the waves.

It was almost as if it had never been there at all.

The WRENS were delighted.

"Does this happen often?" Sub-Lieutenant Tabitha Walpole asked breathlessly.

"Oh, yeah," Capt. Jaxx said. "We do this kind of stuff almost every night."

Jack Cool.

KING DUCK ARRIVED ON STATION ALMOST RIGHT ON time, three miles off the point of land where the VIP resort hotel stood. The submarine action had taken a lot less than the thirty minutes estimated. Duck Patrol made ready to go ashore.

Acting Provisional Sub-Lieutenant Skipper Warthog Finley was talking to Colonel John Randal, who was sitting behind the Browning .50 cal. on the passenger side of Captain Butch "Headhunter" Hoolihan's DUKW—the Headhunter was at the wheel. James "Baldie" Taylor was sitting on the bench seat in the middle.

When Col. Randal exited the DUKW to flank the hotel with his ambush team, Jim was going to slide over and man the big machine gun.

"Ready, Colonel?" Skipper Finley rasped, in his whisky-ruined voice.

"Give the word."

"Permission to disembark," Skipper Finley said to Capt. Hoolihan. "Give 'em hell, Butch."

Capt. Hoolihan put the DUKW into gear and began the sickening drive down the ramp into the Mediterranean. No matter how many times Col. Randal made this descent, he always thought the truck was going to nose-dive straight to the bottom the minute it hit the water.

Through some miracle of flotation, the DUKW plunged in, righted itself as Capt. Hoolihan shifted to Duplex Drive, and started motoring its way toward the beach. It was not possible to see the shoreline at this point. The Headhunter was sailing on a compass heading.

The DUKW bobbed and weaved as Duck Patrol snaked its way toward the objective. Then it was rushing through the surf toward the beach. Capt. Hoolihan shifted out of Duplex Drive and drove up on the sand.

The three trailing DUKWs in the column pulled up on dry land.

In the last vehicle, Sergeant Rex Blackburn offloaded his 81mm mortar. While the two-man crew was setting it up, he untied the rope that was towing a rubber raft with a small outboard motor behind the DUKW. In the event Duck Patrol was unable to egress back across this beach, the raft was their ticket back to the *King Duck*.

While the mortar was being set up, Col. Randal, Captain Billy Jack Jaxx, Lieutenant Clint Hays, and King exited their DUKWs and headed inland, straight toward the hotel. All four were armed with .30 caliber M-1941 Johnson Light Machine Guns.

Col. Randal's initial impression of the weapon was not entirely favorable. The M-1941 Johnson was twice as heavy as his .9mm Beretta MAB-38A, meaning he could only carry half as much .30 caliber ammunition. And the magazine stuck out to the left side, making it seem unwieldy for someone who was a skilled snap shooter.

However, tonight was a field test for the LMG—he decided to reserve judgment.

The moon was up. The night was cool. No one noticed as the four Raiders made their way toward the objective. The ground was firm, what was described in the desert as "good going." Capt. Hoolihan would not experience any trouble reaching the location where Duck Patrol planned to set up a firing position on the objective.

The hotel was a half-mile from the beach. A pebbled path had been created for the guests to follow. Col. Randal and his team followed the pebbles until the hotel came into sight.

The building was not the typical *Beau Geste* mud structure like the remote forts, or a roadside hostel like the *casa stratas* on the Via Balbia. Instead, it looked like a modern roadside motel, built in an L-shape with a swimming pool in the center.

The Nazis had a rigid hierarchy for rest and recreation facilities. This particular retreat was for officers of brigade command and below to the grade of lieutenant colonel. In certain rare cases, it could be used by more junior officers holding positions of exceptional responsibility or who had distinguished themselves in combat.

Captain Alfred Seebohm fell into the rare exception category— though if the truth were to be known, he was more valuable to Afrika Korps than all its brigade commanders together. They could be replaced.

The Hauptmann was irreplaceable, arguably the most valuable asset in Afrika Korps, second only to Rommel.

Nearly every guest had brought his girlfriend or mistress with him for the stay. That fact did not bother Col. Randal. There was a price to be paid for collaboration with the enemy.

The only thing stirring on the objective was a couple having a late-night swim in the pool.

Col. Randal said, "King."

The Merc handed Capt. Jaxx his Johnson LMG. He walked straight to the pool. The two lovers were entwined in the shallow end when he arrived, unnoticed, and shot both of them twice with his silenced .22 High Standard Military Model D.

WHIIICH, WHIIICH, WHIIICH, WHIIICH.

Duck Patrol drove up, making surprisingly little noise. As Capt. Hoolihan pulled into position, Col. Randal and his team moved around the side of the hotel to set up their ambush. It was important they not be in the line of fire once the engagement commenced.

A small structure behind the hotel appeared to be an air raid shelter. Col. Randal and crew took up a position next to it. They had a clear view of the entire back and down the length of the far side of the building. If anyone tried to escape a room from a back window, the ambush party would have a clear shot at them.

Col. Randal took out his flare pistol and fired the signal to initiate the attack.

The instant the parachute flare popped open, a thunderstorm of automatic weapons fire erupted with the 37mm COW booming. The building was almost instantly turned into a cheese shredder, riddled with a hailstorm of .50 caliber and 20mm bullets.

Frank's 37mm COW was pounding the structure methodically—working from one end to the other. The building had not been built to withstand anything like this—it was a pleasure resort. The structure was coming apart.

Then one end caught fire.

People inside were screaming. Some broke out of the back door of what was most likely an entertainment room or the restaurant in the main part of the building. They ran toward the bunker.

Col. Randal said, "Now."

Four .30 caliber Johnson LMGs roared. The group of Nazis were was swept off their feet. Col. Randal had to admit that the firepower was impressive. He decided it might even be possible to figure out some way to get used to the awkward placement of the magazine.

Duck Patrol kept up its high rate of fire. Capt. Hoolihan had brought along a double basic load of ammunition. The roar was continuous.

No more screaming was coming from the building.

The signal for Col. Randal's ambush team to return went up. They moved out quickly, with King leading the way. Studying the objective on the way back to the DUKWs, they could see that it was highly unlikely anyone had survived the onslaught of the massive firepower delivered at point-blank range. Eight 20mm Oerlikons, twelve Browning .50 caliber machine guns, and Frank's 37mm COW had placed an intense, concentrated cone of fire on the target.

The hotel was a burning ruin.

Capt. Hoolihan had Duck Patrol turned around and ready for the return trip to the beach by the time Col. Randal arrived. The DUKWs were rolling before his team had completely climbed on board. The Headhunter had no intention of hanging around any longer than absolutely necessary.

Col. Randal put up the signal for Sgt. Blackburn to commence his 81mm mortar fire mission.

The sound of the first round thumping out of the mortar was almost instantaneous. The next twenty-four rounds to leave the tube were rapid-fire. It seemed like forever, but then the first mortar round slammed home. After it impacted, there was a flurry of mortar rounds exploding on the target in rapid succession. Sgt. Blackburn was one of the foremost 81mm experts in the British army. The barrage was dead on target, and it was deadly.

By the time Duck Patrol arrived on the beach, Sgt. Blackburn had the mortar broken down. His men pitched it in the back of the last DUKW, tied the raft back to the rear bumper, and then the four amphibious trucks were swimming toward the *King Duck.*

Col. Randal fired the signal clearing Wing Commander Ronald Gordon and Captain Pamala Plum-Martin to make their attack. No sooner had the red-over-green flares cracked open than the two Havocs rolled in, each dropping a single 250-pound bomb.

The pair of explosions was earth-shattering. Both aircraft pulled out, circled around, and came in on another attack run to drop the second of their 250-pound bombs with equally devastating effect.

Now out of bombs, the Havocs began making gun runs—firing the four 20mm cannons mounted in their noses. The A-20s continued making strafing runs until both aircraft had expended all of their ammunition. The Havocs pulverized the target.

Duck Patrol arrived on board the *King Duck*. In the distance, the target could be seen burning. It seemed impossible that anyone could have survived unscathed. However, there was no guarantee of that.

The WRENS were on hand when Col. Randal ordered Skipper Finley, "Let's get the hell out of Dodge."

The girls started laughing, giddy with relief—like a lot of other people on board the LCT. The WRENS had been told Col. Randal said that after missions.

Everyone wanted to be able to say they had heard the command. The only way was to go on a raid and be physically present when he did—something the WRENS had never expected to do in their wildest imagination.

Now the girls felt like they were officially a part of Raiding Forces.

7
GODDESS OF LUCK

COLONEL JOHN RANDAL AND MAJOR THE LADY JANE Seaborn were sitting behind A palm in the back of the Gezira Club restaurant. The place was packed. A sprinkling of officers in U.S. uniform was showing up now—mostly Air Corps. Not one person in the restaurant knew about last night's raid.

And that was the way Col. Randal liked it.

Lady Jane was entertaining him with a story about Colonel, then Major, and now Brigadier Orde Wingate. When last heard from in Cairo, he had attempted suicide, been declared insane and returned to England for psychological therapy after being reduced in rank, his career in shambles.

"Orde," Lady Jane said, "wrote a paper about guerrilla operations in his spare time while he was undergoing psychiatric treatment. The Wingate family is exceptionally well-connected. Through their efforts, the paper ended up on the Prime Minister's desk.

"He read it.

"Desperate to find anyone who would fight, Churchill persuaded the doctors to certify Orde as sane again. He sent the paper to the chief of the Imperial General Staff for comment, and he had a copy delivered to Field Marshal Wavell in India."

Lady Jane said, "The General Staff was noncommittal, not overly interested in unorthodox theory about the art of guerrilla warfare penned by a madman."

"Have a point," Col. Randal said.

Lady Jane said, "Wavell, one of Orde's patrons from his days with the Jewish Night Squads, loved the paper. The field marshal requested Wingate be assigned to the China/Burma/India theatre of operations, where his theories could be put into action.

"Overnight, Major Wingate became Brigadier Wingate. He is now Wavell's senior irregular warfare advisor."

"An insane, un-insane, suicidal, guerrilla strategist," Col. Randal said. "That's some story, Jane."

"I have asked you this question before, John," Lady Jane said. "Do you believe we British are taking this war seriously?"

"Sometimes," Col. Randal said, "it doesn't seem like it."

"On another subject . . . and tell me the truth," Lady Jane said, "is there a reason you seem so distant lately? Have I offended you? Do you have another girl?"

"What?" Col. Randal said, attempting to fake surprise and doing a bad job of it. This conversation was not going to end well.

"Distant?"

Lucky for Col. Randal, James "Baldie" Taylor and Brigadier Raymond J. Maunsell appeared at the table in the nick of time.

Jim said, "R.J. and I wanted to drop by to tell you we concur last night's operation was the best-planned, most perfectly executed small-scale raid anyone could ask for. A classic combined arms masterpiece. Nice job."

R.J. said, "We informed Field Marshal Auchinleck of our sentiments."

"Jack and King planned the mission," Col. Randal said. "Pam and Ronnie Gordon coordinated the air assets. Admiral Ransom and Warthog Finley handled the navy side. Butch commanded Duck Patrol.

"Jane had me restricted to light duty," Col. Randal said. "She only agreed to let me go along for the ride."

Lady Jane laughed.

"We all know that not to be *entirely* true," Jim said.

"Unfortunately," R.J. said, "Hauptmann Seebohm was nowhere near the objective when the raid went in."

Col. Randal said, "Not good."

R.J. said, "Y-Service intercepts confirmed the captain canceled his reservations at the last minute—the man has more lives than a cat."

"We've missed him twice," Col. Randal said.

"Nevertheless," Jim said, "Raiding Forces took out a number of key Nazis—caused Rommel actual pain. Officers of the caliber it will not be easy for Afrika Korps to replace."

"Not to forget," R.J. said, "Skipper Finley scored his second confirmed submarine kill. That alone made the operation worthwhile—a bar for his DSO.

"How'd the field marshal take the news," Col. Randal asked, "about Seebohm?"

"Field Marshal Auchinleck," Jim said, "is in a full-blown state of depression—classified information not to leave this table."

"John will get Seebohm," Lady Jane said. "Only a question of when."

For someone under suspicion of being a Nazi spy, she sounded very sure of herself.

THE RANGER OFFICERS WERE ASSEMBLED IN THE MAIN briefing room off the Tactical Operations Center (TOC) at Raiding Forces' Headquarters. Colonel John Randal was providing them the benefit of his ideas about how Raiding Forces planned and carried out their raids and patrols. He was indoctrinating his new troop commanders into his thought process: he wanted them to perform as special operations officers instead of parachute infantry officers—two entirely different schools of thought. A distinction not taught at most military schools, certainly not at the Infantry School at Ft. Benning.

"We combine intelligence with operations," Col. Randal said. "The idea is to have hard intelligence and soft targets. Then we conduct detailed planning for each mission.

"The idea is to strike unexpectedly, usually at night, utilizing the elements of surprise and speed, exercising extreme violence—the trick is to concentrate every ounce of firepower at our disposal on the target, and then disappear back out to sea or into the vastness of the desert.

"Hit and run.

"Then, do it again somewhere else a long way away. Raiding Forces never attacks places with names, and we try to never fight stand-up battles."

Lieutenant Stephanie Fawcett-Tatum, the Royal Marine duty officer, signaled from the back of the room.

"Take ten, gentlemen," Col. Randal said. "Smoke 'em if you've got 'em." He walked back to see what she wanted.

"R.J. is outside in his car," Lt. Fawcett-Tatum said. "He would like a word with you, sir."

"Really?"

"He sent his driver in, John."

"Have Colonel Stone take over here."

"Yes, sir."

Col. Randal went outside to find Brigadier Raymond J. Maunsell sluing in the back of his staff car with the window rolled down. R.J.'s driver was standing under a palm tree away from the vehicle, smoking a cigarette. Col. Randal walked up to the car.

"Colonel," R.J. said, "I need you to do something for me. You shall find it distasteful; however, it has to be done."

Col. Randal clicked on.

"Do you believe in coincidences?"

"Not really, sir."

"Nor I," R.J. said. "In my business, you shall not last long if you do."

"Why do you ask, sir?"

"Seebohm canceled at the last minute?" R.J. asked. "Was he tipped off? Who could have warned him?"

Col. Randal stared hard at the chief of Security Intelligence Middle East—arguably the best spy catcher in the world, not saying a word.

"I want you to arrange for Lady Jane to go to Oasis X," R.J. said. "Do not let her come back to Cairo until you hear from me. She is not to have access to the Phantom long-range radio transmitter."

"Wrap up this spy hunt, Brigadier," Col. Randal said. "Jane already suspects I'm *distant*—whatever that means. You're putting me in a bad situation."

R.J. said, "I realize that."

"Jane has zero interest in politics," Col. Randal said. "She's not your mole."

"My job is to protect the security of the United Kingdom at all costs," R.J. said. "Emotion plays no part in the actions I have to take in order to accomplish that objective.

"Do you believe I would be here having this conversation with you, a man whom I consider a friend, if it were not in the interest of national defense?"

"No," Col. Randal said. "I don't."

COLONEL JOHN RANDAL WALKED BACK INSIDE RFHQ. AS he went past the briefing room on his way upstairs, he could hear the Ranger officers laughing. Lieutenant Colonel Sir Terry "Zorro" Stone was holding court. Since most of the people present would be working for him in the Raiding Regiment, it was a chance for everyone to get to know each other.

It sounded like they were getting off to a rollicking good start.

Lt. Col. Stone said, "Winnie the Pooh—I mean the Prime Minister—has written 'battles are won by maneuver and slaughter. The more one does of the former, the less one has to do the latter' or words to that effect. I was never good at memorization. So that is what we shall expect you lads to do at every opportunity—maneuver."

The Rangers were laughing again as Col. Randal went upstairs to his suite.

Flanigan was on the desk. Major the Lady Jane Seaborn was away in Cairo doing something with Lieutenant Mandy Paige. King was off with Captain Billy Jack Jaxx.

He had the suite to himself.

Col. Randal picked up a list of the proposed assignments that Major Travis McCloud, the commander of Ranger Force, had made to Lt. Col. Stone. He was supposed to be studying it, but in fact he sat, stared at it, and did not read a word.

"Mr. Treywick to see you, sir."

"Send him in."

Waldo came in and took a seat.

Col. Randal said, "We've got a problem."

"What's new about that?"

"The Ranger Patrol TO&E," Col. Randal said, "calls for six patrols—and six patrol leaders. We have enough officers, but it means using green lieutenants.

"I did not intend to do that."

"Ain't real good," Waldo said. "We operate in a mean environment, Colonel. Our AO ain't no place for beginners. A' patrol can go out and vanish—never heard from again."

"I'm penciling you in to break in one of the new Ranger Force patrol leaders," Col. Randal said.

"Ride with him for three or four patrols until you feel he's competent on his own. Like you did with me in Abyssinia when we started hunting man-eaters."

"I hope," Waldo said, "whoever you assign me to babysit shows more initial aptitude for patrol leadin' than you did killin' bad cat."

"If he doesn't," Col. Randal said, "you can whip him into shape.

"What did you want to see me about, Mr. Treywick?"

"Colonel," Waldo said, "you know I ain't real good at talkin' 'bout personal stuff. Ain't had much practice. You're the closest thing to family I got. Emancipated me from slavery, always treated me with respect, allowed me an' Joe to freelance our loot outta' Abyssinia— never said a' word."

"I didn't know what you two were up to," Col. Randal said.

"Yeah, but you knew we was up to somethin'. Let us do it, probably against your better judgment, too," Waldo said. "Didn't ask no unnecessary questions—looked the other way."

"What I'm tryin' to get at, Colonel, is one a' these days you and Lady Jane is goin' to get hitched. I wanna' do somethin' when you do."

"Like what?" Col. Randal asked.

"I checked on that rule a' thumb you told me and Joe about pickin' the exact right size for diamond ear studs—sounded like somethin' outta' the Three Bears. Turns out you was right about two carats bein' the perfect number," Waldo said. "I checked it out.

"But there ain't no limit on the size of the stone in a' engagement ring. I done confirmed that, too. Bigger is better, and I got you a' monster rock."

"Really?'

"Well, actually," Waldo said, "it's your diamond—I been holdin' it for you."

"I don't have a diamond, Mr. Treywick."

"You remember," Waldo said, "the first day when you shot that ras off his mule when you, Butch, and Kaldi parachuted in to invade Abyssinia all by yourselfs?"

"I do."

"When you did, I sent Rita and Lana up to retrieve his weapon and that mean white mule you named Parachute. But what they was really after was the little leather pouch the ras was wearin' 'round his neck."

Waldo reached inside his collar and pulled out a tiny bag he was wearing around *his* neck on a leather string. He slipped it over his head and handed it to Col. Randal.

"Take a' gander at that."

Col. Randal opened the sack and out rolled a diamond the size of a bird's egg. The stone flared when it struck the light.

"Now that particular stone has got itself a' real interestin' history," Waldo said. "The professor and me found it when we come across where all them gold bars and other looted treasure was hid. The diamond was danglin' down from the forehead of a stone statue of a real fine-lookin' woman—and I do mean Lady Jane quality.

"Just about then the ras showed up, captured me, and chased the professor out a' the country like it said in that Chicago newspaper story you read. Since I was holdin' the diamond, that low-life shifta bandit got it.

"The ras claimed the statue was the Goddess a' Luck and the stone would bring whoever possessed it the same."

Col. Randal said, "Wasn't very lucky for him."

"Not after you showed up," Waldo said. "I never told the man, but the professor had said an inscription on the statue identified the woman as the Goddess a' Love—Sheba her own self."

"This the same professor," Col. Randal said, "who thought you found Solomon's lost gold mine?"

"Man had a' colorful imagination," Waldo said. "But that statue could a' been Sheba—like I said—looked a' lot like Lady Jane but not as pretty 'cause she wasn't smilin'. Abyssinians believe to this day the queen was one a' them.

"It's a part a' their oral history."

"So you're giving me a diamond you say already belongs to me, as a wedding present?" Col. Randal said. "Very generous of you, Mr. Treywick."

"Been waitin' for the right time," Waldo said. "I'm thinkin' this is it."

"Jane's married," Col. Randal said. "There's not going to be any engagement, much less a marriage."

Col. Randal could not tell Mr. Treywick about the MI-5 investigation or that Lady Jane was suspected of being an enemy agent and might be going to prison or worse.

"Colonel," Waldo said, "you left me out a' that earring deal you and Brandy done. Hurt my feelins—not that I have hardly any. Kinda came as a' surprise the way it felt.

"When you and Lady Jane do decide to get engaged, I want in on the deal—she ain't gonna stay married to that low-life sailor forever."

"What am I supposed to do with this diamond?" Col. Randal asked.

"That's your problem startin' right now," Waldo said. "Been a' serious main strain totin' it around all these many months. Anyone finds out you got somethin' like that secreted on your person, it'd be like signin' your own death warrant. Cairo's almost as bad as Abyssinia when it comes to somethin' like 'at."

Col. Randal said, "I can see how it would be."

MAJOR THE LADY JANE SEABORN ARRIVED NOT LONG after Waldo had departed. Colonel John Randal quickly slipped the leather thong over his neck and tucked the pouch containing the diamond inside his faded khaki BDU blouse.

Lady Jane said, "I want to take the WRENS to visit Oasis X. And I would like you with us, John."

Col. Randal froze. Was she a psychic? Did she know about R.J.'s visit? Was there an inside source monitoring the spy hunt, briefing her on its progress—keeping her one jump ahead?

"Any reason to go to the oasis right now?" Col. Randal asked.

"Yes," Lady Jane said. "I need a break from being Claude's social secretary. He turned his residence into a bachelor officer's quarters. Made a mistake when he chose not to bring his wife out to Egypt. Though, that is not my real reason."

Col Randal asked, "What is?"

"Between us," Lady Jane said, "not to leave this room?"

"Scout's honor."

"The Auk has lost his confidence," Lady Jane said. "The field marshal believes he cannot beat the Desert Fox. I choose not to be a part of his defeatism."

"Are you serious?"

"Totally," Lady Jane said. "For some reason, our side decided to create the 'Rommel is invincible' myth. Now our own commander believes it."

Col. Randal said, "Propaganda's not supposed to boomerang."

"Captain McKoy claims we created the Rommel legend to make our army look better when we ultimately defeat him," Lady Jane said.

"If that was the plan, it overachieved."

"Rommel is a brilliant tactical commander," Col. Randal said. "That said, he squanders his troops and depletes his equipment by constantly attacking for no long-term gain. Every one of Afrika Korps' offensives ended up right back where it started sooner or later.

"The end result is always the same. The Desert Fox begging Berlin for reinforcements—you read the same intel reports I do."

"True," Lady Jane said.

"Auchinleck's as good a battle commander as Rommel; maybe better," Col. Randal said. "During CRUSADER, he took personal command and turned around a disaster."

"Agreed," Lady Jane said.

Col. Randal said, "If the Desert Fox was a military genius, he would pre-position supply points down the Via Balbia. Then he could win this thing fairly easily. But he doesn't—Rommel attacks, attacks, attacks."

"You make me feel better," Lady Jane said. "Captain McKoy says legend makes bad history."

"He's right about that," Col. Randal said. "OK, let's go to Oasis X."

He had no intention of ever telling R.J. or Jim the trip was Jane's idea.

COLONEL JOHN RANDAL KNOCKED ON THE DOOR TO Brandy Seaborn's suite. She was expecting him. He had called ahead. They sat on the couch in the living area.

Col. Randal took the leather thong off his neck and rolled the Queen of Sheba diamond out onto the coffee table. Brandy gasped in disbelief. It took a lot to impress the golden girl.

He told her the whole story from start to finish—including Jane being the target of an MI-5 investigation, which, unknown to him, Brandy was already aware of.

"Some tale, handsome—Sheba's diamond," Brandy said when he finished, rolling the stone in the palm of her hand. "You were right to come to me with this."

"If anyone finds out what I just told you," Col. Randal said, "my effectiveness as commander of Raiding Forces will be over."

"No one shall," Brandy said. "We can fix part of the problem. The MI-5 inquiry has to run its course. Do not worry, John. It will."

"R.J. better make it fast," Col. Randal said. "I don't like keeping secrets from Jane. She's already suspicious. Says I'm *distant*."

"Counterintelligence proceeds at its own pace," Brandy said. "My guess is R.J. will move to a resolution as quickly as possible. Whoever the Good Source is, he or she has to be shut down . . . and quickly.

"Our primary concern is to make sure when the investigation is over, it is absolutely crystal-clear to Jane you were standing by her the entire time," Brandy said. "Difficult; you and Jane are *too* close. You finish each other's sentences."

"I don't think she's a spy," Col. Randal said.

"Jane will eventually find out she was under suspicion once MI-5 wraps up the case," Brandy said. "It is vital she never dream you doubted her—even for a moment."

"How do I demonstrate support," Col. Randal asked, "for something Jane doesn't know about?"

"What is required, John, is a grand gesture," Brandy said. "One that can only be interpreted as proving your undying loyalty during the period when things were at their darkest."

"I'm for that," Col. Randal said.

"Jane is still married, so you two cannot become engaged," Brandy said. "However, it is not unknown in the Six Hundred for couples to divorce. The process is quite lengthy. Takes years because of the financial entanglements that have to be resolved—even when the proceedings are amicable.

"It is often the custom in the upper, upper class for one side—or even both sides—in a divorce to have a paramour they intend to marry long before the legalities are settled.

"In such cases, it is accepted practice for a ring—called a promise ring—to be exchanged with the intended."

"I see," Col. Randal said, which meant he did not have a clue what Brandy was talking about.

"Sheba's diamond will make a spectacular promise ring," Brandy said.

"You surprise her with it now. The timing will prove beyond any doubt at a later date that you announced your commitment to marry her, even though you were aware she was under suspicion of being an enemy operative.

"Jane will love it—the ring *and* the thought. When you finally *are* married one day, the promise ring sporting the Sheba diamond will serve as her wedding ring."

"Sounds like a plan," Col. Randal said, although he had not expected this turn of events—promised to be married. Then married. Like a string of dominoes bringing the curtain down on his bachelor days. Uh-oh.

"Are you positive you would not rather run away to Kathmandu with me, John?" Brandy laughed. "I want Sheba's sparkler."

Col. Randal said, "We both know there's no proof there ever *was* a queen of Sheba."

"Not true," Brandy said. "The Goddess of Love's diamond is right here. It has Jane's name on it.

"Now remember, John, mum's the word. We have to keep this operation totally secret. The only exception might be to have Dr. Milam standing by, in case Jane goes into cardiac arrest at the moment you make your proposal."

"When should that be?" Col. Randal asked, feeling apprehension kick in. Proposal? How did that happen? *He* might need the doctor.

"I shall make the arrangements for the setting. White gold to match her diamond ear studs—simple, elegant. Present the ring to Lady Jane as soon as it is ready.

"You make my life fun, John Randal."

Col. Randal said, "What if she says no?"

AS THE SUN BEGAN TO GO DOWN AND THE DESERT BEGAN to cool, Raiding Forces was standing in formation at RFHQ. The first one since the unit had been in the Middle East Command. Nearly everyone was present, standing tall. The Raiding Regiment with all its elements, Desert Patrol, Lounge Lizards Patrol, the not completely organized Ranger Force, Sea Squadron, and Royal Marines.

The WRENS were observing, as was Lieutenant Preston Butterfield III.

James "Baldie" Taylor, Brigadier Raymond J. Maunsell, and Colonel Dudley Clarke were standing off to one side.

Sergeant Major Mike "March or Die" Mikkalis called the formation to attention when Colonel John Randal and Major the Lady Jane Seaborn walked out of RFHQ.

Col. Randal ordered, "Stand at ease."

This evening was a badging ceremony. All the Raiding Forces' and Ranger personnel were being presented with the new Egyptian-style parachute wings that Lady Jane had designed. All the British troops were to be awarded U.S. Jump Wings.

U.S. and U.K. personnel were symbolically being forged into one unit by the exchange of badges. It was a solemn affair, there being more to it than pomp and ceremony.

Col. Randal, Lady Jane, and Lieutenant Colonel Sir Terry "Zorro" Stone went to the Raiding Regiment and Sea Squadron commanders. Col. Randal pinned on their wings. They, in turn, badged their patrol commanders. The patrol commanders badged the patrol leaders, who took pairs of wings and pinned them on the men in their patrol.

Lady Jane badged her Royal Marines.

It was a good day. Brave men and true. Raiding Forces was reconstituted.

The mission continued.

BRANDY SEABORN ARRIVED AT RFHQ AFTER THE BADGING ceremony had concluded. Major Lady Jane Seaborn was inside changing. She and Colonel John Randal were going out to dinner alone on her favorite floating restaurant before flying out tomorrow for Oasis X.

Brandy slipped a small green leather box into Col. Randal's pocket. He did not open it.

"What I would give to be a fly on the wall," Brandy laughed. She kissed him lightly on the cheek, then disappeared inside.

Flanigan brought Lady Jane's Rolls Royce around as she was stepped outside. Dressed in a simple black sheath, she was drop-dead gorgeous. The former policeman held the door for the couple, then drove to the restaurant.

Soon the two were ensconced in one of the secluded private dining rooms. If Lady Jane noticed the full-length mirror strategically placed against one wall, she did not say anything. The waiter brought in a magnum of champagne, popped the cork and disappeared.

There was a card. Lady Jane opened it, "Compliments of Joe and Waldo."

Col. Randal could not think of anything to say, so he reached into his pocket, produced the small green leather box and handed it to Lady Jane. She looked puzzled.

Then she lifted the lid and screamed. Laughing and crying at the same time, she said, "Yes, yes, yes . . ."

Col. Randal told her the story about the Queen of Sheba's diamond, leaving out only a few details.

"I am never wearing another stick of jewelry the rest of my life," Lady Jane said, modeling her ring in the mirror. "This diamond is to die for, John!"

Well, Col. Randal thought, people *had* died for it—he had shot one of them.

"I love you," Lady Jane said, making eye contact with him in the mirror with her arms crossed. The brilliant circle-cut diamond blazed in the reflection. It seemed alive—and maybe it was.

Col. Randal wondered if she was the "Good Source."

8
TEN MOST

COLONEL JOHN RANDAL AND MAJOR THE LADY JANE
Seaborn pulled up at the airstrip, with the three WRENS in the back of
their jeep. Captain Billy Jack Jaxx was standing beside the Hudson,
talking to Captain Pamala Plum-Martin and Lieutenant Mandy Paige.
For some reason, the two Royal Marines seemed to be admiring the Colt
1911 Model .38 Super he was wearing in a chest holster.

Sub-Lieutenants Pippa Duncan Sackville, Tabitha Walpole and
Bentley St. Ledger perked up.

"Careful, ladies," Col. Randal said, as he stepped out of the jeep.
"Jack's a life taker and a heartbreaker."

King drove up in another jeep with Rita and Lana and their bags. He
started loading them into the Hudson. There was a festive mood on the
airstrip. Raiding Forces had experienced hard service. More than a few
men had decided to voluntarily return to their regiments, burned out by
the constant pace of high-risk operations behind enemy lines. Others had
been injured too severely to continue.

Now, with the infusion of the 575th Rangers, No. 1 Armored Car
RAF Company, a veteran Foreign Legion officer to lead Blue Patrol,
and the new WRENS, things were beginning to look up.

Lady Jane was as vivacious as anyone had ever seen her. Since she
was always a happy spirit—that meant she was *very* happy today. Her
excitement over the Queen of Sheba's diamond ring was contagious.

She was having fun showing it off. It was a nice change from feeling bitter about Raiding Forces being misused in OPERATION CRUSADER—everyone wanted to see the ring.

Capt. Jaxx said, "I'll be staying here on standby with Brandy and Parker in case a SOLID GOLD mission comes up, sir."

Col. Randal said, "What in the hell is that on your handgun?"

The 1911 Model Colt .38 Super Capt. Jaxx was wearing in a chest holster was sporting transparent grips. Under the right panel was the photo of a spectacular girl in a swimsuit.

"These are Plexiglass. Capt. McKoy had 'em made for me."

"I can see that," Col. Randal said. "Who's the blonde?"

"The University of Texas picks the ten most beautiful girls on campus—they call 'em 'The Ten Most.'" Capt. Jaxx said. "This is Beverly Blackwell, one of the ten, sir — Judge Blackwell's granddaughter."

"The judge who sentenced you to join the Army for leading a panty raid on the Tri Delta Sorority House?"

"Roger that."

"You've got good taste in women, Jack," Col. Randal said, "but if the judge ever finds out about those grips, I'll have to send lawyers, guns, and money to get you out of jail when you get back to Texas."

Capt. Jaxx said, "Don't send the lawyers."

Jack Cool.

THE HUDSON HAD BEEN AIRBORNE APPROXIMATELY AN hour when Captain Pamala Plum-Martin came on the intercom and requested Colonel John Randal report to the cockpit.

"John, we received a priority message from Jim," the Vargas Girl look-alike pilot said.

"Rommel has launched a new offensive. Initial reports sound dreadful. Raiding Forces is to put as many patrols in the field as we can and as soon as possible. Your orders are to concentrate on interdicting supply convoys rushing down the Via Balbia."

The exact same orders that had caused Raiding Forces to suffer such high casualties in OPERATION CRUSADER.

"Do you want to continue on or return to RFHQ, John?" Capt. Plum-Martin said.

"Keep going," Col. Randal said. "We'll see what we can scrape up in the way of patrols when we get to X. Roy Kidd and Dan Morgan will be there after their latest patrol.

"I need you and Wing Commander Gordon to start shuttling people out to the oasis from RFHQ today. Can you make that happen?"

"I am sure we can," Capt. Plum-Martin said. "Ronnie will be able to borrow another Hudson somewhere."

"Contact Admiral Ransom," Col. Randal ordered. "Request him to take command of our sea-going assets—Major Corrigan is new to Sea Squadron and can use the help."

"Roger."

"My guess is Jim has already notified Terry about the offensive," Col. Randal said. "Signal Zorro to start as many of the new jeeps as Chief Rawlston has desert-ready toward Oasis X immediately. Tell him to start prioritizing the personnel for you to air transport.

"Have my Raider Patrol get rolling toward Oasis X immediately and order Captain McKoy's White Patrol to do the same. Strike that—tell Captain McKoy to head straight for his AO. No need for him to divert to X."

"Anything else?"

"Have Blue Patrol personnel cease their training duties and stand by to be flown to Oasis X. Same for the No. 1 Armored Car RAF personnel—Lieutenant Butterfield's Foreign Legion people are to have priority of travel."

"Wilco."

Col. Randal walked back and sat next to Major the Lady Jane Seaborn. "Rommel has attacked. Apparently, no one saw it coming. I've been ordered to put as many patrols in the field as we can cobble together.

"Problem is, we're short at least three navigators."

Lady Jane said, "Trained celestial navigators do not grow on trees."

"Contact the Long Range Desert Group as soon as we arrive at X," Col. Randal said. "They want jeeps. We have jeeps. Trade a few to the LRDG for navigators—the men have to volunteer."

"Consider it done," Lady Jane said. "Is the news bad?"

"According to Pam, the initial reports are dreadful," Col. Randal said. "First word from the battlefield is never accurate, but it's safe to say we've been taken by surprise once again."

Col. Randal felt stupid. He was on a plane mostly full of women, heading to a virtually abandoned base at a remote patrol launch site. Only a skeleton crew was at Oasis X; everyone else had gone to Cairo for R&R following OPERATION CRUSADER. Talk about being caught unprepared.

Sea Squadron would be fine even though it had a new commanding officer (CO). Major Taylor Corrigan, DSO, MC, was a talented leader of men. Col. Randal had no concerns in that department. However, the major did need time to get into the operational rhythm of a unique new command.

The primary concern was Lieutenant Colonel Terry "Zorro" Stone's Raiding Regiment. It was in no condition to take the field. The Lounge Lizards and Desert Patrol would both be stretching it to make four of their six patrols operational. Ranger Force was going to be thrown into the battle with hastily organized patrols composed, for the most part, of men who were virtually untested and who had never operated together as a team.

Col. Randal was left with no other option but to cobble together a gun jeep raiding outfit out of green U.S. troops, RAF personnel who had plenty of desert experience in armored cars but none in gun jeeps, new patrol leaders who were unproven on small-scale, long-range desert missions, and a Raiding Regiment commander who had not fully recovered from a previous wound.

Not a formula for success.

Col. Randal stood up and went back to talk to Rocky. The ice-blonde Norwegian looked up from the magazine she was reading as he knelt in the aisle next to her seat.

"How's Terry been doing on his morning workouts?"

"Steady improvement," Rocky said. "Not quite there. He is trying his best."

"What I thought."

Col. Randal continued down the aisle to speak to Lieutenant Preston Butterfield III, who was sitting with Lieutenant Mandy Paige. The Foreign Legion officer was demonstrating excellent judgment in traveling companions. It spoke well of him.

"Afrika Korps has launched an offensive," Col. Randal said. "Your Blue Patrol personnel will be flown out to Oasis X later today, Lieutenant. As soon as we arrive, I want you to select six gun jeeps from those available. Be prepared to move out on a two-week patrol the moment your people land from RFHQ."

"Yes, sir."

Lt. Butterfield did not seem ruffled by the sudden change of plans. One minute, he was flying out on an orientation tour of a covert Raiding Forces' desert base, chatting up one of the best-looking girls he had ever seen. The next, he was being ordered to take the field during a major enemy offensive, commanding troops he had never met.

Can do.

"Get with Mr. Zargo, our chief of intelligence," Col. Randal ordered. "He'll brief you. One or another of his people will escort Blue Patrol all the way to your AO and stay with you throughout."

Col. Randal walked back up to the pilot's compartment. "Pam, contact Terry to find out where 'Pyro' Percy's Railroad Wrecking Crew is currently located. Have Captain Stirling drop what he's doing and report to X for attachment to the Raiding Regiment.

"Have Billy Jack start his SOG operators toward the oasis with Raider Patrol. I can't afford to have him sitting around waiting for a SOLID GOLD mission during this offensive.

"Notify Travis McCloud that Waldo is available for assignment to a Ranger Patrol element as an advisor. Inform Travis I'm going to want to go over Ranger Force's Table of Organization the minute he arrives at X."

"Anything else, John?" Capt. Plum-Martin asked.

Col. Randal said, "Better have Jack Merritt head toward the oasis from wherever he happens to be. I may need to convert some of his Sudanese into gun jeep patrols.

"I almost forgot—Sergeant Major Mikkalis is to take command of Duck Patrol."

Capt. Plum-Martin said, "Jim signaled he is airborne, en route to the oasis."

Col. Randal returned to his seat next to Lady Jane.

"Start making plans to evacuate RFHQ—everyone to X as soon as we touch down."

"Are things that desperate?"

"How would I know?" Col. Randal said. "I don't feel great about the situation, based in part on what you told me about Field Marshal Auchinleck.

"Why take a chance?"

"I trust your instincts, John."

"Let's hope I'm wrong," Col. Randal said. "Rommel will run out of steam sooner or later like always, but there's no guarantee he won't make it to the Suez Canal before he does."

"'It's Good to have a Plan B,'" Lady Jane said, quoting Raiding Forces' Rules for Raiding.

Col. Randal said, "I wish we had one."

COLONEL JOHN RANDAL AND CAPTAIN ROY KIDD, MC, were standing in the TOC AT Oasis X. They were looking at the map of the Raiding Forces' AO, which ran from west of Alexandria to Tripoli, across western Egypt and all of Libya. There was nothing new for them to see. None of the recent enemy troop movements had been entered— no one had any current information.

Col. Randal said, "Is Lieutenant Morgan ready to lead a patrol?"

"He needs an experienced patrol sergeant and a navigator," Capt. Kidd said. "Dan's going to make an outstanding officer, sir."

"I'm dealing you a bad hand, Roy," Col. Randal said. "Split Scout Patrol in half. You take one half. Give the other to Lieutenant Morgan— he gets your sergeant.

"You can promote one of your corporals to patrol sergeant or pick one from anywhere in the Raiding Regiment. We'll bring in a navigator. Fill up the rest of the vacant slots in the two patrols with Rangers—pick out four more gun jeeps from those in the motor pool here.

"I need both Patrols—Scout I and Scout II—back in the field by tomorrow at the latest."

"Yes, sir," Capt. Kidd said. All things considered, he took the orders well. His Scout Patrol was Raiding Forces' star performer at plinking trucks, the most strategic target in the desert war.

Breaking it up was a crime.

"Give me a list of the personnel you need," Col. Randal said. "I'll have 'em flown in today."

"How do I know which Rangers to select, sir?"

"Talk to King," Col. Randal said. "He spent quite a bit of time training 'em. Go with his recommendations."

Lieutenant Stephanie Fawcett-Tatum, the tall brunette Royal Marine who had been with Raiding Forces since immediately after the Gunfight at the Blue Duck while Col. Randal was recovering from being shot, came over.

"John, we received a signal from the U.S. Military Attaché's office. Colonel Fellers is requesting permission to fly in to visit Oasis X to observe our operations."

"Negative," Col. Randal said. "Inform the colonel this is a restricted site. Tell him to stay the hell away."

"Yes, sir."

"Actually, that was a little harsh of me, Stephanie," Col. Randal said. "Fellers is only trying to do his job."

Lt. Fawcett-Tatum flashed a smile. "I shall inform the colonel you are too busy for visitors."

"Thanks."

James "Baldie" Taylor arrived. He and Col. Randal went into conference.

"Rommel received a shipment of three hundred and fifty panzers," Jim said. "Y-Service intercepts disclosed the Desert Fox had firm orders from his boss 'Smiling Al' Kesselring to use them to set up a defensive line, dig in and stand pat—he immediately attacked.

"The Nazi will not obey orders. He has no comprehension of the operational arts and does not understand the first thing about logistics. On the other hand, he is a truly brilliant tactician and he is driving hard, going for the kill.

"Rommel created a diversion, using a German and an Italian Corps in the north. Then he secretly shifted the German divisions south, concentrated them, flanked the Eigth Army—going around it without slowing down to give battle—and headed for Tobruk, Alexandria, Cairo, and points east.

"The fighting is confused, with the situation in doubt."

"What do you need from us, General?" Col. Randal asked.

"Interdict the Via Balbia," Jim said. "Concentrate on thin-skinned transports. Raid fuel-storage farms. Conduct operations against remote enemy installations to try to force Rommel to draw down his troop strength to guard them.

"Your standard litany of targets, Colonel—only hit more of them."

"We're in the middle of reorganizing Raiding Forces. My people are not ready to undertake anything of this magnitude," Col. Randal said "As you recall, before CRUSADER I warned what would happen if our gun jeep patrols were committed to the main battle area like armored car squadrons."

"Yes, you did."

"This could be worse."

"Colonel, you have your orders," Jim said.

"Yes, sir," Col. Randal said. "I can put three patrols in the field by tonight. Three more patrols within three days. Possibly have as many as fifteen Raiding Regiment patrols two weeks after that."

"That is incredible," Jim said.

"These are going to be weak patrols," Col. Randal said. "Some of them will only have four gun jeeps."

"Even so," Jim said, "the effort will be much esteemed. Harass Rommel 'round the clock, Colonel. Make him suffer death by a thousand cuts—you are good at that sort of thing."

"We're short qualified patrol leaders," Col. Randal said. "I have to make plans to allow for the inexperience of the Rangers."

"Why I flew in," Jim said. "Pencil me in on the roster to advise one of the Ranger Patrols."

Lt. Fawcett-Tatum stuck her head in the door. "Mr. Zargo is here, John."

"Send him in."

The scar-faced intelligence operative entered. It had never been established exactly who he worked for. Rumor had it he was originally employed by the Seven Sisters oil companies before the war. His stable of operatives were mercenaries—guns for hire. What *was* known: Mr. Zargo had a string of agents in place from Cairo to Tripoli who performed long-range reconnaissance for Raiding Forces' patrols.

Mr. Zargo and the hard intelligence provided by his operatives was the magic sauce that made Raiding Forces successful—his value was without measure.

"Rommel has launched a new offensive," Col. Randal said.

"Raiding Forces is undergoing a major reorganization, so it was bad timing for us. Desert Patrol will now be called the Raiding Regiment under Colonel Stone. It will consist of three elements of six patrols each: Desert Patrol, Lounge Lizard Patrol, and Ranger Force.

"The latter will mostly be made up of U.S. Paratroops from the 575th Parachute Infantry Regiment called Rangers," Col. Randal said.

"We haven't recovered from our CRUSADER losses. We're short on experienced patrol leaders. And, we have just been ordered to take the field."

"Same mission as CRUSADER?" Mr. Zargo asked.

"Down to the ground," Col. Randal said. "We need to reorganize our AOs. Currently there are four. Why not cut it to three—you lay out the boundaries."

Mr. Zargo said, "One for each squadron?"

"Exactly," Col. Randal said. "Then I want you to draw a line east to west down the center."

This drew a raised eyebrow from Mr. Zargo.

"Ranger Patrol elements will stay south of the center line at all times," Col. Randal said. "I don't want them going anywhere near the Via Balbia or the series of secondary tracts that parallel it.

"Desert Patrol and Lounge Lizard Patrol will take the western and central AOs. Colonel Stone will make the assignment of who goes where."

"What about the eastern-most AO?" Mr. Zargo asked.

"Captain Jaxx has a team he calls the Small Operations Group—SOG, Captain McKoy's White Patrol, and my old Ranger Patrol—now reflagged as Raider Patrol—will all work it. We need to keep fairly close to X. There's always a possibility of our having to divert to a high-value target if one presents itself."

Mr. Zargo was fully briefed on the priority of operations. His people would most likely have a role in any RED INDIAN or SOLID GOLD mission that developed.

"Let me do a cursory map study," Mr. Zargo said. "I can have Lieutenant Fawcett-Tatum make the changes to the map in the TOC once you approve my recommendations.

"Take your time," Col. Randal said. "Colonel Stone and his three primary commanders will be flying in later this afternoon. We won't need it until then.

"On another subject, there's a Foreign Legion officer, Lieutenant Butterfield. He'll be taking over Blue Patrol. I'd like you to help him plan his mission. He'll be departing today."

"Met him a few minutes ago," Mr. Zargo said. "The Legion's 97th Reconnaissance Group engaged in more action than any mechanized unit in France before it came out through Dunkirk. Their record in Equatorial Africa is unsurpassed. Lieutenant Butterfield is a valuable addition to Raiding Forces, Colonel."

"I don't believe you've ever said that about anyone before, Mr. Zargo," Col. Randal said.

"Your officers often turn out to be excellent leaders *after* they have served with Raiding Forces for a time," Mr. Zargo said.

"Lieutenant Butterfield is a distinguished graduate of the toughest school in the world—Foreign Legion small unit leader, battle-tested."

"We'll see," Col. Randal said.

After Mr. Zargo departed, Jim said, "Good idea redrawing the operational areas the way you described. The new U.S. troops can raid isolated targets, do quite a bit of damage, cause widespread alarm and despondency, and not be drawn into the main battle area."

"I'm trying to learn from my mistakes during CRUSADER," Col. Randal said. "No one is going to give me additional troops to replace the ones I'm about to lose in this FUBAR."

"Granted," Jim said. "The military situation could hardly be worse. Afrika Korps is conducting a full-blown attack. There is a mole in

Auchinleck's inner circle providing Rommel detailed intelligence appraisals about our deepest, darkest secrets. Seebohm's 621st Intercept Company is supplying the Desert Fox our Order of Battle and daily operational orders faster than MEHQ can disseminate them to our own troops.

"And, last, but not least," Jim said, "this is strictly between the two of us, Colonel—Auchinleck has lost his nerve. He is convinced Rommel cannot be defeated in open battle."

Col. Randal chose not to mention that Lady Jane had already informed him of the exact same thing.

"That's not good, General."

"Based on the Y-Service intercepts that come across my desk daily, Afrika Korps is in substantially worse shape than our Eighth Army," Jim said. "Or at least it was before being reinforced with all those tanks.

"By all rights, we should have won this campaign a long time ago. I am hard-pressed for an explanation as to why our generals have not been able to do so.

"No wonder the Prime Minister is so frustrated by developments in Middle East Command. He knows we should have put the Desert Fox down a long time ago."

"That may be the big picture, General," Col. Randal said. "I don't think Rommel sees it the same way. When you roll out, sharpen your bayonet."

Jim said, "I do not have a bayonet."

Col. Randal said, "Neither do I."

"That was some coincidence," Jim said as he was leaving. "You happen to be out of the way flying to Oasis X the morning Rommel launches his attack."

Despite vowing not to, Col. Randal said, "Jane's idea."

Jim said, "Forget I asked."

COLONEL JOHN RANDAL WAS IN THE TOC TALKING TO Major Clive Adair, aka The Mayor of Oasis X. He was also the commander of the Raiding Forces' Phantom Squadron N.

"Can you provide half a dozen Phantom teams for Ranger Force?" Col. Randal asked.

"Yes, sir," Maj. Adair said. "The day the 575th PIR arrived, I requested additional operators from Regiment. They sent me a full Phantom troop. Flew them out from the U.K. within the week. The men have been in the field acclimating to our desert environment ever since they arrived."

"Outstanding," Col. Randal said.

"I had no idea there were going to be so few Five-Seven-Five paratroopers," Maj. Adair said. "I was anticipating supporting a full regiment. We are in first-rate shape for long-range radio communications, sir."

Col. Randal asked, "How many jeeps do you currently have here at X?"

"Not counting the dozen or so that Chief Rawlston left behind," Maj. Adair said, "Phantom has six and there are two more for the Royal Marines HQ staff."

"We may have to use 'em to put patrols in the field right away," Col. Randal said. "Don't worry, Clive. There's plenty of jeeps to issue you replacements."

"Yes, sir."

"Any security problems since I've been away?"

"None to speak of, sir—bearing in mind national loyalty does not exist here at X. The oasis is a tiny little Switzerland. It would not hurt the local's conscience in the least to share information with both sides for the right price," Maj. Adair said.

"Batten down the hatches," Col. Randal said, "with this offensive underway."

Maj. Adair said, "Mandy is already on the case, sir. She has Rita and Lana working the village. If there are any enemy infiltrators, Abwehr plants, or cases of the citizenry selling information to the Nazis, it shall not take long for those three to ferret it out, sir."

After Maj. Adair departed, Lieutenant Stephanie Fawcett-Tatum reported, "An RAF Hudson is making its final approach, John. The Air Force liaison teams Wing Commander Gordon promised are on board.

Col. Randal said, "I'd like to speak to the officer in charge."

"Wilco."

Col. Randal walked upstairs to his quarters in the apartment he shared with Major the Lady Jane Seaborn. She was not there.

Sub-Lieutenant Bentley St. Ledger knocked on the open door behind him, "Stephanie asked me to inform you a U.S. Air Corps C-47 has radioed it is inbound with an ETA of thirty minutes. Blue Patrol is on board."

"Bentley," Col. Randal ordered, "track down Lieutenant Butterfield—you can probably find him with Mr. Zargo. Tell the lieutenant to be standing by at the airstrip with Blue Patrol's gun jeeps when the plane lands. Inform him I expect his Patrol Order to be issued at that time."

"Yes, sir."

"Advise Major Adair to have one of the new RAF liaison parties link up with Blue Patrol at the airstrip. He'll have to coordinate with the RAF officer in charge."

"Roger—John, may I ask a question?"

"Sure."

"Is duty in Raiding Forces always like being swept along in the eye of a hurricane?"

"Actually, Bentley," Col. Randal said, "you got here during one of our slow periods."

RIKKE RUNBORG WALKED OUT ON THE DECK OF COLONEL John Randal's apartment. He was sitting in a canvas chair observing the activity taking place down the escarpment. Jeeps were coming and going, airplanes landing and taking off. Men were on the move.

Rocky said, "You wished to see me, John?"

"I do," Col. Randal said, waving for her to sit down.

"What can you tell me about the British Secret Intelligence Service?"

"MI-6," Rocky said, "enjoys a reputation for being an invisible, implacable force operating in the shadows everywhere worldwide. SIS is envied by its allies and feared by its enemies. In reality, it is run by men of moderate abilities who picture themselves actors in a Kipling novel."

"Really?" Col. Randal said.

"The Secret Intelligence Service values intelligence in proportion to how difficult it is to obtain more than its accuracy," Rocky said.

"MI-6 would attach more value to a scrap of third-rate misinformation smuggled out of Sofia concealed in the fly-buttons of a Romanian pimp than to any intelligence deduced by the simple analysis of foreign press reports."

Col. Randal said, "How about MI-5?"

Rocky studied him closely, certain there was more to this conversation than mere curiosity on Col. Randal's part—the last question always being the primary.

He was not deceiving her.

She was a trained intelligence operative who had worked for, it was thought, the Russians and the Germans. It was rumored Rocky had met both Stalin *and* Hitler. And now the sexy Norwegian ballet dancer was cooperating with the British, maybe.

"The British Security Service is the most effective counterintelligence organization in the world. MI 5 can be as cruel as the Gestapo. I speak from personal experience," Rocky said.

"As bad as the Nazis, huh?"

"Once Security sets their sights on a suspect, they hound their prey to the ends of the earth," Rocky said. "British counterintelligence does not care by what means they obtain the information they desire nor whom they destroy in the process.

"MI-5 has no soul."

It was not the answer Col. Randal wanted to hear.

9
JOHN WAYNE

LIEUTENANT PRESTON BUTTERFIELD III ISSUED BLUE
Patrol its Patrol Order on the airstrip at Oasis X. The patrol had been
augmented by the addition of a Royal Air Force liaison officer and his
radio operator, in a jeep that had been desertized by Chief Warrant
Officer Hank W. Rawlston. The tough ex-Legionnaires and U.S. Army
jeep drivers, formerly of the American Volunteer Group, listened
intently.

The men were not only paying attention to their mission—they were
evaluating their new leader.

Colonel John Randal was observing.

When Lt. Butterfield finished, Col. Randal had a final word with
him before Blue Patrol prepared to move out.

"Raiding Forces isn't the Foreign Legion, Preston," Col. Randal
said. "We don't do the *fight to the last bullet, last man* stuff. Our idea is
everyone who goes in, comes out—hit and run. You're no good to me
dead."

"Understood, sir," Lt. Butterfield said. "I like your approach much
better, Colonel. I'm looking forward to serving in Raiding Forces."

"That was a first-rate patrol order, Lieutenant. You're getting off to
a fast start," Col. Randal said.

"Good luck and good hunting."

One of the captured Italian Ro.63s landed. Drop-dead gorgeous Major the Lady Jane Seaborn disembarked, followed by three bearded Long Range Desert Group troopers in sun-bleached khaki shirts and shorts.

"Major Seaborn reporting, sir," Lady Jane said, flashing one of her patented heart attack smiles. "New LRDG navigators. I traded three jeeps apiece for them."

Col. Randal said, "Way to go, Jane.

"You men volunteer?"

"Yes, sir!"

"Report to Lieutenant Morgan," Col. Randal said. "One of you will be assigned to his Scout Patrol II—moving out before nightfall. The other two will marry up with patrols in the next day or so, as they arrive here at the oasis.

"Welcome to Raiding Forces."

The Hudson carrying Lieutenant Colonel Sir Terry "Zorro" Stone and his three subordinate commanders, Major Jeb Pelham-Davies, DSO, MC, Desert Patrol; Major Travis McCloud, Ranger Force; and Major Baltimore "Mongo" Farquhar, MC—a seasoned veteran of the 12th Royal Lancers (Armored Cars)—came in for landing.

Maj. Farquhar was an officer with extensive combat experience in France and the Middle East. He had been handpicked (shanghaied by his uncle, Sir Terry's father, the Duke) to command the Lancelot Lancers Yeomanry, aka Lounge Lizard Patrol.

The senior officers of the Raiding Regiment repaired to Col. Randal's and Lady Jane's apartment to conduct an intensive strategy session.

Mr. Zargo, James "Baldie" Taylor, Major Clive Adair, and Squadron Leader Johnny Page sat in. As did Lieutenant Mandy Paige— she was not about to be left out.

Lt. Col. Stone chaired.

The atmosphere was informal but strictly professional. Everyone present was experienced. Everyone was aware of Rommel's offensive. No one was under any illusion about the seriousness of the Afrika Korps attack. A sense of hard-edged urgency dominated the conversation.

Col. Randal was confident that no finer group of field grade officers had ever been assembled in one room anywhere, at any time. Raiding Forces had come a long way from the early days, when he and Sir Terry were making it up as they went along.

Sub-Lieutenant Bentley St. Ledger slipped in and whispered in his ear, "Captain Kidd and Lieutenant Morgan to see you."

Col. Randal stepped out of the meeting to speak to them.

"We're good to go, sir," Captain Roy Kidd said. "On your command."

"That was quick," Col. Randal said. "I'm expecting a lot from you studs. Singles and doubles, gentlemen—don't be swinging for the fences."

"Yes, sir!" Scout Patrols I and II were ready to launch.

"Make something happen."

CAPTAIN BILLY JACK JAXX ARRIVED WITH HIS SMALL Operations Group organized into a gun jeep patrol. Lieutenant Clint Hays and Lieutenant Eddy Ryder were driving jeeps. Raider Patrol was married up with SOG.

Colonel John Randal met them when they drove in.

"Made good time, Jack."

Capt. Jaxx said, "You should see what's behind us, sir. A stream of jeeps is headed this way—strung out across the desert from here to RFHQ. Looks like the pioneers. 'Westward Ho, the wagons.'"

"That's what we want," Col. Randal said. "Link up with your new RAF liaison team. Readjust your patrol configuration. Re-up on food, water, and ammunition. Have your drivers perform maintenance on their vehicles. Be ready to pull out at daybreak.

"I'll be traveling with you part way in Raider Patrol."

"Yes, sir," Capt. Jaxx said. "Do we have a plan?"

"Negative," Col. Randal said. "SOG, White Patrol, and Raider Patrol will be going after targets of opportunity—keeping in mind we have to be ready to respond to a RED INDIAN or SOLID GOLD mission if one turns up."

"I like it, sir," Capt. Jaxx said. "Free stylin'."

Col. Randal met briefly with Raider Patrol. Sergeant Ned Pompedous, who had served with him since Swamp Fox Force days in France, was no longer with the patrol. He had been tapped to advise one of the new Ranger Patrols.

Master Sergeant Mack Beckwith, formerly the Sergeant Major (which in the U.S. Army was an honorary title) of the 575th PIR, was assigned to understudy Sergeant Rex Blackburn, the 81mm mortar expert, who would be filling in temporarily as the Raider Patrol sergeant. MSgt. Beckwith had personally picked the Rangers who would fill the vacant slots in the patrol.

Col. Randal said, "Welcome to Raider Patrol, Sergeant Major."

MSgt. Beckwith, who bore a striking resemblance to the movie star John Wayne, said, "Looking forward to working with you, sir."

Raider Patrol was going to have three unassigned Ranger lieutenants attached. Captain Travis McCloud would designate them prior to the patrol departing X. Col. Randal was evaluating the three young officers for future assignment.

The problem was not having enough officers to be patrol leaders—it was having enough *qualified* officers to lead a patrol. Raiding Forces had already weeded out over half of the 575th's company grade officers. Only the best of the rest would be allowed to remain, and they had to earn a slot.

Col. Randal ordered Sgt. Blackburn, "Be ready to pull out at first light.

"Better bring a double basic load of 81mm rounds."

The Railroad Wrecking Crew II arrived at Oasis X. Col. Randal ordered Captain "Pyro" Percy Stirling, DSO, MC, 17/21 Lancers, to report to Lieutenant Colonel Sir Terry "Zorro" Stone for future assignment.

Ranger Lieutenant "Dynamite" Dick Coogan had accompanied Capt. Stirling on his last patrol. The two had been ranging all over the desert, blowing up Rommel's rail lines. The one thing the Desert Fox could never rely on was rail transport.

Col. Randal said, "My Raider Patrol is pulling out in the morning. How would you like to ride with us, Dick?"

"I'd like that, sir."

"Check in with Sergeant Blackburn."

Arriving back at the TOC, Col. Randal found Mr. Zargo talking to Lieutenant Stephanie Fawcett-Tatum. He was showing her the new boundaries of the Raiding Regiments Areas of Operations. Squadron Leader Johnny Page was standing by, unobtrusively observing.

"Johnny, I'd like you to accompany my Raider Patrol tomorrow," Col. Randal said.

"My pleasure, sir."

"Give us time to work out the best way to employ your RAF people," Col. Randal said. "I've got an idea I've been kicking around with Colonel Stone."

James "Baldie" Taylor walked in.

"Any news, General?"

"None you want to hear," Jim said. "Our troops are falling back. Rommel is running amuck. Disaster is imminent—we are all going to die."

Col. Randal said, "We've heard that before."

"Yes, we have," Jim said. "This time feels different. MEHQ has the wind up. There is talk of evacuating all non-essential personnel from Cairo."

Col. Randal and Jim locked eyes. The two had worked together under extreme pressure and hostile conditions long enough to be able to read each other's thoughts. Now, both men were thinking the same thing: The Allies were fighting all over the world, and they were losing everywhere they were fighting.

Neither said a word.

Lieutenant Mandy Paige came into the TOC. Col. Randal said, "Round up Rita and Lana. I want to talk to you, the WRENS, and the girls—in my apartment in fifteen minutes."

"Yes, sir."

Lt. Col. Stone arrived with Major Jeb Pelham-Davies, Major Travis McCloud, and Major Baltimore "Mongo" Farquhar. They gathered around the giant wall map. Lt. Col. Stone briefed the new boundaries and pertinent features of each of the AOs before assigning one to each officer.

Col. Randal observed the discussion, well-satisfied. He did not contribute or interfere. Now that the Raiding Regiment's primary troop commanders were studying a map, tension from the earlier meeting ratcheted down.

Conversation ceased.

The officers stood wrapped up in their own thoughts, beginning to formulate preliminary plans, thinking out their options, contemplating which patrols to assign to various parts of their AOs.

They could all read a map. They all knew the desert. They were all capable tacticians.

While the COs studied the wall map, Lt. Col. Stone and Col. Randal stepped off to the far side of the TOC. Sir Terry offered Col. Randal a Player's Navy Cut from his elegant, sterling silver cigarette case.

Col. Randal pulled out his battered U.S. 26th Cavalry Regiment Zippo lighter. "Tell me about Major Farquhar."

"Grew up in the Regiment as a boy," Lt. Col. Stone said. "Knows everyone by name, including most of the new replacements. That's why Father selected him—Right Man, Right Job.

"Splendid record fighting in armored cars in France, screening the withdrawal at Dunkirk. Mongo has been in almost nonstop action out here with the 12th Royal Lancers for the last two years."

"So," Col. Randal said, "you would have picked him yourself?"

"My favorite cousin, old stick," Lt. Col. Stone said. "I would have picked him myself."

Col. Randal said, "Good enough for me."

Major the Lady Jane Seaborn had arranged for a pitcher of iced tea to be delivered to the apartment for Col. Randal's meeting. She was sitting out on the deck with the WRENS, Lt. Mandy, Rita, and Lana when he arrived.

The girls were admiring her Queen of Sheba promise ring for the thirtieth or fortieth time—having fun.

Lady Jane stood up to leave. Col. Randal said, "Stick around, Jane."

He was rewarded with his second full-on heart attack-grade smile of the day, which was getting close to the lethal limit.

Col. Randal said, "There's a lot of activity here at the moment, ladies. However, in a few days the oasis will be almost abandoned. It won't be safe for any of you to be out alone.

"So, starting right now, none of you, to include Lady Jane, are to go anywhere outside of the TOC unless Mandy, Rita, or Lana accompany you. Carry your weapon at all times. Always travel in pairs.

"Any questions?"

Sub-Lieutenant Bentley St. Ledger asked, "Is it true Rita and Lana are your slaves?"

"Roger that," Col. Randal said. "And, it's going to be your job, Bentley, to beat 'em for me once a day while I'm away on patrol."

Thus concluded a fruitful and rewarding session with the female contingent of Raiding Forces currently stationed at Oasis X.

Col. Randal decided it was way past time for him to get back to the desert.

BRANDY SEABORN AND CAPTAIN PENELOPE "LEGS" Honeycutt-Parker arrived on the last flight of the day from RFHQ to Oasis X.

Colonel John Randal immediately pulled the women aside. "SOG and my Raider Patrol will be operating in the AO nearest Oasis X. We'll never be more than two hours away from a location where a plane can land in the desert to extract a team for a SOLID GOLD or RED INDIAN mission."

Brandy said, "The situation is so fluid at the moment, John, I seriously doubt that shall be necessary."

Capt. Honeycutt-Parker said, "Y-Service has gone dark, but not quiet. The signals boffins are finding it impossible to sort out the intelligence we need from the chaos and hysteria clogging the airwaves."

Col. Randal said, "Well, if you do develop a target, ladies—we'll hit it for you."

"Thanks, John," Brandy said.

"Glad you two high-risk thrill seekers decided to ride it out here with Lady Jane and her crew," Col. Randal said. "Won't have to worry about you now."

"Cairo has gone quite mad," Capt. Honeycutt-Parker said. "What a relief to be here."

"Agreed," Brandy said.

Wing Commander Ronald Gordon and Captain Pamala Plum-Martin came in from the airstrip after a long day's flying. They immediately went into conference with Col. Randal.

W/Cdr. Gordon said, "RAF is going to place a flight of four A-20 Havocs in direct support of Raiding Forces. The aircraft will be operating off of the auxiliary airstrip at RFHQ. Easier to perform ground support and maintenance there than out here at Oasis X."

Capt. Plum-Martin said, "We need to establish a protocol for how to best utilize the A-20s, John. If this test Ronnie arranged is a success, the Air Vice Marshal has agreed to consider developing a wide-reaching plan for providing close air support to the rest of Eighth Army."

Col. Randal said, "What brought that about?"

"After working here with Raiding Forces," W/Cdr. Gordon said, "I became convinced of the need for cooperation between air and ground maneuver elements if we ever hope to defeat Afrika Korps—not a popular concept in some circles. I lobbied my boss until he caved in.

"There is more than a little resistance to the idea from some quarters in the RAF. It is imperative we succeed, Colonel."

"In that case," Col. Randal said, "don't get the Havocs shot down."

Capt. Plum-Martin asked, "How would you propose we go about preventing that, John?"

Col. Randal said. "Fly night missions exclusively."

W/Cdr. Gordon said, "I agree."

"Set up a strict protocol," Col. Randal said. "The only targets worthy of an airstrike might be stationary tank or armored car formations laagered for the night—maybe a really large convoy. You two work it out."

"We are on the same page, Colonel," W/Cdr. Gordon said. "Patrols provide coordinates and mark the direction to the target with flares. The Havocs fly in and hot it up."

"Word is," Col. Randal said, "Rommel has three hundred and fifty new Panzer Mark IIIs—let's see how many your people can kill, Wing Commander."

"Locate the tanks, sir," W/Cdr. Gordon said. "My lads shall take the fight to the enemy."

"I'll go over the details with Terry," Col. Randal said. "You two brief the RAF liaison teams on priorities tonight before patrols start moving out in the morning.

"Let's use the identifier 'FLASH BANG' for the Havoc's targets. For the duration of Rommel's current offensive, the only two missions with a higher priority are RED INDIAN and SOLID GOLD—if one of those comes up, there's a good chance I'm going to ask you to support it."

"Consider it done," W/Cdr. Gordon said, having no idea what a RED INDIAN or a SOLID GOLD mission was, not possessing the Need to Know.

Capt. Plum-Martin said, "If only the RAF Air Vice Marshal and Eighth Army's Lieutenant General Ritchie would work together the way you two do, we would put paid to the Desert Fox in short order."

Col. Randal said, "Good luck with that."

COLONEL JOHN RANDAL ISSUED HIS WARNING ORDER TO Raider Patrol as the sun was going down in a blaze of scarlet. Normally a six-jeep patrol, an extra gun jeep had been assigned to this mission to carry all the straphangers. Smaller is nimbler; however, this was not simply an operational patrol.

The idea was to have a live-fire field-training exercise with real bad guys.

The plan was to evaluate the new Ranger personnel assigned to Raider Patrol, the RAF liaison team and three unassigned lieutenants, and to introduce Squadron Leader Johnny Page to the mystery of a gun jeep patrol. And to determine whether Lieutenant "Dynamite" Dick Coogan was ready to form his own patrol.

Raider Patrol had a lot of new faces, and it was missing some of the old familiar ones. The one constant in war is that nothing stays the same. Col. Randal wrapped up the order, "Line of Departure time is zero-six-hundred."

Veronica Paige, the Chief of MI-9 (Escape) was standing by to give Raider Patrol a short briefing on the "blood chits" she had ordered produced for Raiding Forces.

"We have agents spread out across the desert who have made contact with the various Arab tribes. They promised a cash reward, payable in gold, to anyone who aids in safely returning to friendly lines an Allied airman or soldier in possession of one of these chits."

Brandy Seaborn appeared and stood next to Col. Randal at the back of Raider Patrol, where he was listening to Veronica explain Raiding Forces' new Escape and Evasion plan. The golden girl put her arms around his neck, pulled his head down and placed her forehead against his—looking into his eyes.

"Worried about you, handsome," Brandy said. "You have to be distracted by the MI-5 investigation. The Western Desert is no place to be preoccupied for an instant, especially with Rommel in full blitzkrieg."

"I need to get away," Col. Randal said. "Keeping secrets from Jane is not my idea of a good time."

"Understood," Brandy said. "Stay focused, John."

Lieutenant Mandy Paige ambushed Col. Randal on the candlelit steps carved into the cliff of the escarpment outside his apartment, as he was returning from Raider Patrol's briefing.

"I was coming to listen to Mother make her pitch," Lt. Mandy said. "What's the story with you and Brandy?"

Col. Randal said, "Brandy's worried about me going on patrol. She's been emotional ever since her husband was killed."

"Something is going on, John," Lt. Mandy said. "You're not telling me everything—not fooling me."

"I liked you better when you were a simple horse girl," Col. Randal said. "Before you turned into Miss Sherlock Holmes."

"You told me that once before in Cairo. It was funny back then," Lt. Mandy said. "Now you're hiding something from me and no one is laughing.

"Do not make me beat it out of you with a rubber hose, John."

Col. Randal said, "Brandy wants me to go back to Abyssinia—shoot another bandit with a big diamond."

"Knock one off for me while you are at it. I want a stone with a legend like Lady Jane's," Lt. Mandy said. "What a love story!"

"Mandy," Col. Randal said. "I'm counting on you to take care of Jane for me while I'm gone. Watch out for the WRENS too—they're babes in the woods."

"You know I shall," Lt. Mandy said. "You're not going to tell me the secret, are you?"

"No."

10
ON PATROL

RAIDER PATROL, FOLLOWED BY SOG, PULLED OUT OF OASIS X at sunrise. A lot of people were on hand to see them off. Colonel John Randal was eager to get back to the desert. Brandy had been right—he was distracted by the MI-5 investigation.

"You're restricted to X or Cairo," Col. Randal ordered Lieutenant Colonel Sir Terry "Zorro" Stone. "Is that clear?"

"Crystal," Lt. Col. Stone said. "Happy hunting."

Major the Lady Jane Seaborn gave him a kiss. "Be safe, John—love my ring, love you."

He felt guilty for wondering if she was the Nazi mole.

Rita and Lana stood so close by the jeep they were rubbing up against him like cats. Col. Randal felt the sudden urge to tell them to hop in the back like the old days in Abyssinia.

Things were a lot simpler then. All he had to worry about then was navigating a sea of shifta bandits who had a tradition of hacking off their enemies' precious body parts, surviving in a country where murder is the national sport, and dealing with a population explosion of man-eating lions.

Lieutenant Mandy Paige gave him a hug, which was not normal. The WRENS waved good-by. Even Rikke Runborg placed her cheek against his—a show of emotion he never expected. Col. Randal never thought Rocky had any.

Sub-Lieutenant Bentley St. Ledger said, "You *were* teasing about beating Rita and Lana?"

Col. Randal said, "I never tease, Bentley."

The well-wishers were clearly troubled about the gravity of the situation. Rommel was tearing up the desert. Eighth Army was imploding. While everyone else was falling back in disarray, Raiding Forces was driving straight at Afrika Korps.

"Let's roll," Col. Randal ordered Lieutenant David Granbury, one of the unassigned Ranger officers attached to Raider Patrol. The lieutenant was starting out as his driver. The other two Ranger officers would rotate through the position.

The idea was to give Col. Randal a chance to get to know them, meaning he wanted a chance to evaluate the young lieutenants for future duties.

The moment the jeep cleared the top of the escarpment, Col. Randal began to feel better. He liked the sensation of heading into the great unknown. Always on the move, always looking for targets of opportunity. And always experiencing the heightened sense of awareness danger brought.

A patrol leader is constantly observing, gauging, estimating, making a stream of life-and-death decisions. Rolling the dice. Mistakes could— and most likely would—be fatal.

Raider Patrol drove for ten hours, pushing hard. Today would be the only time they traveled during daylight hours. From sundown on, the patrol would laager by day and move by night under cover of darkness. Enemy air was the big threat. Fortunately, neither the Luftwaffe nor the Regia Aeronautica flew desert sweeps after last light.

Finally, as the horizon was swallowing up the setting sun, Col. Randal ordered a halt. He walked back to talk with Captain Billy Jack Jaxx in SOG Patrol.

"I'm turning north, Jack," Col. Randal said. "We'll try to make it to the Via Balbia tonight. You keep pushing west."

"Yes, sir," Capt. Jaxx said. "My boys are ready for action."

"I'm sure you'll find some, stud."

Sergeant Ned Pompedous, who had been with him since the Swamp Fox Force days in France, walked up.

"I thought you were advising one of the new Ranger patrols."

"SOG *is* a new Ranger patrol, sir." Jack Cool had stolen his patrol sergeant.

"Bring 'em back alive, Sergeant," Col. Randal said.

"Same to you, Colonel."

"All right, Jack . . . do your stuff," Col. Randal said, feeling a twinge of unease. SOG was out to make a name for itself.

"SOG's going to kick ass," Capt. Jaxx said, "and take names, sir."

Exactly what Col. Randal was worried about.

While SOG drove off into the desert, Raider Patrol dismounted for a brief frag order.

Col. Randal said, "What we're about to do is attempt to drive to the Via Balbia and engage enemy convoys running at night. We have to exert extreme caution making our approach march.

"While the Via Balbia parallels the coastline, sticking close to it, there's secondary dirt tracks up to fifteen miles or so inland. Could be tough for us to cover those last miles to the hardball if the bad guys are running on the secondary roads at night.

"Follow my lead. Keep your eyes peeled. Teamwork, teamwork, teamwork."

Col. Randal climbed in the driver's seat. Master Sergeant Mack Beckwith was in the passenger seat, and King was manning the twin Vickers K .303 machine guns pedestal-mounted in the back.

Once it started to get dark, it turned dark fast. Driving without headlights, only using the "cat's eye" running lights copied from the Germans, there was just enough moonlight for Col. Randal to have the impression, more of a sixth sense really, that they were approaching one of the parallel dirt roads. He immediately stopped.

Lovat Scout Lionel Fenwick dismounted from the jeep immediately behind the command jeep and made his way forward according to plan. King climbed out of the jeep, and the two men moved up to recon the dirt road.

They came running back.

"Convoy coming, Chief," King said. "Moving left to right."

The odds against encountering a convoy at this point in the patrol were astronomical—at least they had been in the past. Col. Randal had only seconds to react.

"King, pass the word for the patrol to pull up on line, twenty-yard spacing between jeeps. Fire on my command."

Every jeep in the patrol had a number. When coming on line, even-numbered gun jeeps went to the right of the command jeep and odd-numbered went to the left—Raider Patrol had trained for it.

There was no explaining why an enemy convoy would be traveling this far south in the desert, headed east toward the front on a remote secondary track that was barely a road except in name. Col. Randal wondered if the truckers had become disoriented.

The cat's eye lights were turned off. Drivers gunned their engines as the gun jeeps pulled into position. Raider Patrol was approximately fifty yards from the dirt track. Lights flashed off to the left. The truck drivers were running fully lit up.

And, as commonly happened on night convoys, the spacing between the Afrika Korps vehicles had closed up. Not only was it dark but there was a cloud of dust kicked up by the lead vehicles enveloping the convoy, which reduced visibility to practically zero. The trucks were running bumper to bumper.

Raider Patrol was in perfect position to execute a linear ambush—the most basic, classic type of surprise attack since the beginning of organized warfare.

Col. Randal had no way of knowing how many trucks were in the column, what they were transporting, or if there were armored cars providing security. There might be a hundred trucks all carrying combat infantry who could dismount and gobble up Raider Patrol.

Ambushes always carried a certain element of risk to those doing the ambushing.

He let the lead truck pass until he estimated it was even with the last gun jeep on his right flank. At that moment, he curled his finger around the trigger of the twin .303 Vickers Ks on his side of the jeep, took up the slack and ordered, "Commence fire."

King had such quick reflexes it was difficult to tell who fired first. However, the initial burst from the rest of Raider Patrol was ragged.

Then, like a sputtering motor that finally caught, the machine guns roared into a synchronized, full-throated, mind-numbing crescendo of concentrated fire.

The machine gun drums on the quick-firing .303 Vickers Ks were loaded one tracer every six rounds. The cyclic rate of the weapons was so fast, the effect was like turning a solid beam of light on the convoy. The volume of fire was insanely loud. Everyone in the jeeps felt like they had been body-slammed by the noise.

There were seven jeeps, with six machine guns per jeep, including Gun's twin 20mm Oerlikon. Anyone not manning a machine gun was firing one of the .30 cal. M-1941 Johnson Light machine guns.

Raider Patrol packed an enormous amount of firepower. The trick was for Col. Randal to get the men to concentrate their massed fires. They trained for it. The gunners had all been taught to aim low, fire short bursts of six, shift their fires to new targets, and keep firing in short bursts until ordered to stand down.

At least fifteen trucks of various models and makes, many captured from the British, were caught in the immediate killing zone of the ambush, with others trailing behind. The lead truck burst into flames and crashed. The second truck ran into it, crashed, and caught fire.

The wreck sealed the fate of the remaining vehicles. They stopped and the drivers bailed out, causing an accordion effect on the trucks to the rear of the column. Tracers vectored in on the silhouettes of the trucks.

The dancing flames of the burning vehicles illuminated the convoy. One truck's gas tank exploded, sounding like a 500-pound bomb.

Col. Randal put up a green parachute flare—the signal to cease fire. Shouting the command would have been a waste of time. Gradually the firing died down. The keyed-up machine gunners wanted to keep hammering the targets, getting in a few late bursts.

Then the night was perfectly still, eerily silent. The only sound was the crackling of the burning enemy truck's small arms rounds they were transporting. And everyone's ears ringing.

The air smelt of cordite.

Col. Randal cranked up the engine. He led Raider Patrol on a wide arc around the tail of the convoy to avoid the possibility of running into any of the truckers or their passengers in the dark. There were almost as many trucks that had not reached the ambush's killing zone sitting empty—abandoned by their drivers.

Raider Patrol fired on them as they drove past. Down the length of the dirt track as each gun jeep crossed over, they could see a line of wrecked and burning trucks extending for nearly 200 yards.

"Trained my entire career for a night like this, sir," MSgt. Beckwith said. "Worth the wait. Have to admit, sir, I had my doubts at first about breaking down the Five-Seven-Five into patrols."

It was one of the best small-scale ambushes Col. Randal had ever conducted. A classic example of what can happen when a disciplined body of men operates far behind enemy lines with evil intent.

The question was, why was the convoy there?

Raider Patrol continued north toward the Via Balbia. An hour later, the patrol came to another parallel dirt track. As Col. Randal was trying to decide what to do next, a motorcycle rider drove past traveling west.

"Take the wheel, King," Col. Randal ordered, stepping out of the jeep. "Follow him and report back. That rider may be looking for a convoy."

Lovat Scout Munro Ferguson had moved forward from the second jeep in the patrol again. He hopped in the back to take over the pedestal-mounted machine guns. King drove out onto the dirt road, following the direction the motorcycle had disappeared. He was driving with the cat's eye lights on, like the Germans used during blackout. Hopefully any enemy personnel who saw them would think it was a Nazi vehicle.

Col. Randal sat on the hood of the second gun jeep in the column, clenching one of Waldo's unlit cigars in his teeth and waiting for what happened next. Thirty minutes went by. He was beginning to become concerned. Then he saw the cat's eye lights coming back.

Slipping off the hood of the jeep, Col. Randal stepped out in the road so King would know where the patrol was parked.

"Truck laager up the road about a mile, Chief," King reported. "Munro and I dismounted and checked it out. Hard to say exactly, but my estimate is in the range of fifty-plus vehicles."

"Any armored cars?"

"None we could identify," King said. "That does not mean there could not be a few there somewhere."

"Yeah," Col. Randal said, running through the combination of possibilities in his mind about what to do next.

His natural inclination was to drive up there, shoot up the truck park, then head north again for the Via Balbia.

Or, he could call in an airstrike—except the protocol for air attacks stipulated they only be committed to tanks, armored car formations, or large convoys. From the sound of it, this laager did not qualify.

Col. Randal walked back to the last jeep in the column. "Sergeant Blackburn, we've got approximately fifty enemy trucks parked up the road about a mile. I need you to do a mortar shoot. What do we have to do to make that happen?"

"Ideally, sir," Sergeant Rex Blackburn said, "we should cut the distance in half and I would like to lay eyes on the target so I know how to configure my sheath."

"Can do," Col. Randal said. "King will run you up there in the command jeep to do a quick recon. Then when you get back, we'll move the patrol up the track to within five hundred yards of the target."

"Perfect, sir," Sgt. Blackburn said. "Pasting a laagered convoy of trucks is a mortarman's dream—sitting ducks, provided I know how to properly plan the beaten zone of the mortar rounds."

While King and Sgt. Blackburn were making their reconnaissance, Col. Randal gathered Lieutenant "Dynamite" Dick Coogan, Squadron Leader Johnny Page, and the three Ranger lieutenants to explain the situation. He wanted to brief them on the thought process of what Raider Patrol was about to do next.

When the jeep returned, Col. Randal climbed into the driver's seat and drove parallel to the dirt track until he had cut the distance to the laager in half. Then he stopped. In the distance, small fires could be seen where the convoy was parked.

The mortar crew set up the 81mm tube.

Col. Randal gave the order, "Fire when ready."

Sgt. Blackburn said, "Hang it."

The mortar pumped out the first round immediately, followed by two more. Then Sgt. Blackburn adjusted the elevation knob and ordered, "Hang it."

By the time the third round was leaving the tube, the first round was impacting the target. There was a loud explosion, immediately followed by two more. Sgt. Blackburn continued to traverse the target, adjusting the vertical sheath of the shells slamming into the beaten zone, dropping a total of fifteen 81mm rounds on the truck park.

In the distance, trucks could be seen blazing.

Col. Randal ordered, "Saddle up."

Taking the wheel of the command jeep, he drove out on the track and turned right, heading toward burning trucks—three of which were cooking off, belching secondary explosions. The sound was something everyone liked to hear.

It sounded like victory.

The rest of Raider Patrol followed, all machine guns cocked and locked.

"Open when you come to bear on the first truck you see," Col. Randal ordered MSgt. Beckwith. He swiveled his pair of twin Vickers K's hard to the right as far as the stop would allow. His finger was on the trigger.

Up ahead, the enemy convoy came into view. There were at least a dozen trucks burning. The drivers had not set up a defensive perimeter, they had merely pulled off to the side of the road and camped for the night.

That was a mistake. Raider Patrol drove by, guns blazing at point-blank range—meaning it was almost possible to reach out and touch an enemy truck as the patrol traveled the length of the convoy. Each gun jeep engaged as they came past. Firing with one hand as he drove, Col. Randal felt the urge to speed up, but he kept it slow to give the gunners more time to hose down the target.

Engaging this close was exhilarating, but it was also high risk. What if one of the trucks exploded?

The parked vehicles were strung out for about half a mile. While only three more vehicles caught fire from the strafing, the devastation was catastrophic. Every lorry parked alongside the road was riddled by a blizzard of armor-piercing rounds, turning them into cheese shredders.

This convoy was not going anywhere.

The command jeep ceased fire as it passed the last truck. The crescendo of massed machine gun fire died out down the line as the other jeeps drove past the last truck in the convoy one by one. Then with the storm of machine guns silent, the night became unnaturally quiet.

As far as Col. Randal could determine, not a single round had been fired at Raider Patrol. That was how he liked it. Arrive unannounced and unexpected, never fight fair, hit and run, then disappear into the night, swallowed up in the vastness of the desert.

Do it again somewhere else.

11
SHOOT ANYONE

RAIDER PATROL WAS IN A LAYING UP POSITION (LUP) under camouflage netting in a wadi approximately twelve miles from the Via Balbia, the hard-topped highway that ran along the Mediterranean coastline. Colonel John Randal was well-pleased with his patrol's performance. If they turned around right now and returned to Oasis X, it would be classified as a highly successful mission. On the first night out, an estimated seventy-five-plus Axis trucks had been damaged or destroyed.

During an offensive like Rommel was waging, *damaged* scored as high as *destroyed*. In fact, damaged vehicles were more of a drain on Rommel's resources.

Afrika Korps maintenance crews would attempt to recover and repair trucks they believed could be salvaged and put back in service. That would tie up drivers, recovery vehicles, motor pool maintenance facilities, and mechanics who could otherwise have been used for something else if Raiding Forces had not arrived unannounced in the dark of night and shot up the trucks.

The idea was to overload Rommel's support services system, one pinprick at a time.

Col. Randal was sitting under camouflage netting, next to his command jeep at a small camp table with a blanket spread over it, cleaning his weapons with a shaving brush. He had his .9mm Browning

P-35—aka High Power—disassembled. On patrol, he was careful to clean only one weapon at a time.

Raider Patrol was in defilade, strung out along a wadi in hiding. Enemy air had been active since sunrise. However, there was no sign the Luftwaffe or Regia Aeronautica was actively searching for them in particular.

Squadron Leader Johnny Page, who had served with him during the siege at RAF Habbaniya, was leaning back in a folding canvas chair. The three Ranger officers, Lieutenant David Granbury, Lieutenant Jake Hannity and Lieutenant Charles Duffield, were sitting cross-legged on the ground. King was outside the netting on air guard.

Col. Randal said, "So, why did I have you gentlemen knock down one of the banks to the wadi?"

"To give us something to do, sir?" Lt. Duffield said.

"True," Col. Randal said. "Not the right answer, though. We're in a desert, sitting in a narrow ravine. What happens when it rains?"

"We get wet, sir?" Lt. Hannity said.

"Also true," Col. Randal said, "wrong again.

"In the desert, when it rains, these wadis can turn into rampaging rivers in a matter of minutes. With no way out, we could drown or lose all our jeeps."

The Ranger lieutenants nodded, as if to say "Got it." He knew they did not. You actually had to experience how fast a wadi could flood to appreciate it.

Col. Randal said, "I had you men knock down a section of the bank so in the event a rainstorm does blow in we'll have a way to drive out.

"That's called a Plan B, and Raiding Forces' Rules for Raiding stipulate, 'It's always good to have a Plan B.'"

More nods from the Ranger officers. They had all been required to memorize the rules as part of their Blood in the Sand training.

Col. Randal said, "The purpose of having you do the work yourself was because I wanted you men to never forget the importance of contingency planning—*always* have a Plan B. When you get your own patrols you'll have to be thinking three moves ahead at all times."

Lt. Granbury asked, "How often does it rain in this part of the desert, sir?"

"About every fifty years."

COLONEL JOHN RANDAL WAS A MASTER OF SMALL-SCALE hit-and-run warfare. He was in his element out in the middle of nowhere, far behind enemy lines. Guerrilla raiding was what he lived for, and it seemed like he had been doing it all his adult life.

The primary reason men in the Long Range Desert Group, Special Air Service, and Raiding Forces voluntarily returned to their units after prolonged desert service was because they eventually felt like prey after long stints behind enemy lines.

Col. Randal never felt like prey. He was a predator. Right now, he was planning his next move.

The idea occurred to him this might be a good opportunity to impart to Lieutenant "Dynamite" Dick Coogan, Squadron Leader Johnny Page, and the Ranger officers how a Raiding Forces' patrol leader's thought process worked—a teaching point.

"Here's the situation," Col. Randal said. "My original intent was to drive to the Via Balbia. The idea being to locate tank carriers transporting German Mark IIIs to the front and call in an airstrike.

"While the highway is only a dozen miles due north from here, shooting up the two convoys last night took so much time we were forced to find a LUP before daylight. We'll stay in place here until after sunset, when we can move out under cover of darkness.

"The question is, where do we go?

"Now, I've never seen the desert so crowded or as much Afrika Korps traffic this far inland," Col. Randal said. "Rommel is clearly pushing everything he has east toward Tobruk as hard and fast as he can.

"All the traffic on the secondary tracks complicates our chances of reaching the Via Balbia. It also increases the chances of our being discovered during the day. And limits our ability to hit-and-run at night.

"Now if you were me, what would you do next? Bear in mind, Raider Patrol has to stay within two hours of a suitable landing site at all times to be extracted for a strategic mission with a higher priority."

No one said anything. This was one of those Officer Candidate School, "What are you going to do now, lieutenant?" questions that the leadership committee instructors liked to spring on aspiring officers. Only the Rangers were 200 miles behind enemy lines—not in a classroom at the Infantry School.

Lieutenant Jake Hannity asked, "Sir, could you provide a little more intel on what to expect from the enemy?"

"Good question, Jake," Col. Randal said. "The convoys will be roadbound. All the drivers will be interested only in pushing on to the front and dropping their loads. At this point, the truckers may have already traveled as far as a thousand miles and they're probably exhausted.

"There's not much chance of Afrika Korps ground troops actively searching for us unless our LUP is spotted by enemy air or betrayed by local Arabs."

The Ranger lieutenants sat there digesting that information. No one came up with an answer. What seemed like a simple question was a lot more complicated when you were hiding in a wadi.

Finally, Col. Randal said, "King, what should I do?"

Answering from outside the netting, where he was on air guard studying the sky, the Merc said, "Reaching the Via Balbia was a *goal* . . . not an objective, Chief.

"As long as we continue killing rolling stock on the secondary tracks, keep doing it."

The lieutenants looked embarrassed. The Merc had given a short, concise analysis of the situation, followed by a clear, logical answer that none of them had managed to think of.

"So, gentlemen," Col. Randal said, "Raider Patrol is concealed from enemy air. How do we prevent the local Arabs from turning us in for a reward in the event they spot our LUP?"

Lt. Hannity said, "Shoot anyone who comes in sight."

Col. Randal stuck one of Waldo's thin cigars between his front teeth. "Even if it's an eight-year-old girl herding goats?"

Ahaaaaaaaa—being a Raiding Forces' patrol leader might turn out to be a little trickier than first thought.

COLONEL JOHN RANDAL SAID, "JOHNNY, I'VE BEEN considering what to do with your Number 1 Armored Car Company."

Squadron Leader Johnny Page said, "An armored car company no more, sir. Those vehicles we turned in were older than our drivers' fathers."

"You put 'em to good use," Col. Randal said. "They sure worked when we conducted our last raid at Habbaniya. Sir Terry informs me your people performed magnificently when you chased the Iraqi rebels out of Baghdad, and during subsequent follow-up operations against the Vichy French."

S/Ldr. Page said, "Taking Baghdad was a walkover. We gained the initiative and never let up. The Iraqis did not put up much resistance, sir. Their heart was not in it. I doubt the average soldier ever understood what they were fighting for.

"The Syrian Campaign, now that is another story entirely, Colonel. We had no air support. The Luftwaffe was able to fly out of Vichy French airfields and attack us at will."

Col. Randal said, "Terry's brother was commanding the Lancelot Lancers. He and the brigadier in command of the column both suffered nervous breakdowns. Were things that rough?"

"Not really, sir. It is no walk in the park being caught in the open desert by enemy air," S/Ldr. Page said.

"However, while the column did take a number of casualties killed and wounded, other than a handful of trucks destroyed, there was a surprising lack of actual damage caused by all the aerial bombing and strafing."

Col. Randal asked, "So why the mental collapse of two highly regarded officers?"

"I wonder about that question, sir," S/Ldr. Page said. "Haunts me, actually. Nothing in the campaign was as bad as what we faced being surrounded by ten thousand bloodthirsty Iraqis at Habbaniya, Colonel."

"Here's what I've been thinking," Col. Randal said. "After we return to Oasis X, how would you feel about forming an RAF Patrol with your Number 1 Armored Car people?"

"I should like that," S/Ldr. Page said, "very much, sir. Gun jeeps provide more flexibility than our old armored cars. Desert raiding will appeal to my troops—it certainly does to me, Colonel."

"Good," Col. Randal said. "I'm going to expect a lot out of you, Johnny."

"My lads will not let you down, sir."

KING SAID, "I HAVE BEEN WATCHING ALL THE ENEMY AIR activity, Chief. My guess is the Luftwaffe has established a forward air base in the vicinity. All I am seeing is Me-109s—fairly short-range aircraft."

"Makes sense," Colonel John Randal said. "Move fighters up to airstrips close to the front to provide air cover. You have an azimuth to where you think the base might be located?"

"One hundred-seventy degrees," the Merc said. "No idea of distance."

"The second road we crossed ran roughly that direction," Col. Randal said. "We should ride up there tonight and take a look."

"Want me to make a reconnaissance, Chief?"

"Let's take the patrol," Col. Randal said. "Might run into another convoy on the way."

At 2025 hours Col. Randal gave a brief Frag Order, "We're going back to the last road we crossed, drive west, and develop the situation."

Raider Patrol rolled out fifteen minutes later. The command jeep led the way with Col. Randal driving and King sitting on the hood with a .30 caliber Johnson M-1941 Light Machine Gun—a weapon he had quickly come to prefer. Lieutenant "Dynamite" Dick Coogan was in the passenger seat. Lovat Scout Munro Ferguson was on the pedestal-mounted twin .303 Vickers K machine guns.

The patrol reached the dirt track after driving cross-country for a mile. Col. Randal glanced at his Rolex—2105 hours. The night was pitch-dark. However, a full moon was supposed to come up later.

Anticipation was running high. Anything could happen. The Raiders were on high alert.

Col. Randal pulled up on the road, turned right and rolled out, traveling about twenty miles per hour. He had the cat's-eye blackout lights on, which gave him barely enough light to see but did not destroy his night vision completely. The jeeps had traveled less than two miles before a sentry stepped out in the road and signaled "Stop."

It was an Italian soldier.

King slipped off the hood and walked up to speak with the sentry. Col. Randal put the jeep in park and, leaving it running, stepped out. He walked up and shot the sentry in the back of the neck with his silenced High Standard Military Model D .22—*WHIIICH, WHIIICH.*

The Fascist collapsed to the ground dead. Col. Randal and King dragged him into the shadows on the side of the right-of-way.

"He was telling me where to park," King said. "A convoy is pulled over on the right-hand side of the road about fifty yards ahead."

"Hop in the back with Ferguson," Col. Randal said. "Let's light 'em up."

One of the advantages of operating so far behind enemy lines was that no one expected you to be there. The Italians were particularly lax about security. Their biggest concern was for an isolated sentry walking his post to have his throat slit by nomadic desert Arab scavengers. It happened from time to time.

Lone sentries seldom actually walked their post at night. They hid. And, that was good for Raider Patrol.

Italian troops performed most of the noncombat tasks for Afrika Korps. Running convoys, guarding fixed installations like airfields or isolated fuel tank storage farms etc.—the types of targets Col. Randal liked to raid.

"Convoy parked on the right," Col. Randal said to Lt. Coogan and Scout Ferguson, as he climbed back in the driver's seat. "Fifty yards— be ready."

King went down the line of jeeps to give them the word. Then he came back and climbed in the back of the command jeep.

Col. Randal swiveled the pair of .303 Vickers Ks mounted in front of the steering wheel as far to the right as the stop would allow, let the clutch out and the jeep began to roll forward slowly. Up ahead could be seen what appeared to be cooking fires scattered along the side of the road.

"Mention how big this convoy was?" Col. Randal asked over his shoulder.

"We never got that far before you interrupted our conversation," King said.

The command jeep drove past the first parked enemy vehicle. It was simply pulled off to the side of the road. The truck appeared to be a captured British Bedford.

Col. Randal did not open on the truck, though the temptation was strong. He wanted to keep driving until all of the gun jeeps were parallel to the parked convoy before commencing fire. The idea was to maximize the element of surprise, cause as much initial damage as possible, and increase the shock of the opening salvo.

"Check over your shoulder and tell me when, King."

"Roger."

Col. Randal adjusted his 45mm Brixia shoulder-fired mortar mounted beside him. He was only going to be able to get off one round, not being able to reload while driving. However, he wanted it handy in the event the right target presented itself.

No one paid Raider Patrol the slightest attention as the jeeps slowly drove by. Why should they? The convoy was two hundred miles or so from the front. Who could possibly bother them?

"Now, Chief!"

The six .303 caliber machine guns and King's .30 caliber Johnson LMG commenced fire as one, putting out a massive wall of firepower at point-blank range, shattering the solitude of the night. No matter how many times he had experienced it, Col. Randal was always momentarily stunned by the sheer volume of fire a gun jeep put out.

Since Col. Randal had waited until everyone could bear on a truck to initiate the attack, all six jeeps in trail opened almost in unison. The sound was ear-shattering. Night vision was instantly destroyed by the muzzle blasts of all the automatic weapons.

The effect of the unexpected attack was devastating. Most of the truckers were sitting around campfires on the far side of the trucks off the right-of-way so they were partially shielded. However, the suddenness and violence of action caused them to automatically go prone or curl up in a fetal position. Some scurried away.

The idea of fighting back never occurred to a single man.

Trucks started to burn as tracers laced through the canvas tops. A fuel tanker went up in an orange mushroom of flame. The heat seared the occupants of the follow-on gun jeeps as they rolled past, firing as they came.

Col. Randal kept the speed down but he was beginning to get anxious. The end of the convoy was not in sight. To the rear, one of the trucks exploded—*KAAAAABOOOM*—as the flames reached its fuel tank.

Lt. Coogan was struggling to change the magazines on his Vickers Ks. Lovat Scout Ferguson had already recharged his. He was putting rounds into the engine of every truck as it came to bear. King was firing his Johnson M-1941 LMG from the shoulder in short, crisp bursts.

The end of the convoy was still not in sight. It seemed to Col. Randal as if the action had been taking place for an hour. In fact, it was something less than sixty seconds.

Everything was in Technicolor. Tracers ricocheted off the engine blocks of some of the trucks, creating a light show as they screamed skyward. Hot brass was ricocheting off hats, shoulders, burning bare arms, bouncing off the seats. You could feel the heat from the weapons. The roar of all the machine guns was mind-numbing.

Then Col. Randal was driving by the last parked truck. He was out of ammo in his pair of machine guns, but everyone else in the jeep shot it up as they rolled past, as did the rest of Raider Patrol. There had not been a suitable target for his 45mm Brixia.

Col. Randal glanced over his shoulder. All he could see was burning trucks lining the killing zone.

"King, did you get a count?"

"Forty-two, Chief."

"Dick?"

"I counted forty-one, sir."

"Ferguson?"

"Too busy to get a good count, Colonel."

"I wasn't counting either," Col. Randal said. "Good job, men."

Raider Patrol drove a mile down the road, then pulled over. Col. Randal dismounted and walked back to check on each jeep. The troops were euphoric. The only injuries were minor scrapes, abrasions, and burns caused by overheated machine gun barrels coming into contact with unprotected skin.

At this point, Raider Patrol had damaged or destroyed over one hundred of Rommel's trucks. Unless the Desert Fox could capture more from the British Army to replace his losses, at this rate in a couple of weeks he was going to start feeling the pinch for wheeled transport.

Col. Randal knew Rommel was going to be able to seize replacement vehicles. He always had in the past. The field marshal was a master of improvisation. Lend Lease was supplying the Eighth Army *and* Afrika Korps.

He did not mention that thought to anyone.

"Lock and load," Col. Randal ordered the crew of each jeep. "Prepare to move out in zero five."

A strange thing about the desert—it appears flat but it's not. Looking back, there was a faint glow in the sky where the convoy was burning but it was not possible to see any flames.

And, the desert swallowed up sound. If any of the truck's gas tanks or cargos were cooking off back there, the explosions did not carry this far. Possibly the prevailing wind caused that to happen.

Raider Patrol continued driving west on the dirt road. After a while, the moon came out full, as predicted. It cast a mellow, bluish glow on the desert.

Eventually Col. Randal could see a checkpoint swimming into sight up ahead. There was a striped barber pole impeding entry to another dirt road that ran off to the south.

"Stay in the jeep this time, Chief," King said. He climbed out and walked up to the checkpoint.

A lengthy conversation ensued between the Merc and what appeared to be the sergeant of the guard, making everyone in Raider Patrol anxious. The men wanted to get the action started.

King walked back and climbed in the jeep. "Keep going straight. That track is the turnoff to the Luftwaffe airfield. A squadron of Me-109s is down there, operating off an improvised airstrip like we thought.

"Fairly well-guarded, according to the sergeant. However, ten aviation fuel tankers are laagered on the north end of the strip to refuel the German fighters. Approximately a quarter mile off this track."

"Nice work," Col. Randal said. "We'll pass on the aircraft. Let's go shoot up the tanker trucks. Those are strategic targets."

Lt. Coogan asked, "Who did that Italian think you were, King?"

"A Nazi *Feldgendarmerie* patrol officer," King said. "Military Police keeping the convoys running and checking on security procedures. I reported all was quiet on the track behind us."

Lt. Coogan said, "Nice going!"

Raider Patrol drove up the road until they were out of sight of the Italian security post. Col. Randal pulled off to the side and parked. "King, you and Munro locate those fuel tankers."

The Merc and Scout Ferguson disappeared into the desert like phantoms.

"Dick," Col. Randal ordered, "take some of the camel chip mines and put 'em out on the road behind us. We won't be coming back this way—make sure everyone knows you're doing it."

"Yes, sir."

Time stood still. No matter how many patrols he had led, when Col. Randal had to wait for someone else to perform a task and report back, the waiting was excruciating. He stood out in the middle of the dirt track and walked back and forth.

That might not have been the wisest thing to do—in fact, he knew full well it was not. An Italian Bersaglieri dispatch rider wearing a plumed helmet roared up on a Moto Guzzi motorcycle with a Breda 30 machine gun mounted on the handlebars. He stopped to talk to Col. Randal.

Since Col. Randal did not speak a single word of Italian, he shot the Bersaglieri three times with his silenced .22 High Standard Military Model D. The motorcycle toppled over, pinning the dead rider.

Lieutenant Jake Hannity, Master Sergeant Mack Beckwith, and Lovat Scout Lionel Fenwick jumped out of their jeep. They rushed out in the road to help Col. Randal lift the Moto Guzzi and push it off the side of the track. Then they dragged the dead dispatch rider out of the right-of-way.

"How many people are you planning to shoot tonight, sir?" Lt. Hannity asked, as he was appropriating the dead man's Beretta pistol.

"Not supposed to be like this, Jake," Col. Randal said. "This track is almost never traveled."

King and Scout Ferguson appeared.

"We located the fuel transporters," King reported. Parked about four hundred yards straight that direction."

"Guards?'

"Not that we could observe, Chief," King said. "The tanker trucks are not set up in a perimeter. The drivers parked them side by side for refueling."

"What's your recommendation?" Col. Randal asked, as he stuck one of Waldo's unlit cigars between his front teeth.

"We can ride in and do a gun run," King said, "or, if we have prepared explosives, it would not be difficult to slip in and place charges—which would give us time to clear the area before the tankers start going up."

Col. Randal walked over to the command jeep, "Dick, do you have enough explosives to make charges to blow ten aviation fuel tankers?"

"Sir, I have a canvas bag full of Nobel 808 cut in quarter-pound blocks," Lt. Coogan said. "Pyro Percy always warned me to be ready to blow up airplanes if we came across a Nazi landing ground.

"Tell me how long you want the fuses, and it'll only take a few minutes to have ten charges ready to go."

Col. Randal ran through his options. He preferred to ride in with all guns blazing and shoot up the aviation gas fuel tankers and be gone.

On the other hand, sneaking in and setting the charges would allow Raider Patrol to be a long way off before the trucks started blowing.

"Fifteen-minute fuses," Col. Randal ordered. "Dick—you, Fenwick, Ferguson, King, and I will infiltrate the truck park and place the charges. Two trucks each.

"Then we'll get the hell out of Dodge."

"I'm on it, sir," Lt. Coogan said.

Col. Randal said to Squadron Leader Johnny Page, "Pull the jeeps off the road on the left side about fifty yards. You're in charge. If we're not back within two hours, take command of Raider Patrol and continue the mission."

"What is the mission, sir?"

"Anything you want it to be," Col. Randal said. "Operate for two weeks or until you run out of ammo—then return to X."

"I do not like the sound of that, sir."

"Well, neither do I," Col. Randal said. "Just do it, Squadron Leader."

The demolitions party assembled by the side of the road. Lt. Coogan passed out the charges—two per man.

He said, "Place this against the side of the aviation fuel tank and pull the ring on the fuse lighter. Any questions?"

Col. Randal said, "King and Ferguson will guide us to the objective. When we reach the Release Point, Ferguson will lead out and take the first two trucks. King will then assign each of us two trucks. Then he will follow on and take the last two.

"The Release Point will also be the Objective Rally Point—after you place your explosive devices, rendezvous back there.

"Time is of the essence. We've already spent way too long in this immediate vicinity for my liking.

"Questions? Lead out, King."

The moon was bright. The desert was flat and sandy with a few scrub bushes here and there. It was easy to travel the distance to the Release Point in absolute silence.

King halted and the demolitions team all went down on one knee. Tension ratcheted up. This was the moment of truth—the point of no return.

The shadows of the giant fuel tankers could be seen less than fifty yards away. There was nothing moving—not even any truckers around campfires. They must have parked the big trucks and decided to spend the night under canvas with the Luftwaffe ground crew.

After driving those heavy rigs on an isolated dirt road for a thousand miles, who could blame them for wanting to sleep on a cot when they got the chance?

Scout Ferguson moved out first, floating on the sand as silently as a butterfly.

King pointed out two trucks to Lt. Coogan, and he disappeared. A hunter who had grown up in the hills of Georgia, he was almost as stealthy as the Lovat Scout.

Scout Fenwick went next, then King silently indicated two trucks to Col. Randal, and he was away.

The night was cool. There was not the slightest sign of a breeze.

Col. Randal made his way to the first of his targets. It was spooky silent. The ten-ton aviation fuel tanker seemed out of place sitting alone in the desert. He pulled the paper off one side of the 808 and slapped the sticky side against the truck.

Col. Randal put his finger in the ring of the ignition fuse lighter and pulled it. There was a faint *POP,* then he could smell a whiff of burning.

A cloud drifted across the moon. Col. Randal waited for the shadow, then followed it across to the next truck. He slapped the charge on the side, pulled the ring, and headed back to the Rally Point.

He had not seen any sign of a guard.

Col. Randal was the last man to arrive.

"Move out," he ordered, when he saw he had a good count.

Raider Patrol was a long way from the Luftwaffe airstrip, driving toward the safety of the Great Sand Sea, when the sky behind them lightened. Night turned to day off in the distance as the tankers detonated, sending giant orange mushrooms of burning aviation gas skyward.

Col. Randal pulled over to let his men watch the show. It was a good feeling. They had accomplished something significant. Airplanes cannot fly without fuel.

If Rommel wanted close air support from this squadron of Me-109s, he was going to have to truck in more aviation gas and a Raiding Forces' patrol just might be lying in ambush somewhere along the way—it could happen.

RAIDER PATROL WAS SITTING BESIDE A LONG STRETCH OF perfectly white, hard-packed desert on the edge of the Great Sand Sea, that was as flat as a pool table and stretched as far as the eye could see. It was the kind of place desert explorers had been known to tie their steering wheel in place, wedge a brick against the accelerator and take a nap while their car drove by itself. At least Captain "Geronimo" Joe McKoy had made that claim in the distant past during a late-night bull session while on patrol.

Who knew whether the story was true, but the terrain made the perfect landing strip. The Phantom team had received a FROGSPAWN prefix message that an aircraft was en route. It was due to arrive at 0330 hours.

There was no explanation as to why.

12
THE MOLE

SIGNAL FLARES WERE OUT. THEY GLOWED BRIGHT RED ON the empty desert floor. The night was cold. Colonel John Randal was sitting in his jeep wearing his leather bomber jacket with the fur collar.

He had no idea why anyone was flying out from Oasis X.

The pair of Raiding Forces' IMAM Ro.63 short landing and takeoff airplanes captured from the Regia Aeronautica flew in and touched down in a remarkably short distance. Col. Randal walked to the lead aircraft. The door popped open as he arrived.

Brandy Seaborn was alone in the small passenger compartment.

"Hello, handsome," Brandy said. "Climb in. We need to talk."

Col. Randal clicked on. "OK."

"R.J. unmasked Rommel's Good Source," Brandy said. "We have finally established the identity of the Nazi penetration agent."

"Really?"

"Colonel Bonner Fellers," Brandy said. "The U.S. Army Military Attaché."

Col. Randal said, "You're kidding?"

"It's Bonner," Brandy said. "He sends daily reports to the War Department. Your president has them immediately delivered by courier to his office.

"Unfortunately, so does Field Marshal Rommel." Brandy laughed. "He had them before the president."

"This is a joke, right?"

"No, John," Brandy said. "Colonel Fellers was using the U.S. State Department Black Code, as per his specific orders. The Germans cracked it. Poor Bonner has been working for two masters."

Col. Randal said, "Unbelievable."

"Not his fault," Brandy said. "No one is blaming him. However, he is effectively through in Middle East Command."

"Does this mean Jane's off the hook?" Col. Randal asked.

"Jane was never actually under suspicion. Who could take that idea seriously?" Brandy laughed. "MI-5 vets everyone when a mole hunt is underway. Counterintelligence is relentless and thorough—as they should be."

Col. Randal asked, "What about her husband, Mallory, agreeing to sign a statement saying Jane was a fascist?"

Brandy said, "Now *that* was a joke. Lady Astor assured MI-5 Jane never attended a single political session during any of the visits to her estate for the Gods Truth Ltd. weekends. She spent her time riding, playing tennis, and lounging by the pool. "

"That squares with what Jane told me," Col. Randal said. "She said Mallory was flirting with joining the Blackshirts before the war."

"Mallory," Brandy said, no longer sounding amused, "was a card-carrying member of the British Union of Fascists before it was disbanded in 1940. He shall be required to pay a price for the lie to MI-5 about Jane. Making a misstatement to Counterintelligence in time of war is a serious felony."

"Lied about Jane to get a transfer," Col. Randal said. "That's cold."

"It shall cost him," Brandy said. "Not only is Mallory in legal trouble, he will be cashiered from the navy and banished from the Six Hundred. His club memberships will be revoked and he will be a social outcast for the rest of his life. His friends and former military associates will cut him dead."

"Well," Col. Randal said, "he shouldn't have tried to frame Lady Jane."

"Agreed," Brandy said. "Turn over Raider Patrol to your No. 2. Come back to Oasis X with me so we can explain everything to her immediately. We have to make sure she never feels you suspected her, even for an instant.

Col. Randal said, "I don't have a second in command. And the desert is crawling with Afrika Korps convoys. There's no way I can leave now."

King rapped on the side of the fuselage. "Need anything, Chief?

"Go tell Squadron Leader Page to saddle up," Col. Randal said. "He's headed back to X."

"Roger."

"How long before Raider Patrol returns to the oasis?" Brandy asked.

"At the rate we're burning through our ammo," Col. Randal said, "we won't be able to stay out longer than another four or five days."

"In that case," Brandy said, "I shall see to it Jane does not learn about the cloud she has been under until you are back—but do hurry."

"Thanks, Brandy," Col. Randal said.

"Pam would like for you to say hello."

Col. Randal stuck his head in the cockpit. The Vargas Girl look-alike Royal Marine pilot was filing her scarlet nails. She had a foot-long, platinum blonde ponytail sticking out of the back of the black baseball cap she was wearing—a gift from one of the Rangers.

"Ronnie asked me to inform you," Lieutenant Pamala Plum-Martin said, "that the Havocs have flown three highly successful direct support missions. One for Captain McKoy and two for Billy Jack—the Wing Commander is beside himself."

Col. Randal said, "That's good news, Pam. We need the Wing Commander's experiment to be successful."

"Working well so far, John."

Squadron Leader Johnny Page arrived.

"You sent for me, sir?"

"You're flying back with Mrs. Seaborn," Col. Randal said. "Report to Sir Terry. Start organizing RAF Patrol. I need your men in the field as soon as possible—if not sooner."

"Yes, sir!"

RAIDER PATROL WAS IN A LUP ON THE EDGE OF THE GREAT
Sand Sea. It was hot. Mirages rippled in the distance. A man on a camel
appeared. He was dressed in a flowing robe.

Lieutenant Jake Hannity said, "He's no eight-year-old girl, Colonel.
Want me to shoot him?"

"Why don't we wait and see what the man wants first," Colonel John
Randal said.

King was studying the rider through a pair of field glasses, "I believe
that's Heart."

"What makes you think so?"

"He has a playing card pinned on the front of his robe. Not able to
make out the suit at this distance, but it looks like him."

"Who's Heart, sir?" Lt. Hannity asked.

"One of Mr. Zargo's men. For security reasons they identify
themselves as either face cards or suits," Col. Randal said. "If Heart's
looking for us, things could get interesting in a hurry."

The camel rider pulled up in front of the camouflaged gun jeeps.
Heart said, "Fancy meeting you here, Colonel."

"I thought you'd be working with one of the new Ranger Patrols,
Mr. Heart," Col. Randal said.

"On the way to link up with one now," Heart said. "It's about a day
out. I believe Mr. Treywick will be with it.

"When I learned Raider Patrol was in the area I decided to swing by
to let you know about a target you might find of interest."

Heart made it sound like it was no big deal for him to appear out of
nowhere in the middle of the desert and ride straight to Raider Patrol's
LUP. In fact, it was a feat of land navigation so incredible as to be almost
supernatural. Mr. Zargo's men did that sort of thing on a regular basis.

Col. Randal spread out a map on the small camp table. Lieutenant
"Dynamite" Dick Coogan, Lieutenant Charles Duffield, Lieutenant
David Granbury, and Lt. Hannity gathered around to observe.

"Show me."

Heart said, "As you know by now, Rommel is pushing everything
he has east—clogging the Via Balbia—forcing him to use all the
secondary tracks as well. The Luftwaffe is leapfrogging improvised

landing grounds forward to provide his panzer elements close air support—Ju-87 Stuka flying artillery.

"Afrika Korps has to supply those landing grounds with fuel. There are no large fuel tank farms this far inland, and there are not any pipelines. Captain Stirling blew up every one the Nazis tried to build."

Col. Randal said, "A problem for the Desert Fox."

"The Luftwaffe," Heart said, "has begun loading up ten-ton fuel trucks at the tank farms, then pre-positioning them in parks in a central location to dispatch to the forward landing grounds as needed.

"I understand you blew up ten of them last night."

Col. Randal thought there was no way Heart could know that piece of information. He said, "Roger that."

Heart said, "If you like, I can show you where Afrika Korps has approximately a hundred more of those fully topped-off fuel transports staged."

"You men interested?" Col. Randal said to his lieutenants, as he stuck one of Waldo's thin cigars between his teeth.

There was a buzz of excited "Roger thats" and "Hell yesses" from the group. These young officers were handpicked, hard-charging paratroopers. They had gotten a taste of Raiding Forces' style of hit-and-run tactics.

The Rangers wanted more.

Col. Randal said, "I guess we are, Mr. Heart."

Zargo's man pointed to a spot on the map. Since there were virtually no terrain features, it being all reasonably flat desert, the target was nothing more than a grid coordinate on a mostly blank section of map approximately thirty miles from Raider Patrol's LUP.

"You've been there," Col. Randal asked, "eyes on target?"

"Affirmative."

"Run it down for me."

"The fuel tankers are parked under camouflage netting with ten- to twenty-yard spacing between trucks. No security element of any significant size. The truck drivers are living under canvas in tents. There is a small administrative HQ. When additional fuel is required at a certain landing ground, the senior Luftwaffe officer at the airstrip contacts the HQ and trucks are dispatched to deliver the aviation gas as needed."

"Good report, Heart," Col. Randal said. "Twenty-yard spacing—pretty big parking lot. So, gentlemen, how do we take it down?"

Lt. Duffield said, "This might be a good time to call in an airstrike, sir."

Lt. Granbury said, "Sergeant Blackburn could mortar it, sir. He's like a surgeon with his 81mm."

Lt. Coogan said, "I think the fuel tankers are too spread out to use explosives, sir. Placing approximately one hundred charges is a lot. Too many not to expect to be discovered."

Lt. Hannity said, "Sir, why don't we just roll in with all guns blazing and light 'em up?"

Col. Randal said, "I like that plan, Jake."

RAIDER PATROL WAS IN ITS OBJECTIVE RALLY POINT (ORP) for the raid on the staging area of Afrika Korps' aviation fuel tanker trucks. Mr. Heart had guided them to the target and was standing by to take the patrol the rest of the way. The plan was for an attack starting at 0200 hours. The scheme of maneuver called for the seven gun jeeps to drive in, come on line, and cruise through the truck park, shooting up every ten-ton fuel truck they came across.

While they waited for the appointed hour, Colonel John Randal was taking the opportunity to explain to his junior officers why the fuel tankers were classified as strategic targets.

"Rommel only has so many of the ten-ton fuel tankers. Afrika Korps can't conduct mobile operations without them. Every one we destroy is one he is forced to replace.

"The only way to do that is to ship another ten-ton tanker truck from Italy to Tripoli. The rail lines that carry them to the ports are under unrelenting air attack on the Continent. And the merchant ships that transport them are under constant attack around the clock from Allied air, submarine, and surface warships.

"If a ship goes down carrying a fuel tanker, then the process has to start all over. Another has to be shipped to replace the replacement for the truck we shot up."

"Get the picture?"

"Wow!" Lieutenant Jake Hannity said. "So we're not just joy-riding around the desert in our gun jeeps raising hell, sir—this is serious strategic stuff."

Col. Randal said, "Glad you figured that out."

Lieutenant David Granbury said, "No one ever explained our mission as clear as that, sir. Puts a whole new light on what we're doing."

Lieutenant "Dynamite" Dick Coogan said, "Tanks can't roll and planes can't fly without fuel—it's Afrika Korps' lifeblood. Rommel has to transport every ounce of it all the way from Tripoli by truck to support his troops at the front. I hear he uses up about half of his fuel allocation just hauling it."

"I wondered why we went after those fuel trucks instead of the Me-109s, sir," Lieutenant Charles Duffield said.

Col. Randal said, "Raiding Forces attacks the targets that cause Rommel the most pain. When you men get your own patrols, remember that.

"Before you take your troops—meaning *my* troops—in harm's way, make sure the value of the target justifies the risk. Is that clear?"

"CLEAR, SIR!"

Col. Randal, accompanied by Master Sergeant Mack Beckwith, made his way around to every jeep in Raider Patrol. The sergeant was performing well in understudying the role of patrol sergeant.

He was everywhere—inspecting weapons, checking under the hoods of jeeps, making sure everyone had full canteens of water, and a million other details. MSgt. Beckwith was constantly looking out for the welfare of the troops.

Col. Randal was coming to the opinion that the former Sergeant Major of the 575th PIR was one of the most valuable additions to Raiding Forces in quite some time.

Guns was making a last-minute inspection of his twin 20mm Oerlikons. The ace gunner was expecting to be busy when the attack went in. Experience had taught him to never leave anything to chance when it came to his weapons.

He never did.

"How's the 20mm ammo holding out?" Col. Randal asked.

"Not good, Colonel," Guns said. "Most of our firefights in the past have been of short duration. On this patrol, they have lasted longer.

"Be running low after tonight, sir."

Col. Randal said. "Use short bursts but don't hold back. I want to take out every fuel tanker we can."

"Aye, aye, sir."

When they came to Sergeant Rex Blackburn's jeep, Col. Randal said, "Any problem putting up parachute flares from the back of your jeep on the roll like we talked about?"

"Negative, sir."

Col. Randal said, "When I pop a green flare, you start illuminating the target area."

"On your command, sir."

Waiting in an ORP always seemed to make time stand still. Col. Randal glanced at his Rolex, wondering—as he often did at times like this if it was broken. The watch was a present from Major the Lady Jane Seaborn. Every time he looked at it, he thought about her. In confidence, Brandy had explained that it was why she gave it to him— if true, it had worked.

Col. Randal was relieved the MI-5 investigation was over. He had never wanted to believe Lady Jane was an enemy agent. However, he also did not believe in coincidences. There had been more than one or two, and they had not looked good for his drop-dead gorgeous girlfriend.

Like a lot of men who had seen heavy combat, he did not experience emotional highs and lows. However, that did not apply to Lady Jane. Col. Randal had been more concerned than he would have wanted anyone to ever know.

"Saddle up," Col. Randal said, giving the same preparatory order that commanders had given their troops for centuries.

There was a rattle of weaponry and the bustle of men climbing into their gun jeeps. Col. Randal was at the wheel of the command jeep. Heart was in the passenger seat, behind the twin .303 Vickers K machine guns, to guide him the rest of the way to the objective. King was on the pedestal-mounted pair of Vickers Ks in the back.

Col. Randal turned the starter switch. The jeep came to life, followed almost instantaneously by the rest of the vehicles in the patrol. All the drivers had been poised to crank up. Anticipation was in the air.

Col. Randal let the clutch out and rolled out slow. The staging area was a mile away. At this point in the desert, between the scrub brush that belted the coastal region and the high sand dunes that made up the Great Sand Sea, the ground was firm and flat.

The seven gun jeeps were surprisingly quiet. However, to the men in Raider Patrol they sounded as loud as a freight train. The moon was out and visibility was good. The drive took only a few minutes. In the distance, dark humps began to take shape.

Camouflage netting can conceal things from the air and sometimes hide them from a distance. But at moderate to short range on the flat desert floor, all it does is draw attention. That was of little or no concern to the Italian truck drivers in the park. They were 200 miles behind the fighting at the front.

What could possibly go wrong?

Col. Randal was driving with all the lights off. He tapped the brakes three times in succession to signal the patrol to come on line. Behind him, the first three jeeps speeded up and pulled up on his right, while the second three came up on his left.

Raider Patrol was committed now.

Heart had described the layout of the laager. The tankers were parked at random, with ten- to twenty-yard spacing between trucks. Raider Patrol had its work cut out for it.

Col. Randal picked a hump and drove straight toward it. When he felt like he was about to ram it, he opened fire with the pair of Vickers's Ks mounted on the hood in front of his steering wheel. The tracers, armor piercing, and incendiary rounds ripped into the ten-ton tank, and it exploded in a huge fireball.

The raid was on.

Heart was focused on another truck and King another. The instant Col. Randal touched the trigger, they opened on their targets. Two more trucks went up in flames.

The rest of Raider Patrol engaged. Trucks were blowing up left and right. Then Col. Randal was weaving his way through the leading edge of the staging area, dodging burning vehicles.

The flames lit up the night sky. He fired at every camouflaged truck he encountered. The result was always the same—a strange soft *WHOOOSH BOOOM*, followed by an orange fireball.

All the gun jeeps were seeking out targets. The gunners had been ordered to home in on individual trucks—not all firing at the same one. Detonations were going off left and right.

Col. Randal reached for the flare pistol hanging from his seat by parachute cord. He triggered a green flare into the air. Within seconds a parachute flare cracked open, followed by a second one illuminating the parked trucks. Sgt. Blackburn had delivered, as promised.

Night turned to day.

Things seemed to be happening in slow motion as the jeeps weaved in and out. The attack seemed surreal. Trucks were exploding, brightly colored tracers converged on new targets, and parachute flares swayed overhead as more trucks went up in fireballs.

Sounds were distorted. The massed machine guns were roaring but no one seemed to notice the noise. Booms were going off continuously when fuel tanks exploded.

It was a dreamlike experience.

The truck park was approximately 1,000 yards by 200 yards. Raider Patrol had intentionally come in on one of the narrow sides. It was relatively easy to sweep through the entire target area. No one was shooting back.

However, it was taking a long time to travel those 1,000 yards.

The rule of thumb for strafing a target, as more than one combat pilot had explained to Col. Randal, was to make one showy pass and be gone. He always tried to adopt the same policy for gun jeep attacks. But tonight he was determined to destroy every single fuel truck. He was willing to make a second pass and violate the principle of not going back if necessary.

However, when Raider Patrol drove out of the target area and assembled to get a quick after-action report from each of the jeeps, the ammunition situation was so critical that the idea of making another gun run was a nonstarter.

Behind them, the desert was littered with burning trucks as far as the eye could see. Did they get them all? It sure looked like it, but probably not—there was no way to know.

Col. Randal gave the order, "Time to get the hell out of Dodge—let's go home, boys."

Not counting the trip out, Raider Patrol had only been able to stay in the field three nights. However, based on the value of the targets engaged, it was one of the most successful patrols on record.

Col. Randal was pleased to note that the patrol had not suffered a single enemy-inflicted casualty. A number of men had burns, scrapes, and abrasions. None were serious.

After dropping Heart off where he had left his camel tethered, Col. Randal called his officers together.

"It's not always going to be this easy."

RAIDER PATROL ROLLED IN TO OASIS X. THE PLACE WAS bustling with activity. Patrols were forming up, preparing to pull out. Nearly everyone from RFHQ had arrived. Raider Patrol was the first to return from the field.

Colonel John Randal ordered Master Sergeant Mack Beckwith to take charge of the patrol and have it ready to move out again within forty-eight hours.

He ordered the three Ranger lieutenants to report to Lieutenant Colonel Sir Terry "Zorro" Stone for assignment. Col. Randal was going to recommend they be made assistant patrol leaders to get more time on operations before being allowed to command patrols.

Lieutenant "Dynamite" Dick Coogan was another story. Col. Randal said, "Dick, I want you to form a demolitions patrol along the lines of Pyro Percy's. You'll be under my direct command. Be in the field operating as soon as you can get organized."

"Sir, yes, sir!"

Major the Lady Jane Seaborn, Brandy and Lieutenant Mandy Paige were standing by, impatiently waiting for Col. Randal to dismiss his men. They proceeded straight to the apartment above the operations room the moment he did.

Brandy immediately broke the news to Lady Jane about the investigation by MI-5 into the possibility of her being the mole at GHQ—Rommel's Good Source. It was a tense moment waiting for Lady Jane's reaction.

She burst out laughing. "How fun! Me—a Nazi spy? Seriously?"

Col. Randal wondered, "What the hell was I so worried about?"

13
LIFE IS A DREAM

JAMES "BALDIE" TAYLOR WAS AT OASIS X. AS SOON AS Colonel John Randal had a chance to take a shower and change into a fresh uniform, the senior MI-6 officer pulled him aside.

"How did Lady Jane take the news?"

Col. Randal said, "She's still laughing."

"You never actually believed she might be the Good Source?" Jim asked.

"Did you?"

"A lot of coincidences."

"Yes, there were."

"On another case," Jim said, wanting to shift away from the dicey subject of Major the Lady Jane Seaborn, "Colonel Bonner Fellers, the U.S. Military Attaché, was using the State Department code he had been instructed to use, even though he protested that it might be compromised. He was ordered to continue using it, did continue using it, and is now going to be sent home.

"We allowed Col. Fellers unfettered access. He proved to be an extraordinarily diligent officer. Everyone liked and respected him.

"His daily reports were brutally honest. They outlined our strengths, weaknesses, positions, losses, reinforcements, supply situation, plans, troop morale; evaluated our equipment; and provided a scathing assessment of the shortcomings of our senior officers."

Col. Randal said, "Rommel was reading those messages on a daily basis?"

"That's right," Jim said. "At breakfast."

"Well, that made his job a lot easier."

"Yes, it did," Jim said. "So much for the Desert Fox having a crystal ball.

"Col. Fellers informed Washington he believed we were going to lose the war in the Middle East. But he recommended the U.S. provide us maximum support under Lend Lease anyway. When America came in, he lobbied for the War Department to immediately send the 1st Armored Division to Egypt.

"Hard to fault the colonel. He was working for our side as hard as he could—we received a substantial amount of the things he asked for."

Col. Randal said, "Rommel's going to miss him."

"Yes, he is," Jim said. "In one batch of messages, Fellers described a series of raids the Special Air Service was about to undertake. The Germans were waiting. The SAS has been virtually wiped out—again."

"Someone in the Plans Division at GHQ," Col. Randal said, "must have briefed Colonel Fellers on those classified missions—bragging in advance—and good men died."

"On another subject," Jim said, "the United States renamed the Office of Coordinator of Information. Now it's called the Office of Strategic Services—OSS.

"Colonel 'Wild Bill' Donovan has been confirmed as its head, as we hoped. I have been ordered to Washington immediately to confer. Unfortunately, I shall not be available to advise one of the Ranger patrols."

Col. Randal asked, "What do they want to talk to you about, Jim?"

"My new title is Special Operations Liaison. The job description is to coordinate direct action missions between the British Secret Service, Special Operations Executive, and OSS. Plus, I am to advise Donovan on the organization and training of OSS field units."

"That's great, General."

"Off the record, Colonel, my primary responsibility at this point is to ensure Raiding Forces remains a joint U.S./British operation available to carry out special projects on request for MI-6 and the Naval Intelligence Division.

"I would like you to travel to Washington with me. You need to meet Colonel Donovan face-to-face. The three of us are going to be working together extensively."

"You know I can't leave right now," Col. Randal said. "Rommel's new offensive caught Raiding Forces in the middle of a complete reorganization. I've got green troops going on patrols they're not ready to handle, led by officers not fully qualified to lead them.

"This is not going to end well for us."

"I knew you were going to say that," Jim said. "My mission to the U.S. will last something over a month. The instant you feel you can break away, I need you and Lady Jane to fly to the States. It is critical we establish a relationship with Donovan and OSS early on."

"I'll be there, General," Col. Randal said. "You have my word on it."

Jim said, "Lady Jane is going to be an enormously valuable asset. Wild Bill is a man who came from a poor Irish Catholic background. He clawed his way to the top through sheer guts, determination and talent. The colonel is a tireless self-promoter and an unrepentant social climber.

"He and Lady Jane met when he was here in Cairo while you were MIA in Abyssinia. Lady Jane has agreed to allow me to put forth the suggestion she introduce him to British society—the unofficial Raiding Forces' social liaison to OSS."

"So," Col. Randal said, "it's a good thing Jane turned out not to be a Nazi spy."

"Yes it is, Colonel," Jim said. "Now hear this, loud and clear. Other than the fact R.J. and I interviewed you about Lady Jane as part of our official duties, the three of us never *EVER* had as much as the scintilla of a hint of a conversation to the effect that the idea Lady Jane might possibly be an enemy operative was anything other than ludicrous— bordering on sheer lunacy—dreamed up by a crazy person while dead drunk."

Col. Randal said, "Well, I don't remember it like that."

Jim said, "That's my story and I am sticking to it. I strongly recommend you do too."

"Roger that," Col. Randal said. "In spades."

Jim said, "Lot of coincidences."

"Yeah."

LIEUTENANT COLONEL SIR TERRY "ZORRO" STONE AND Colonel John Randal met in private to discuss Raiding Regiment's progress.

"Desert Patrol took No.1 priority," Lt. Col. Stone said. "We were only able to pull together four patrols after our losses during CRUSADER. Patrol Leaders are Captains Airey McKnight, Cord Granger, and Jack Masters. They are all en route to their assigned area of operations at this time.

"Captain Tall-Castle is organizing another from scratch.

"Ranger Patrol has already deployed two patrols—one under Captain Duke Slater, the other under one of the former Five-Seven-Five C Company commanders, Captain Douglas Wilson. We have the personnel to form four—provided we can identify quality patrol leaders.

"The main holdup has been Chief Rawlston not being able to desertize enough of the new jeeps fast enough. He and his team are working around the clock, but it takes time to do the job to our standards. We are about caught up now.

Col. Randal said, "Good."

Lt. Col. Stone said, "Squadron Leader Page has four patrols in the process of rolling out. His troops are old hands at operating in the desert. All he needed was one navigator, four Phantom teams, and Rangers to drive the jeeps. Took him about ten minutes to have RAF Patrol completely organized—good man.

"Pam did us a favor."

Col. Randal said, "You'll probably want to revert back to our original four AOs now that RAF Patrol is taking the field."

"Quite right," Lt. Col. Stone said. "I came to that decision as soon as Squadron Leader Page informed me you had authorized him to form RAF Patrol."

"Excellent."

"The Lounge Lizards will be last out," Lt. Col. Stone said. "My idea is to give Major Farquhar as much time as possible to familiarize himself with his new command. You might like to sit in on Mongo's Operations Order at 1800 hours."

"I'll be there," Col. Randal said.

"By the time Dynamite Dick's plane landed," Lt. Col. Stone said, "he had already drawn up a list of the men he wanted. I assigned him one of the former LRDG navigators. Clive Adair provided a Phantom team. TNT Patrol was ready to go and gone within twenty-four hours."

"Coogan's a stud," Col. Randal said. "Keep your eye on him. Dick's going to make a good patrol leader."

"The Raiding Regiment," Lt. Col. Stone said, "shall have four patrols in the field on operations at all times. Four patrols will be traveling to, or returning from, their AOs—they will be cleared to attack targets of opportunity en route both ways—so actually that makes eight patrols. Four patrols will be here at Oasis X, refitting and making preparations to return to the field.

"And, Raiding Regiment shall always have two patrols on ten days' leave once we survive this current flap."

"You should be able to keep that rotation up indefinitely," Col. Randal said. "Depending on casualties. If the time comes we have to start cannibalizing patrols, you'll have to come up with a new plan."

"I am already anticipating that eventuality," Lt. Col. Stone said. "Keep in mind the rotation I described is exclusive of Raider Patrol, SOG, the Railroad Wrecking Crew, TNT Patrol, White Patrol, and Scout Patrols I and II, which are under your direct command. If the going gets tough, you may have to share."

"Understood," Col. Randal said. "Sounds like you have things well in hand, as usual, Terry."

"On another subject," Lt. Col. Stone said, as he took out his elegant sterling silver cigarette case—with the family crest embossed—and extracted a Player's, "we have been provided a Y-Service radio-intercept intelligence report indicating that Raider Patrol knocked out over one hundred fuel tanker trucks. Rommel has literally gone berserk over the extent of the loss. He is even threatening to execute one of the Regia Aeronautica generals for failing to adequately protect them.

"How did you manage to run up such a fantastic score on what amounted to a training patrol?"

"The desert is crawling with Afrika Korps convoys," Col. Randal said. "It was like shooting fish in a barrel."

Lt. Col. Stone said, "Raider Patrol definitely made an impression on the Desert Fox, old stick."

"He made one on me," Col. Randal said. "I couldn't get close to the Via Balbia. We've never seen anything to match this offensive."

Lt. Col. Stone asked, "What would you like me to do with the three lieutenants who accompanied you?"

"They go to Ranger Force to be assigned as assistant patrol leaders," Col. Randal said. "I'll take Lieutenant Hannity.

"Don't make it look like I picked him."

"Consider it done," Lt. Col. Stone said. "I shall have a quiet word with the Ranger Force patrol leaders, allow them to select who they want. If anyone selects Lt. Hannity, I shall say he has already been spoken for."

"That works."

"On another subject, old stick," Lt. Col Stone said, "the Duke picked up on the fact that our reorganization has turned out not exactly the way it was initially described to him."

"He is unhappy the Lounge Lizards became a Patrol instead of the Raiding Regiment?" Col. Randal asked.

"Took the news quite well, actually," Lt. Col. Stone said. "One never knows with the Duke. He petitioned the College of Arms to grant a name change, 'Lancelot Lancers Raiding Regiment.' Happy as a clam—loves the sound of it."

"Make sure to use that title to describe the Raiding Regiment in all correspondence with your father," Col. Randal said. "We want to stay on his good side."

"Shall do."

Col. Randal went in search of Rikke Runborg. He found her sunning on the deck of the apartment she shared with Veronica Paige. The sexy ice-blonde Norwegian was oiled and glistening.

Rocky loved the sun.

"Still conducting your morning workouts?" Col. Randal asked.

"I am, John. Naturally, we had to eliminate our swim. Instead we run the perimeter of the oasis—approximately five miles."

"How's Sir Terry doing?"

"Still improving."

THE OPERATIONS ROOM AT OASIS X WAS A MADHOUSE. Field phones were clattering, Phantom operators were taking after-action reports from patrols in the field, Royal Marines and WRENS were passing them to the appropriate officer to evaluate. Signals were coming in from the RAF. Women were sticking new pins in the big wall map or moving others, based on patrol situation reports and/or the latest intelligence updates from Middle East Command Headquarters—none of the MEHQ reports were good news.

Wing Commander Ronald Gordon, aka "Flash Bang", was at a desk evaluating requests from patrols for airstrikes on potential targets later that night. He advised Col. Randal that after the success of the first three called in by SOG and White Patrol, the RAF had decided to commit to major air interdiction operations against convoys on the Via Balbia during daylight hours. If that worked, they would consider expanding the cooperation.

This was a first—direct air support for the army.

All four Raiding Regiment commanding officers were present: Major Jeb Pelham-Davies, Major Travis McCloud, Major Baltimore "Mongo" Farquhar and Squadron Leader Johnny Page. Each of them was briefing one of his patrol leaders individually on an upcoming mission.

Colonel John Randal stood in the back of the room. He stuck one of Waldo's thin cigars in his teeth and observed what was going on. He had provided the necessary command guidance; now what he needed to do was stay out of the way, keep an eye on things, and let his subordinate unit commanders get on with the job.

Not easy to do.

Col. Randal thought of himself as a tactician, but along the way he had become a special operations strategist. How did that happen?

As he saw it, his role as the commander of Raiding Forces involved three specific elements: (1) he needed to know and be able to communicate to his subordinate commanders what Raiding Forces was expected to accomplish; (2) he needed to ensure adequate resources were available for his troops to accomplish the mission; and (3) he had to understand the limitations of his men and equipment.

The last was the reason Col. Randal required all his senior officers to lead patrols before moving up to a command position—the exceptions being Maj. Farquhar and S/Ldr. Page, who both had years of desert experience commanding armored cars . . . which was the same thing. The only way to truly understand the workings of Raiding Forces' patrol operations was to have led them.

And that need to evaluate officers was the reason why he continued to lead Raider Patrol—or at least that was what he told himself.

Sub-Lieutenant Bentley St. Ledger breezed past. "Exciting!"

Lieutenant Mandy Paige, standing next to Col. Randal, said, "I think Bentley has a crush on you, John."

Col. Randal said, "I've already got three girlfriends."

"Three?"

"Lady Jane, Brandy, then there's you, Mandy," Col. Randal said.

"*I* am one of your girlfriends?"

"Well, yeah," Col. Randal said. "Jane has the money and connections, Brandy—she's a one-off original. You I keep around for your looks."

"If it were not for me, John Randal," Lt. Mandy said, "you would go on patrol without your toothbrush."

Col. Randal said, "You're probably right."

A few minutes later, Lt. Mandy said, "That was a nice thing for you to say."

Col. Randal said, "What—about the toothbrush?"

It was not easy to put one over on Lt. Mandy.

Major the Lady Jane Seaborn arrived. "Ready, John?"

The three left the Operations Room and went down the white steps carved in the side of the embankment to the stretch along the river where the patrols were making their last-minute preparations. Even though a third of Raiding Regiments patrols were already out, Oasis X was packed with men and jeeps. Everywhere, troops were mounting machine guns, making radio checks, loading supplies, pulling maintenance on their vehicles, studying maps, making ready.

Col. Randal wanted to see for himself how the reorganization was shaping up. Lady Jane, who was deadly serious about her role as the patroness of Raiding Forces, wanted to make sure the troops had enough of everything they needed. And Lt. Mandy did not want to miss anything.

Lady Jane said, "Teddy is flying out from England to take charge of camouflage here at the Oasis. With as many patrols as Raiding Regiment has created, there shall always be several here at any given time. We want to make sure the jeeps are always well-concealed from enemy air reconnaissance."

"Good idea, Jane," Col. Randal said. "I've had concerns myself."

There was very little likelihood enemy air would ever overfly Oasis X because neither the Luftwaffe nor Regia Aeronautica pilots cared for long-distance flying across the vast remoteness of the Great Sand Sea. But why take a chance? The Great Teddy was a genius at making things appear and disappear.

Lt. Mandy said, "Mr. Zargo and I are stepping up our surveillance activities. Rita and Lana circulate through the village day and night, when not performing their duty as bodyguards. We intend to guarantee all this increased activity does not attract unwelcome attention from outsiders.

"At night, acting on our suggestion, Terry has been setting out four-man ambush parties around the oasis."

"Keep it up," Col. Randal said. "Be harsh with anyone you believe to be an infiltrator."

"We shall," Lt. Mandy said. "Lady Jane asked Captain Chatterhorn to review security procedures. He suggested we build watchtowers around the perimeter of the oasis to see who is coming and going during the day.

"And, he recommended Major Adair declare a dusk-to-dawn curfew. Anyone moving outside the perimeter of the oasis during the hours of darkness will be summarily shot."

"In that case, Mandy," Col. Randal said. "I can quit worrying about security at Oasis X. You have it well in hand."

Lady Jane and Lt. Mandy both rewarded him with million-dollar smiles.

The inspection tour lasted an hour. Col. Randal spoke briefly with each of the patrol leaders and joked with the men but made sure not to interfere with their work. He wanted to get a feel for the morale of his troops.

It was high.

Col. Randal told each of the patrol leaders the same thing, "Never fight fair. Strike unexpected and unannounced under cover of darkness. Maximize the element of surprise. Utilize extreme violence and concentrated firepower—hit and run.

"Move on to the next target and do it all over again."

Everyone had heard him say the exact same thing at least a dozen times already—even the new men. Col. Randal knew he was repeating himself. He was a firm believer in repetition, repetition, repetition when it came to Raiding Forces' tactics.

The Raiding Regiment of today was a far different outfit than the original Small-Scale Raiding Company.

Raiding Forces had evolved light-years from the early days when it was made up of polo-playing guardsmen from the Life and Horse Guards regiments. Now, over half of the troops were Americans, with a quarter of the patrols soon to be commanded by U.S. Army officers. Some of the patina of professionalism had been lost. However, it was more than compensated for by the enthusiasm of the new GIs.

Col. Randal knew rapidly expanding a small, tight-knit military unit could have bad results. However, it is a given in a fighting outfit during wartime that nothing ever stays the same. The only constant is change. Men get killed, wounded, or transfer away.

New ones arrive.

The jury was still out on how the infusion of the U.S. 575th Parachute Infantry Regiment into Raiding Forces was going to work.

Only time would tell.

Col. Randal did not have the luxury of introducing the new Ranger Force patrols to desert raiding gradually. The 575 men were going to be thrown into the crucible of a full-bore Afrika Korps *blitzkrieg* counterattack. The Rangers were about to be tested.

Live-fire, on-the-job training.

Col. Randal pulled the Ranger Force Commander, Major Travis McCloud, aside. "Make sure to emphasize to your patrol leaders to stay south of the northern border of their AO at all times. I don't want them tangled up in the secondary dirt track network—is that clear?"

"Yes, sir."

"One of Mr. Zargo's men will guide your patrols to preselected targets," Col. Randal said. "No freelancing—that's an order."

"Understood, Colonel."

"It's dangerous out there, Travis," Col. Randal said. "Worse than CRUSADER."

"I picked up on that, sir—CRUSADER was no cakewalk."

"You might not want to mention I said so."

"Roger."

"Comfortable with the Ranger officers you picked to be your patrol leaders?"

"Negative, sir," Maj. McCloud said. "My guys are green as hell."

MAJOR BALTIMORE "MONGO" FARQUHAR WAS ISSUING HIS Patrol Order to the officers of Lounge Lizard Patrol. He had taken the extraordinary step of ordering all other ranks to attend the briefing as well. Colonel John Randal was standing in the back of a packed room with Captain "Geronimo" Joe McKoy. White Patrol had just arrived at Oasis X after a highly successful patrol.

They both had one of Waldo's thin cigars in their teeth.

Maj. Farquhar appeared to be the archetypical British Yeomanry officer: beautifully tailored uniform, scarf at his neck, knobbed stick, mildly eccentric, comfortable talking to his troops—calling out his officers and men by name, joking with them before the briefing started.

The Lounge Lizards were laughing. Everyone was enjoying themselves, though this was serious business. It would not have been difficult to imagine Maj. Farquhar as Robin Hood, briefing his merry men before going out to hound the wicked Sheriff of Nottingham.

Col. Randal liked what he saw.

Maj. Farquhar said, "Situation: This is WWII. We are in it. The wily Desert Fox has launched a counterattack headed for points east, etc. etc. etc.

"Poor bloke, eh, what!"

Everyone laughed.

"Mission: Lounge Lizard Patrol is taking the field to attack strategic targets—priority to fuel tank facilities, ten-ton fuel carriers, tank carriers, thin-skinned rolling stock, etc. etc. etc.

"Execution: Lounge Lizard Patrol shall deploy four jeep patrols to conduct raids, ambushes, engage targets of opportunity, etc. etc. etc. Our mission is strategic—prevent Rommel's fuel and supplies from reaching the maneuver elements of Afrika Korps at the front by destroying the old boy's means to transport it, etc. etc. etc.

"Raiding Regiment has a flight of four A-20 Havocs in direct support. Find a worthy target—preferably tanks, armored cars etc. etc. etc. Call for an airstrike—bash the bloody Huns for six, what!"

"Concept of the operation: Starting tomorrow morning at zero-four-hundred hours, Gecko Patrol will lead out, followed every hour by the remainder of the patrols, staggered in the order briefed, etc. etc. etc.

"Administration and logistics: Standard vehicle load out, double basic load of ammunition, rations, water, fuel, etc. etc. etc.

"Command and signal: "Chain-of-Command SOP, etc. etc. etc. Phantom teams to make daily situation reports, flares to mark targets for airstrikes, smoke grenades, flare pistols, etc. etc. etc.

"Before I reported in to Raiding Forces, I was given a classified briefing by the senior logistics officer of Middle East Command. Here are the relevant parts you lads need to know.

"Rommel has one of the longest supply lines in modern history—about twelve hundred to fifteen hundred miles as the crow flies. However, the Desert Fox is not a bloody crow. He has to bring all his fuel, ammunition, food stuffs, etc. etc. etc. with him when Afrika Korps attacks.

"Trucks—whether they be tank carriers, fuel tankers, or simple ordinary, everyday rolling stock—are our target of choice. Rommel requires five thousand of them to keep his fighting elements supplied. Reports indicate about a third of his wheeled vehicles have to be in for maintenance at any given time. He uses up over fifty percent of his total fuel allocation simply hauling fuel to the front.

"When you factor in losses due to enemy action—meaning us—the math simply does not work for the Desert Fox. Not that I was ever very bloody good at math, what!

"So, in conclusion, the Lounge Lizards—I mean the Lancelot Lancers, ha ha—shall do everything in our power to reduce Rommel's flow of supplies and fuel, etc. etc. etc. to a trickle by destroying his means to deliver it.

"Now, remember this when you lads take the field," Maj. Farquhar said, "strike hard for King, Empire, and the *Regiment!*"

Capt. McKoy said, "Ol' Farquhar sounds like he has the makin's of a' real good patrol commander. Where'd you get em'?"

"Terry's father," Col. Randal said. "The Duke's his uncle. Grew up in the Lancelot Lancers—commanded armored cars in France and he's been out here with the 12th Royal Lancers for two years."

"You seem a little tense," Capt. McKoy said, "What's got you so riled up, John?"

"Ranger Force," Col. Randal. "Western Egypt and Libya—no country for amateurs. How do you think they're going to do?"

"It's hard to predict the future 'cause it ain't happened yet—so lighten up. In a perfect world, you'd be able to ease the Rangers into the raidin' game real slow and easy-like," Capt. McKoy said.

"But this *ain't* a perfect world."

Col. Randal said, "That is true."

AT TWENTY-TWO HUNDRED HOURS, COLONEL JOHN Randal and Major the Lady Jane Seaborn were sitting out on the deck of their apartment over the Operations Room—the highest spot in the oasis.

He always became super-relaxed when he was alone with her. Lady Jane took away his pain.

Oasis X was a magical place after dark. Candles lined the steps down the escarpment. Torches burned along the narrow banks of the river that surfaced from beneath the desert and cascaded downhill until it disappeared underground again.

A million stars twinkled overhead.

Col. Randal had been in an endless series of meetings from the moment he had returned from patrol. Now, for the first time, he and Lady Jane could spend time together.

They did not have long.

He had ordered Raider Patrol to be ready to move out at first light—advancing their departure by twenty-four hours.

Col. Randal told Lady Jane what Capt. McKoy had said about predicting the future.

She said, "I am fairly certain someone famous made that statement first."

Col. Randal said, "The captain claims it was Socrates."

Lady Jane giggled, "Captain McKoy quoted Socrates?"

"Yeah—that's what he said."

Lady Jane asked, "Were you concerned I was Rommel's Good Source, John?"

"Negative," Col. Randal lied. "Didn't like keeping the secret you were being investigated by MI-5—felt bad about it. Still do."

"Every one of us has been vetted at one time or another," Lady Jane said. "Even you. Though, in your case, that was an accident."

"I didn't know that—knew I got vetted," Col. Randal said. "Volunteered to do it again because of all those women SOE ran at me. But that was long before you showed back up."

"Jim informs me there was a substantial amount of incriminating circumstantial evidence that did not portray me in a favorable light," Lady Jane said. "Mallory certainly did not help matters.

"He shall pay for his lie."

"Good," Col. Randal said. "I'd like to shoot the son-of-a-bitch."

"So would I," Lady Jane laughed. "Let's not."

"Maybe I thought you *could* be a spy," Col. Randal said.

Lady Jane said, "Nevertheless, even in the face of the allegation, you gave me this fabulous ring as a promise—Sheba's diamond. Love the ring, but I shall always cherish the public vote of confidence more, John.

"Well . . ."

"I know you had to be troubled," Lady Jane said, "What a tangled web we find ourselves in. Sometimes it feels as if the world is spinning out of control."

"Roger that," Col. Randal said. "The war's just getting started now, with the U.S. in. Feels like it's been going on forever.

"And we've been losing the whole time."

"Mr. Treywick told me a haunting story I cannot get off my mind," Lady Jane said. "The professor he was guiding in Abyssinia claimed the ancients believed life is nothing more than a dream.

"Could they be right, John?"

"I have no idea."

Col. Randal was glad Lady Jane was not the Nazi mole.

14
TARGET-RICH ENVIRONMENT

RAIDER PATROL ROLLED OUT AT DAWN. IT CONSISTED OF A slightly different configuration than the last time Colonel John Randal took the field. Lieutenant Jake Hannity was the assistant patrol leader. Master Sergeant Mack Beckwith was now officially the patrol sergeant. And Captain Hawthorne Merryweather, the happy psychological warrior, had decided to come along as a straphanger.

Raider Patrol was operating under its third name, having been Violet Patrol and Ranger Patrol previously, but the core troop complement was basically the same. The Phantom team from Abyssinia, Lovat Scouts Lionel Fenwick and Munro Ferguson, the fitters, Guns, the American Volunteer Group drivers now back in U.S. uniform, GG and King—nearly all the old hands were on board. The patrol was back to being a six jeep formation.

Col. Randal would have liked to have Captain "Geronimo" Joe McKoy, Waldo, or Captain Billy Jack Jaxx along, but they were performing vital missions elsewhere. Other than that, he was completely comfortable with the makeup of his patrol. With the exception of Lt. Hannity, MSgt. Beckwith, and three 575th Ranger replacements, the men had all served together for a long time.

Lt. Hannity was the wild card. The lieutenant needed to get more combat experience under his belt. Everyone knew Col. Randal would not have allowed him to be the assistant patrol leader if he did not have the right stuff. So, that was a plus in his favor. Raider Patrol troops were used to help break in new officers. However, everyone hoped nothing happened to the colonel.

For his part, MSgt. Beckwith was a seasoned professional soldier. He had melded with the patrol as if he had been a member from day one. Raider Patrol respected him right from the start.

MSgt. Beckwith did not suffer fools lightly. It was claimed (out of his earshot) by the Rangers that he "ate captains for breakfast"—which was another way of saying he was fearless in the pursuit of excellence. An officer better know his stuff before he crossed MSgt. Beckwith.

If there was anything Col. Randal liked better than talented junior officers, it was tough, capable NCOs. In the parlance of Raiding Forces, MSgt. Beckwith was a "good fit."

Capt. McKoy had once mentioned how the commander of the Frontier Battalion, Texas Rangers, had traveled up and down the length of Texas inspecting his Ranger Companies operating against the Comanche Indians. Col. Randal decided to do the same—traverse the length of the Raiding Regiment's AO, checking on his patrols.

The route he intended to take ran along the northern boundary of Raiding Regiment's AO. Using it as a base line, he could check in with Mr. Zargo's operatives, who would be working with the patrol operating in their sector. And Col. Randal would be able to drive north to interdict a secondary track, or even attempt to reach the Via Balbia, if the opportunity presented itself.

It was an ambitious plan.

Shortly after Raider Patrol departed Oasis X, they encountered Capt. Jaxx's SOG Patrol returning to base. Col. Randal pulled up beside the lead jeep Capt. Jaxx was driving. The two vehicles were facing in opposite directions with the drivers sitting less than a foot apart.

"Give me a report, Jack."

Capt. Jaxx said, "Rommel's driving east hard and fast. We intended to stay out two weeks. Only made it five days, sir."

"Heard you called in a couple of airstrikes," Col. Randal said.

"Yes, sir," Capt. Jaxx said. "Second day out, we worked our way to the Via Balbia. Just about dark, we set up a two-man road watch and happened to be in the right place at the right time. A battalion of German

Sd. Kfz. 231 armored cars rolled up and pulled into a laager almost directly in front of our two observers.

"The team beat feet back to where the rest of SOG was parked in defilade, sir. We got on the horn to Wing Commander Gordon. He informed us it would take two hours for the airstrike to arrive.

"No problem," Capt. Jaxx said. "We had time, sir."

"After waiting the two hours, we put out flares in the shape of a directional arrow a quarter mile from the target. A pair of Havocs arrived on station promptly, as promised, sir."

"Very good." Col. Randal said.

"Lit 'em up big time," Capt. Jaxx said. "Adios Sd. Kfz. 231s. Those Havocs can bring smoke, sir!

"The next night, we were sitting on the side of the Via Balbia when a company of Panzer Mark IIIs being transported on tank carriers came by, running down the hardball, sir. We waited for the last one to pass, then swung in behind and tagged along on the tail end of the convoy.

"When the drivers finally stopped for the night—same thing, sir. We called in a *Flash Bang*. The Havocs arrived on station and went straight into the attack. Tanks not destroyed were damaged when their transport carriers burned.

"Unfortunately, the AO was so active, sir, there was no way we could conduct a bomb damage assessment either night. So, I don't know what our final tally was, exactly."

"Outstanding, Jack!"

Capt. Jaxx said, "Everywhere we went, it was the same thing, Colonel—what they described as a *target-rich environment* at the Infantry School."

"I had the same experience," Col. Randal said.

"We had a turkey shoot on thin-skinned vehicles too, sir—just kept coming. Ran out of ammo and used up all our camel chip mines," Capt. Jaxx said.

"Good job, stud. You did a lot better than us. We weren't able to make it anywhere close to the Via Balbia," Col. Randal said. "What's your plan now?"

"SOG is going to re-up on everything, pull maintenance on our jeeps—same for our weapons. Double up on camel chip mines and ammo, then be back in the field in the next forty-eight hours, sir—maybe less.

"This can't last forever, sir. Don't want to miss out."

"Perfect."

"Heads up, Colonel," Capt. Jaxx said. "Afrika Korps is headed east with bad intent. Lock and load, sir."

"That I know."

Capt. Jaxx said, "Hey Jake, you the CO's new APL? Keep him out of trouble for me."

Col. Randal glanced over at Lt. Hannity, who was riding shotgun. He was green with envy after hearing the SOG report. The lieutenant was two years older than Capt. Jaxx and he was clearly chafing to have his own patrol—wanted to go kill Nazis—and that was possibly his biggest flaw. Col. Randal thought he might be a trifle trigger-happy—although that was not much of a blot on anyone's record in Raiding Forces.

For his part, Lt. Hannity aspired to have his commanding officer treat him as an equal and call him "stud." He did not fail to notice that Col. Randal had not issued Capt. Jaxx one single order.

Col. Randal put his jeep in gear, and the two patrols each went their own way. King said, "Nicknames like 'Jack Cool' are not passed out lightly in our outfit."

Col. Randal said, "That is a fact."

Based on Capt. Jaxx's report, he began to consider the idea that Rommel's offensive might be worse than originally thought.

RAIDER PATROL DROVE FOR TWELVE HOURS. COLONEL John Randal had the gun jeeps pull into a laager after dark. Master Sergeant Mack Beckwith reported to him immediately, as was his practice every time the patrol stopped.

"Have everyone pull weapons maintenance first, Sergeant Major. Have the fitters inspect the jeeps, drivers perform vehicle maintenance, then chow," Col. Randal ordered. "After that, tell everyone to get an hour's sleep—I'll pull security."

"Are we going out tonight, sir?"

"Roger that," Col. Randal said. "We're about two miles south of the farthest dirt track south of the coast. I want to see if there is still enemy traffic this far inland."

"Yes, sir."

As Col. Randal was cleaning one of his 1911 Colt .38 Supers in the dark with a shaving brush, a Phantom operator arrived at his command jeep with a message from Oasis X.

"Tell it to me, Wilcox," Col. Randal ordered. "I don't want to use a flashlight."

"RED INDIAN coordinates WRZ 697350. Standing by for instructions, sir."

Col. Randal asked, "You sure that message is secure?" The broken State Department Code, Colonel Fellers' fall from grace, and Rommel having a daily brief of high-level intel handed to him on a silver platter was fresh on his mind.

"This is a one-time-only-pad message, sir," the Phantom operator said. "No one can break the code since we throw it away at the end of every day and start all over with a new pad the next. It does not get any more secure than that, Colonel."

"Fair enough," Col. Randal said, knowing even without breaking out the map that the grid coordinates were to a location somewhere deep in the Great Sand Sea. "Send the following: "RE: RED INDIAN STOP JAXX COMMANDS RAID TEAM STOP EXPEDITE STOP.""

"Sir!"

"What's a RED INDIAN, sir?" Lieutenant Jake Hannity asked.

"A high-priority classified mission," Col. Randal said. "Need to Know only, Jake—when you have the need, you'll know."

"Yes, sir."

Raider Patrol rolled out at 2200 hours. At this point, the ground was described on the maps as "good going"—meaning it was firm, not soft sand, though there were treacherous patches from time to time. Col. Randal drove cautiously until he came to the dirt track.

Without hesitation, Raider Patrol turned left on the road and started driving west. Under normal conditions, they could have traveled all the way to Tripoli—over 1,000 miles away—without meeting a single enemy vehicle. These were not normal conditions.

After traveling less than five miles, a convoy consisting of a gypsy mishmash of German, Italian, British, and U.S. trucks, appearing out of the dark, met them driving east in the opposite direction. The convoy had cat's eye blackout lights on. Since Raider Patrol utilized the exact same headlamps, the enemy drivers saw no reason for alarm.

"Try to get a count, Jake," Col. Randal said as he swiveled his twin Vickers K .303 machine guns toward the oncoming convoy. He guessed the convoy had been traveling eighteen to twenty hours a day for the last three or four days. The dirt paths this far from the coast were not much more than ruts—not worthy of being described as secondary roads. Since the tracks were never maintained, they made for difficult driving.

The drivers had to be exhausted.

Those in front had a hard time seeing the road with only the dim cat's eye lights to drive by. But they were the lucky ones. The truckers from about the third vehicle back had to fight through a never-ending cloud of dust,which reduced visibility to virtually zero. Breathing was miserable.

Driving conditions only got worse toward the end of the column.

Col. Randal pulled over to the far side of the road but did not slow down. He could not drive off the track because of the sporadic patches of soft sand. And he had no intention of stopping.

The truck drivers did not move over to allow the oncoming vehicles extra room to pass by. Apparently they thought the gun jeeps were Volkswagen *Kübelwagens*. Germans drove *Kübelwagens*. Most Italians soldiers despised their Nazi counterparts as much as the Nazis despised them.

The truck drivers were not yielding.

Col. Randal managed to get the goggles dangling around his neck up and on before his jeep was past the first three trucks and plunging into the massive cloud of dust. When he estimated all six gun jeeps were parallel to the convoy, he commenced fire with his pair of Vickers K .303 caliber machine guns. King and Lt. Hannity opened simultaneously, as did the five jeeps behind them. Everyone had been anticipating the signal to commence fire, and the gun jeeps engaged as one, right on cue.

The burst of firing from the massed machine guns and Guns' pair of 20mm Oerlikons was thundering. The trucks were soaking up the automatic weapons fire. The dirt track was narrow and the convoy was hogging the road, making the range point-blank—eighteen inches or less.

The dust cloud was so thick that the drivers in the middle and rear of the convoy had a difficult time seeing the muzzle flashes of the weapons, but they could hear the firing. The Italians did not immediately understand what was taking place.

Near the front of the convoy, one of the panicked drivers slammed on his brakes. That was a mistake.

Since the trucks had closed up due to the poor visibility, the convoy was running almost bumper to bumper. Trucks slammed into each other in an accordion effect. Some caught on fire from the tracers and incendiary rounds. Luckily, none of them had exploded—yet.

Toward the rear of the column, one driver veered out of line directly in front of the command jeep. Col. Randal swerved to miss it, but that was impossible. The truck's heavy bumper clipped the left rear quarter of the jeep, flipping it. The gun jeep rolled at least three times—maybe four—throwing everyone out.

Col. Randal landed on the side of the road, slamming against a scraggly semi-petrified bush. He had the wind knocked out of him and for a moment thought he was dying. King, standing at his pedestal-mounted machine guns in the back of the jeep, was thrown clear and landed in sand virtually unscathed.

The Merc ran over and pulled Col. Randal to his feet. The rest of the gun jeeps continued on past to shoot up the tail end of the convoy before circling back to provide covering fire for the command party.

Tracers were slamming into trucks. Some rounds caromed straight up into the sky. The sound of the massed automatic weapons fire was a bone-jarring din. Confusion and the fog of war, which in this case was a dust cloud, had both sides firmly in its grip. Chaos reigned.

Raider Patrol continued to rake the convoy while the machine guns and equipment were being recovered from the wrecked command jeep.

The firefight—if you could call it that since no one in the convoy was firing back—was at point-blank muzzle contact range. The firing was furious.

"Where's Jake?" Col. Randal shouted at King, over the roar of the machine guns.

After a frenzied search, they found him. Crushed. He was dead.

Col. Randal and King carried Lt. Hannity's body to the Phantom jeep. After a quick check to make double sure nothing of military value had been left behind, Col. Randal was in the act of placing an incendiary grenade on the hood when Master Sergeant Mack Beckwith roared up in his jeep and jumped out.

"Stand back, Colonel," MSgt. Beckwith shouted over the gunfire.

He hooked a tow rope to the bumper of the command jeep. Everyone mounted up and Raider Patrol departed the area with the wobbly jeep in tow, firing everything from machine guns to pistols.

Behind the patrol, the gas tanks of the burning trucks began to cook off, sounding like 500-pound bombs, sending flames leaping high into the sky. This was one convoy that was not going reach the front.

No one in Raider Patrol felt very good about it.

Five miles later, the jeeps pulled off the track on a flat stretch of ground. A shallow hole was hurriedly dug. Lt. Hannity was placed in it and covered with sand and dirt.

There was no time for fanfare.

Col. Randal stood over the grave, "Lt Hannity showed promise. He went down fighting. I believe he would have made a good Raiding Forces' officer."

Then, following orders, MSgt Beckwith drove one of the jeeps over the grave several times to conceal the existence of the burial. Col. Randal did not want Arab scavengers finding the site and digging it up.

There was no reason to mark the location on the map. No one was ever coming back. Lt. Hannity died a soldier's death. He was buried in a soldier's grave.

There was a war on.

Col. Randal said, "Let's get the hell out of Dodge."

RAIDER PATROL WAS IN DEFILADE UNDER CAMOUFLAGE netting in a wadi, hiding during the daylight hours, waiting to go out again as soon as it became dark.

King said, "Chief, I believe there's an airfield over to the west."

Colonel John Randal said, "What makes you think so?"

The Merc said, "Three aircraft have suddenly appeared, one after the other, at low altitude, traveling east and gaining altitude. Me-110s I believe."

Col. Randal crawled up on the bank of the wadi next to him with the pair of Zeiss binoculars he had captured off a senior officer of the 10th Panzer Division at Pas-de-Calais. King pointed out the location and, sure enough, in a few minutes another airplane appeared at low altitude in the sky.

"You could be right."

"Need me to go check it out, Chief?"

"Roger," Col. Randal said. "Want one of the Lovats to go with you?"

"Negative."

King liked to work alone whenever possible. He walked out into the desert and disappeared. One minute he was there, and then he vanished. When it came to solo reconnaissance work, the Merc had no equal.

Two hours later, he reappeared.

"Airfield, all right," King said. "Set up like this."

He took his Commando knife and scratched out the layout of the landing ground in the dirt at the bottom of the wadi.

"Improvised airstrip," King said. "Most likely, one of the Italian emergency landing grounds. Including the four planes that took off, I make it nine twin engine Me-110s. The pilots and ground crew are living under canvas.

"No real security. However, there is a battery of twenty-millimeter anti-aircraft guns. Not worried about ground attack but they definitely have the RAF on their mind.

"Four fuel tankers are parked on the runway.

"Now, here is what you are going to be interested in, Chief. They built a big—and I do mean big—sand-bagged bunker for shelter in the event our air force shows up."

"Really?"

"Located adjacent to the tents."

"Good work," Col. Randal said. "Hit the rack, King. I need you rested for later."

"My pleasure."

Col. Randal summoned the Phantom operator who had the duty on radio watch. "When you make your next scheduled radio check, include a signal for Capt. Plum-Martin. Message to read, "EXECUTING BOMBSHELL TONIGHT STOP."

"Sir!"

As the sun went down, Col. Randal issued a frag order to the men of Raider Patrol. The plan was in accordance with Raiding Forces' Rules for Raiding to Keep it Short and Simple. Preparations for the night's work began immediately.

While King and Master Sergeant Mack Beckwith prepared a satchel charge, Col. Randal cleaned his weapons for the second time. With a mission imminent, the morale of the patrol spiked. Time to get payback.

Everyone wanted some.

At 2400 hours, Raider Patrol pulled out. They left behind the skeleton of the command jeep. It had been stripped of every removable part.

MSgt. Beckwith said, "Waste not, want not," and that was certainly true operating this far behind enemy lines.

After reshuffling personnel to make up for the loss of a jeep, Col. Randal drove, with King in the right seat doing the navigating. Captain Hawthorne Merryweather was on the pair of twin .303 Vickers K machine guns in the back. It was hoped they would not have to be used during this part of the mission.

The desert was good going—mostly flat, which made the movement to the ORP an easy but cautious drive. Upon arrival, Sergeant Rex Blackburn set up his 81mm mortar.

A quarter of a mile away, the shadows of Messerschmitt Bf-110s, aka Me-110 heavy fighters, could be seen parked in a neat row. As far as enemy aircraft went, the Me-110 was at the top of the most dangerous list. While not an impressive fighter in the air-to-air role, armed with a pair of Oerlikons 20mm cannon, five Rheinmetall 7.92 machine guns, and two 250-pound bombs, it was a deadly ground attack threat.

Had this been a regular Luftwaffe landing ground, it would not have been possible for Raider Patrol to approach so close in its gun jeeps. However, this was an improvised airstrip. There were no watch towers or any other elaborate airfield ground security, and this late at night, it was doubtful anyone would notice five shadows appearing out of the desert in the distance.

If anyone on guard duty did notice, they were not likely to be alarmed. At this range in the dark, the jeeps could—and probably would—be mistaken for a herd of camels. Besides, if Italian troops were providing the airfield security, as was generally the case, the plane guards would probably be asleep by this time of night.

Col. Randal had his troops gather around to go over their orders one last time. "King, the Sergeant Major, Ferguson, and I are going to infiltrate the airfield. Captain Merryweather will be in command in the ORP until we return. Sergeant Blackburn will wait thirty minutes from the time we depart, then he will fire ten 81mm mortar rounds at the parked Me-110s.

"When the initial mortar rounds impact the air strip, the pilots and ground crew in the tents should believe the base is being bombed and make a run for the bunker. Once they're inside, King is going to move to a position next to the entrance and toss in a satchel charge.

"At that point, the assault team will exfil back to the ORP, mount up and Raider Patrol will disappear into the night.

"Questions?"

There were no questions, but the tension level ratcheted up. Col. Randal and Sgt. Blackburn synchronized their watches.

Col. Randal gathered the assault team around him, "King will lead out, followed by me, the Sergeant Major, and Ferguson. No firing unless absolutely necessary.

"Let's do this."

King led out with the satchel charge in one hand and his .22 High Standard Military Model D with silencer affixed in the other. Col. Randal came behind him, carrying his .9mm MAB-38A submachine gun, with his Brixia 45mm shoulder-fired mortar slung over his shoulder; MSgt. Beckwith was behind him with a .30 caliber Johnson M-1941 LMG; and Scout Ferguson pulled rear security armed with a .30 caliber M-1 Grand rifle he had traded one of the Rangers a .45 cal. Thompson submachine gun for.

The assault team moved swiftly toward the landing ground. King could see in the dark like a cat, but tonight he was helped by the fact that the moon was out. The Merc halted when the tents came into view.

Without a word being spoken, King led the team on a wide circuit of the small tent city until they were in a position where they could see the sand-bagged bunker up ahead. It had been built with typical Teutonic efficiency. The shelter was constructed aboveground, out of telephone poles and multiple layers of sandbags.

The structure was squat and sturdy. The sandbags would protect those sheltering inside from shrapnel and bomb blast. However, the bunker would not withstand a direct hit from an aerial bomb. Almost nothing would.

Like all air raid shelters, it was a death trap if attacked by enemy ground troops. There was only one entrance. No firing ports. And, once inside, there was no way for the occupants to defend themselves.

No one in their right mind was going to stand guard outside the door during an air raid.

Not to worry—the base was nearly 200 miles behind the front line. There were no British ground troops anywhere within that distance. Nomadic desert Arabs did not attack fixed positions.

Life was good.

Raider Patrol's assault team silently approached to within twenty yards of the bunker, at a right angle to the tents. At that point, they lay down and assumed firing positions. Col. Randal looked at his Rolex. The lime green hands showed five minutes to wait before Sgt. Blackburn initiated his mortar barrage.

Out of the dark, a German shepherd appeared. The dog started licking Col. Randal's face. It was a heart attack moment.

Col. Randal tried to shoo the animal away. The German shepherd thought he was trying to play and started dancing on his forepaws, head down, nuzzling him. It was a friendly dog.

Finally, Col. Randal reached out, pulled the animal down, cradled him under his arm, and rubbed between his ears. The dog liked that.

One of Raiding Forces' Rules, which had been quietly done away with because it never worked in practice, was to Expect the Unexpected.

No one would have expected a sociable attack dog.

The other three Raiding Forces' troopers were snickering at Col. Randal's predicament.

KAAAAABOOM! KAAAAABOOM! KAAAAABOOM!

Men started shouting in German and a mass exodus from the tents ensued. Nazis were bailing out of their cots and running for the bunker on autopilot, half-dressed, half-asleep—self-preservation kicking in. Caught completely by surprise, the men—some highly decorated combat pilots—were panicked.

KAAAAABOOM! KAAAAABOOM!

One of the Me-110s exploded. Two others were on fire. Then the fuel tankers began blowing up, one after the other. Big orange mushroom-shaped balls of fire lit up the night, casting a pale, flickering glow over the area. Sgt. Blackburn was methodically traversing the line of targets with his 81mm mortar.

The dog lying next to Col. Randal seemed to enjoy watching everyone run, yelling and shouting, to the bomb shelter. In seconds, there was no one left in the small tent city.

The place was a ghost town.

KAAAAABOOM, KAAAAABOOM!

Col. Randal took his arm from around the German shepherd, raised his Brixia 45mm, and loosed off a round that slammed inside the door of the bunker. *WHUUUUUPH!*

The almost instantaneous detonation of the little mortar round was muffled, but the screaming from the men trapped inside the bunker could be heard distinctly.

King dashed to the bomb shelter. He pulled the ring on the igniter––a five-second fuse. Then he leaned inside and tossed in the satchel charge, needing to get it around the blast wall. As the Merc raced away, Col. Randal pumped another 45mm round through the door to discourage anyone from trying to be a hero and throw the satchel back out.

The *WHUUUUUMP* of the Brixia round was followed almost simultaneously by the muffled *KEEEEEBLAAAAM!* of the satchel charge. A tongue of fire shot out the entrance. The sandbags on the tops of the bunker lifted slightly into the air. The bomb shelter made a weird, yawning sound, then in slow motion, the entire structure caved in, creating a massive cloud of dust.

No one made it out.

Col. Randal ordered, "Let's go."

Four more 81mm mortar rounds impacted the airstrip in rapid sequence, which served as great covering fire for the team to make their way out of the area undetected.

Belatedly, the air defense gunners climbed out of the slit trenches where they had been crouching. The Italians opened with their fast-firing 20mm Oerlikon antiaircraft guns with a passion. Blazing away at phantom RAF bombers in the sky.

It was a spectacular light show.

The dog followed Col. Randal all the way back to the ORP.

15
H. E. ON THE DECK

WALDO TREYWICK SAID, "WHERE'D YOU GET THAT DOG?"

Colonel John Randal was sitting in his pink, yellow, and pale green camouflaged gun jeep, having just linked up with A Patrol. Ranger Force used letters A through F to identify their patrols, the way the U.S. Army did their companies. Waldo was sitting in his jeep on the passenger side, parked about six inches away. The jeeps were like horses. No one ever got off them unless they had to.

Col. Randal said, "He just showed up and stuck around."

"Looks like a' dog that could gnaw your leg off," Waldo said.

"Looks can be deceiving," Col. Randal said. "How goes it, Mr. Treywick?"

"We've been ridin' around the desert, blowin' stuff up," Waldo said. "Joker had a' plan all doped out—a' whole list a' targets. A Patrol's just been followin' his marchin' orders. Kickin' ass and takin' names *very* carefully."

The two were having a private conversation. The rest of the troops were putting up camouflage netting. The sun would be up full shortly and the two patrols needed to be under cover.

Waldo reached over and gave Col. Randal a handful of his custom-rolled cigars. "Put these in your pocket, Colonel. Don't want you runnin' short."

"Thanks, Mr. Treywick," Col. Randal said. "How's Major Beauchamp doing?"

"Everard is a' fine Southern gentleman," Waldo said. "Louisiana National Guard—still mad at the damn Yankees for burnin' down the ol' family plantation house in 1865. You done struck pay dirt when you got him."

"Good," Col. Randal said, knowing Waldo was a tough grader. He was quick to point out a flaw in anyone—especially officers in positions of command authority.

The old ex-ivory poacher had voiced more than a few concerns about Col. Randal's own shortcomings during their long association—most of which had been spent behind enemy lines. Col. Randal valued his opinion.

"Getting ready to head in," Waldo said. "We done expended most a' our ordnance. "Why don't we let the major take A Patrol on back to X and I'll marry up with you—looks like you're short a jeep."

"Beauchamp ready for that?"

"As he'll ever be."

"OK," Col. Randal said. "The Rangers riding with you can continue on with A Patrol. Put Ferguson and Fenwick in your jeep—or maybe GG. Your call."

"What's that dog's name?"

"He doesn't have one."

MAJOR EVERARD BEAUCHAMP MADE HIS REPORT. HE AND Colonel John Randal were sitting in folding canvas camp chairs under camouflage netting, smoking Waldo's cigars. The dog was on the ground next to Col. Randal, seeming to enjoy the conversation. Except for air guards, the men of the two patrols were sleeping.

"Have to admit, suh," Maj. Beauchamp said, "I was bitter when you broke up the Five-Seven-Five and dispersed it out around Raiding Forces the way you did."

Col. Randal said, "That's what Sergeant Major Beckwith told me, too."

"Now I realize a half-strength parachute infantry battalion would be practically useless in the desert," Maj. Beauchamp said.

"Paratroopers trained and mentally prepared to jump behind enemy lines and fight, suh—take 'em and mount 'em in heavily armed, highly mobile gun jeeps operating independently in small patrols—now that's another proposition altogether.

"Reminds me of the Confederate cavalry raiders in the nonfiction Civil War books I like to read, suh."

"True," Col. Randal said, "Lot of similarities to gun jeep patrolling."

Maj. Beauchamp said, "Most of my Rangers aren't regular army. The majority are draftees or National Guardsmen who were mobilized and volunteered for the paratroops for the extra jump pay. They're here to win the war and go home, suh. The one thing they have in common is baseball."

"Baseball?"

"Every last man," Maj. Beauchamp said, "understands the concept of 'hitting 'em where they ain't.'" They're taking to Raiding Forces' gun jeep operations like ducks to water, suh."

"Glad to hear it," Col. Randal said.

"Strange thing, Colonel, some of my worst rascals in garrison are turning out to be my best field troopers. Some of my strictly GI, by-the-book men are not performing," Maj. Beauchamp said. "Little disappointed in a few of my boys, suh."

"Always be prepared to get rid of the weakest man in your patrol so you can bring in new talent," Col. Randal said. "Let your people know that's your policy. You'll find they like the idea only the best make the grade. Wondering who's the weak man gives your people something to think about—keeps 'em on their toes."

"Makes sense, suh," Maj. Beauchamp said.

"That policy," Col. Randal said, "will produce the professionalism and cohesiveness I demand in Raiding Forces."

"As I recall, suh," Maj. Beauchamp said, "you did not seem as concerned as I expected when the Five-Seven-Five first arrived, looking like a bunch of tramps."

"Yeah, well, I was a little anxious, actually," Col. Randal said.

"Lady Jane—she took one look and said the 575th PIR was a 'splendid little regiment.'"

Maj. Beauchamp said, "Lady Seaborn saw something I didn't at that point, suh. We *were* a fine battalion before the Airborne Mafia at Fort Benning dumped all their ash and trash on us.

"The 575th Rangers won't let you down—just might not be as many of 'em left after the final shakeout, suh."

"That's fine," Col. Randal said.

"Here's what's about to happen, Major. You lead A Patrol minus one jeep back to Oasis X. Waldo and Joker are staying with me. Engage targets of opportunity on your way home.

"Replace the jeep I'm commandeering, refit, and resupply. Do a quick turnaround. Be started back here to your AO within forty-eight hours of arriving at X."

"Yes, suh."

"Remember, Everard, never, *ever* fight the bad guys when they want to fight you," Col. Randal said. "Hit and run."

"Yes, suh."

"Think of it this way," Col. Randal said. "Pretend you're Colonel John S. Mosby."

"The Grey Ghost," Maj. Beauchamp said. "Read everything ever written about the 43rd Battalion, Virginia Cavalry—Mosby's Rangers—at least twice, suh.

"Are you suggesting I imagine what Mosby would do in a given situation, then ape it?"

Col. Randal said, "Works for me."

COLONEL JOHN RANDAL WAS IN HIS CANVAS CHAIR UNDER the camouflage netting where his command jeep was concealed, talking to Mr. Zargo's "Murder, Inc." (Mandy had given them the nickname) intelligence operative who went by the *nom de plume* of Joker. The two had worked together before.

They'd always had excellent success.

Joker said, "That's a good-looking dog."

Col. Randal said, "I think he's a lover, not a fighter."

The tough mercenary said, "World needs those too, Colonel."

"That's the truth," Col. Randal said. "What kinds of targets do you have for me tonight, Joker?"

"A radio relay station about twenty miles east of here. Half a dozen Italians manning it," Joker said. "Soft target.

"Then, there is an emergency Regia Aeronautica landing ground five miles north of the radio station. Italians have a dump of one-hundred-pound bombs pre-positioned there, and a small cache of aviation fuel in drums. In addition to serving as an emergency strip, the Regia Aeronautica occasionally use it as a staging base—truck in ground support prior to their missions."

"A lot of these small targets?" Col. Randal asked.

"Colonel," Joker said, "if you maintained a patrol stationed here permanently and raided every night for the next three years, there is no way we could attack all the isolated posts the Italians have scattered around the desert in this AO alone."

"Let's hit both targets," Col. Randal said. "Then, if we have time left, we'll push north out of the A Patrol AO and see if we can ambush a convoy running toward Tobruk on one of the dirt tracks."

Joker asked, "What are you planning to call your dog?"

"The Rangers want to name him Ranger, but then they want to name everything Ranger, including a tree they put a sign on. My patrol wants to call him Raider," Col. Randal said.

"I'm going to let Lady Jane name him—I don't believe he knows he's a dog."

The German shepherd looked up, without moving his head from his paws. He knew they were talking about him.

Joker said, "Seems like he wants to be friends."

Col. Randal said, "Wasn't very loyal to those Nazi pilots."

"Possibly," Joker said, "he did not care for them—dogs do not always like their masters."

As the sun began to sink into the desert in a blaze of screaming colors, Raider Patrol and Ranger Patrol struck camp. The patrols were traveling in opposite directions.

This far south of the Mediterranean, on the very edge of the Great Sand Sea, the ground was still solid, but there were large swaths of soft sand that needed to be avoided. It was faster to try to spot the bad patches and drive around than traverse them using the sand channels the jeeps carried—which was considerably more difficult after dark.

Raider Patrol did not have to worry about bumping into the enemy. The Germans and the Italians almost never traveled this far south of the Via Balbia road network. The Nazis hated and feared the Great Sand Sea, while the Italians were not comfortable operating south of the coastal road network—even though they had occupied Libya for decades.

King rode on the hood of the jeep, staring into the dark, while Joker jogged ahead. They rotated positions every mile. The night was cold. Col. Randal was wearing the leather bomber jacket that the bandit, Cheap Bribe, had captured from a Regia Aeronautica pilot and given him in Abyssinia. At this time of the year, there was not much middle ground in the desert—the weather was either burning hot or freezing cold.

After two hours of herky-jerky driving, Joker stopped and turned back to face the patrol. Col. Randal pulled up beside him.

"Target dead ahead, Colonel, three hundred yards."

Col. Randal said, "Mr. Treywick, go tell Sergeant Blackburn to set up his mortar. Bring the rest of the jeeps on line."

Waldo disappeared in the dark. Soon the patrol began pulling up on each side of the command jeep. Master Sergeant Mack Beckwith appeared on foot. Col. Randal stepped out, and the two trooped the line, making a last-minute check with each vehicle commander to make sure everyone understood exactly what was about to take place.

This was redundant. He had issued a frag order before the patrol departed their LUP. Everyone knew what to do. Raider Patrol was made up of seasoned veterans with a sprinkling of new Rangers who were learning fast.

Waldo returned to his place in his jeep. King climbed in the vacated right hand seat of the command vehicle and Joker manned the pair of pedestal-mounted .303 Vickers Ks in the back. Directly behind the jeep, Sgt. Blackburn set up his mortar and hung a round, sliding the fins part way down the mouth of the tube. The 81mm mortar was a smooth bore, muzzle-loaded, high-angle-of-fire weapon.

It hit hard.

"Ready, sir, on your command—one round HE on the deck."

"Do it!" Col. Randal ordered.

The mortar thumped, the round was away. Sgt. Blackburn was not actually trying to drop the shell on the radio relay station since all he had to go on was a direction and distance to target. The idea was to get close. The highly-drilled mortar team immediately broke down the weapon, pitched it in the back of their jeep, mounted up, and pulled on line with the rest of the patrol as the 81mm round arched high into the sky.

As soon as Sgt. Blackburn's jeep was in place, Col. Randal let out the clutch. All six jeeps started rolling toward the objective, which they still could not see in the distance. The plan, as briefed, was to move forward until the 81mm mortar shell impacted.

When it detonated, all the gunners would use the explosion as the signal to commence firing and a gun jeep cavalry charge would ensue.

The idea was for the incoming round to scare the handful of Italians manning the radio relay station into taking cover or fleeing for their lives—not realizing what was happening—except that it was bad.

Col. Randal had no interest in killing them.

He needed panicked survivors to be able to report back to their higher headquarters what had happened. It does not accomplish anything to conduct a pinprick raid in the middle of nowhere if the word does not get out about it.

Col. Randal did not want to chance a firefight over what was a basically a worthless target of no real military value. The mortar round was an improvised feint. The idea was to distract the enemy long enough for a violent, high-speed ground attack to close on the objective unopposed.

At least that was the plan.

CRUUUUUMP!

Up ahead, the 81mm round screamed down out of the sky and slammed home, shattering the night. There was a brilliant flash of light. Now the men of Raider Patrol could see the objective. Thirty-four .303 Vickers K machine guns and one pair of 20mm Oerlikon cannons opened with a mighty roar. A massive stream of tracers vectored in on the radio station.

Col. Randal was firing and driving. The roar of all the automatic weapons was deafening. He could not see the objective. All the muzzle blasts from the machine guns on his jeep had destroyed his night vision.

If it was this bad in the jeep, he wondered how bad it must be on the receiving end.

As hoped, the instant Sgt. Blackburn's mortar round impacted, sounding like the end of the world to the sleeping Italian radiomen, they jumped out of bed and ran off into the desert in different directions, panicked out of their minds. No one bothered wasting time getting dressed.

Most of the Italians were under the impression the radio station was being bombed. The Blackshirts did not have a bunker to hide in. They had never bothered to dig slit trenches—digging being hard, hot work in the desert. No one ever dreamed this remote station would be attacked.

Out of the dark, the shape of a small one-story mud building materialized. The cone of machine gun fire vectored in on it. Col. Randal switched on his cat's eye lights. That was the signal for the other jeeps to do the same. As the patrol pulled close, the objective was illuminated in the mellow glow of the six jeeps' blackout headlamps.

Col. Randal fired a red parachute flare. The firing ceased.

Lovat Scouts Lionel Fenwick and Munro Ferguson and the Phantom team dismounted on the run. They made entry into the bullet-pockmarked building. Their red-lens flashlights were turned on, pistols at the ready. All five men were trained to look for classified enemy signals' intelligence information.

The Raiders appeared to be moving in slow motion but that was deceptive—slow equals smooth, smooth equals fast. Every move was choreographed, well-thought-out in advance, exactly as Captain "Geronimo" Joe McKoy preached to the troops at every opportunity: "Take your time in a hurry."

This simple concept formed the basis of virtually everything Raiding Forces did tactically.

Col. Randal followed them inside. The building was completely empty. Surprisingly—or maybe not—he found six pistol belts containing Beretta M-1935 .32 ACP caliber handguns in their holsters, hanging on a rack by the front door. Five M-91 6.5X52mm Carcano carbines were in a wooden stand.

There was not going to be any firefight tonight. The signalmen had departed the area in all due haste—without their weapons. Col. Randal scooped up the gun belts. The Berettas came in handy to trade to the rear echelon armchair commando types at the Puzzle Palace, who preferred to carry them instead of their issue .455 Webley revolvers. Captured enemy sidearms added to the edgy desert warrior image the armchair commandos loved to cultivate.

He left the rifles. The Italian signalmen might need them later to defend against Arab marauders. If the Italians were left completely unarmed, the bandits would murder them all.

"All clear, sir," Scout Fenwick reported.

"Other than operating instruction manuals and the codes for the next month, nothing significant of interest here."

Master Sergeant Mack Beckwith arrived, carrying a pair of small charges made out of 808 explosives. He placed one of them on the radio, then disappeared up the stairs to the roof where he put a charge at the base of the radio antenna.

When he came back down, he said, "Fire in the hole!"

Col. Randal tossed him one of the pistol belts, "Here's a souvenir, Sergeant Major."

"Thanks, Colonel," MSgt. Beckwith said as he pulled the ring on the fuse igniter attached to the charge on the radio. "Fire in the hole!"

Everyone cleared the building, moving fast but *not* running—the ironclad rule being to never run away from explosives with the fuse lit. You might trip, fall down, injure yourself, and get blown up. Everyone was shouting "Fire in the hole!" Five-minute fuses on the demolitions were burning and some of that time had elapsed. Raider Patrol was pulling out of the area when the sound of the explosions reached them.

The small charges were not very loud.

By Col. Randal's standards, this was the picture-perfect small-scale raid: No friendly casualties. Some intelligence gained. Military equipment at the target destroyed.

A message had been sent to Afrika Korps—Raiding Forces could attack any time, any place it wanted to and there was nothing Rommel could do about it.

And, they might be back.

The Italians at the relay station were radio specialists. Once they got up the nerve to return to investigate what had happened, they should be able to improvise communications. No doubt they would be contacting their higher headquarters, screaming for help.

Would anyone come to reinforce them? Col. Randal was of the opinion probably not. But Afrika Korps would be unable to ignore the fact Raiding Forces were operating deep in their backyard. That would give Rommel one more thing to think about at a time when his offensive required all his attention. Reports of raids would be coming in from Tobruk to Tripoli.

Not exactly "death by a thousand cuts," Col. Randal thought, as Raider Patrol rolled into the dark. But absolutely "maddening distraction." He had seen classified Y-Service intercepts that suggested the Desert Fox fixated on Raiding Forces' strikes against his remote rear areas in the desert and along the coastline. They disturbed him far more than the materiel damage should have.

Intelligence also claimed that Hitler obsessed over reports of the raids.

Enemy personnel and equipment losses—minor. Attack on the enemy commander's psyche—priceless.

THERE HAD BEEN A CHANGE OF PLANS. RAIDER PATROL WAS in concealment in a patch of scrub brush along one of the eastbound desert tracks. Colonel John Randal had decided to head north to set up an ambush for wheeled traffic, then turn around and travel back to the Italian landing ground Joker had identified as a target. The idea occurred to him that the last place enemy air would look for them after an ambush would be on their own auxiliary airstrip—hiding in plain sight.

His plan was not without risk. Raider Patrol would be making at least part of the drive to the Regia Aeronautica landing ground during daylight. The gamble was that they could carry out an ambush and be gone before the word got back to Afrika Korps and enemy air came looking for them.

It might work.

Col. Randal loved setting up ambushes. It was a skill that is as much an art as a military science. He had been at it since his prewar days in the U.S. 26th Cavalry Regiment. Back then, he had been detached to command a flying squad of Philippine Scouts tasked with hunting elusive communist Huk guerrilla bandits deep in the jungle.

Ambushes can be broken down into two main categories. The first alludes to distance: Near ambushes and far ambushes. The second goes to the configuration of the ambush—linear, L-shaped, V-shaped, etc. The list is only limited by the imagination.

Over the years, Col. Randal had come to prefer simple tactics. Tonight, or more accurately, this morning, though it was still pitch dark, he had deployed Raider Patrol in a close linear formation. Close, meaning the gun jeeps were approximately fifty feet off the dirt track hidden in the brush. The vehicles were spread out about ten yards apart.

This complied with Raiding Forces' Rules for Raiding: Keep it Short and Simple. The thirty-five Vickers K machine guns and the pair of 20mm cannon fires would be concentrated, giving Col. Randal tight control.

The signal to initiate the ambush was to be a 45mm round fired from his Brixia shoulder-fired mortar. Col. Randal could have chosen to utilize a parachute flare or blow a whistle. However, he preferred his signal to commence firing to be one that inflicted immediate casualties—not one that alerted the intended target an attack was about to take place.

Even a split second's warning can give the enemy time to react. One of the unwritten rules Raiding Forces lived by was: Never Fight Fair. Surprise and shock were paramount. A properly planned, prepared, and executed ambush should only last a matter of seconds.

Violent in the extreme.

There is no defense against an ambush unless the target that enters the killing zone is superior in size to the party doing the ambushing. In that case, the enemy can assault into the ambushers or roll up the flanks.

Militarily speaking, that is officially not good, though there is no way to guarantee it will not happen. Complacency can get the ambushing party killed.

Col. Randal was running all those combinations of things through his mind as he stepped out on the track to walk the length of the kill zone—with the dog trotting alongside—to inspect it from the bad guys' point of view. The paramount rule to remember when setting up an ambush is to never, ever hold your enemy in contempt. They *can* fight back—particularly the Germans.

Never leave anything to chance.

Trooping the length of the ambush site, what Col. Randal saw was nothing. Which was exactly what he wanted to see—perfect. The dog seemed to enjoy the stroll.

Then it was time to wait. The waiting in an ambush site is the worst part. Unless there is specific intelligence about an enemy movement, there is no guarantee a target will present itself. Which happens as often as not.

The sun came up. The desert went from cold to hot with no in-between. One minute it was cold; the next it was hot.

Three hours and nothing happened. Sitting in an ambush can be as boring as watching paint dry. It should not be that way, but it is.

The dog was sleeping on the floorboard between the bucket seats of the jeep. His ears pricked up but he did not raise his muzzle off his paws. Both eyes came open.

Col. Randal clicked on. He did not know what, but something had happened. King moved in behind his pair of .303 caliber Vickers K machine guns.

The dirt track ran over the horizon to the west and disappeared into the patch of sunbaked thicket Raider Patrol was concealed in to the east. In the distance, five motorcycles appeared. An Italian *Bersaglieri* motorcycle patrol running in trail came into sight.

Col. Randal raised his Zeiss binoculars.

"Guzzi Alice 500s each with a 6.5X52 mm Breda 30 machine gun mounted on the handle bars," he said, to no one in particular. King was studying the riders through his own binoculars. Captain Hawthorne

Merryweather was on the pair of pedestal-mounted Vickers Ks in the back.

The dog cocked his head, seemingly interested in the comment about the composition of the Italian patrol.

"Let's capture 'em," Col. Randal said.

King went left and he went right to notify the other jeeps of the change in plan. On the far right flank, Col. Randal found MSgt Beckwith. "Five Italian motorcyclists heading this way. We're going to try to take 'em prisoneR.J.ust before they get to you, Sergeant Major, initiate the ambush by pulling your jeep out and blocking the road."

"Yes, sir!"

"Be careful," Col. Randal said. "The riders have machine guns mounted on their handlebars. If any of *Bersaglieri* so much as touch one, let 'em have it."

"Wilco," MSgt. Beckwith said. "You hear that, men?"

The two Rangers in the jeep chorused, "Roger, Top."

Col. Randal and the dog trotted back to the command jeep. He climbed in and waited. The German shepherd sat up straight, fully alert. Things were no longer boring.

Capt. Merryweather said, "Since we have no way to deal with prisoners and barely enough food and water for ourselves, why did you decide to try for a capture, sir?"

"I have no idea," Col. Randal said. "Seemed like the thing to do at the time.

"King, stand ready with your Johnson LMG. Shoot anyone that even appears to make a move for a weapon once we stop the motorcycles."

"Count on it, Chief."

Then the motorcycles, swishing past, were in the killing zone of the ambush. Out of nowhere, MSgt. Beckwith pulled his jeep out in front of the lead rider, blocking the road.

The *Bersaglieri* are an elite military unit and world-class motorcycle riders. The lead cyclist coolly put his cycle down on its side and skidded into the side of the jeep. MSgt. Beckwith stuck a .45 cal. Thompson submachine gun in his face.

The rest of the patrol pancaked, with the drivers doing their best not to crash into each other and making a good job of it. All five Guzzi Alice

500s were down on the track, with not much damage to riders or bikes. Raider patrol swarmed out of their jeeps and piled on the startled Italians.

They never had a chance.

The prisoners were terrified of the dog when Col. Randal walked out to inspect the results. The animal did not try to lick any of them. He seemed ambivalent to Italians.

Waldo said, "What're we gonna do now? We ain't got room for prisoners, Colonel."

MSgt. Beckwith said, "We can use these motorcycles, sir."

"All right," Col. Randal said. "Search the *Bersaglieri,* collect their weapons, then turn 'em loose. Detail our best motorcycle riders to the Guzzis and let's get out of here, Sergeant Major. If the motorcycles can't keep up, we'll put 'em in the back of the jeeps."

"Yes, sir."

GG explained the situation to the *Bersaglieri.* He told them they were free to leave on foot. The men seemed depressed to learn they were not going to be taken prisoner. For them, the war was not over.

The Italians wanted it to be.

They seemed shocked to find one of their countrymen serving in Raiding Forces. A *Bersaglieri* blurted, "Have you killed anyone?"

"Probably," GG said. "I'm the cook."

RAIDER PATROL WAS UNDER CAMOUFLAGE NETTING IN A LUP on the auxiliary Regia Aeronautica landing ground. The plan was to blow it up as soon as it got dark. Colonel John Randal was sitting in a canvas folding chair talking to Waldo, King, and Captain Hawthorne Merryweather.

The dog was at his feet, seeming to keep up with the conversation. However, Col. Randal had been giving that some thought—how would a German shepherd know English?

One of the Phantom operators arrived with a FROGSPAWN message:

TOBRUK HAS FALLEN STOP MOVE TO A
LOCATION TO BE EXTRACTED BY AIR STOP
SIGNAL COORDINATES ASAP STOP AIRBORNE
YOUR WAY AT THIS TIME STOP EXPEDITE
STOP
SIGNED J. STOP

Col. Randal said, "Get our grid coordinates from Joker. Provide them with the response we are standing by on a deserted Italian landing ground."

"Sir!"

"Rommel has overrun Tobruk," Col. Randal said. "I've been ordered to return immediately by air. King, you and Waldo will come with me.

"Captain Merryweather, take charge of Raider Patrol. Lead it back to Oasis X. You are authorized to engage targets of opportunity en route."

"Sir!"

"Nothing fancy, Hawthorne."

"Yes, sir," Capt. Merryweather said. He had never expected to be given command of a patrol. Not in his wildest imagination.

The news about Tobruk was a shock. No one knew what to say. Now Rommel might drive all the way to the Suez Canal. Nothing stood in his way except Alexandria and Cairo, and they were virtually undefended. Things had been so desperate that the troops assigned to protect both cities had been pulled out and committed to the main battle. The Royal Navy had up-anchored and pulled out of Alexandria.

There were no reserves.

Pearl Harbor, Singapore, Bataan, and now Tobruk—a string of demoralizing defeats coming one after the other in rapid succession. Like Major the Lady Jane Seaborn had said, 1942 was shaping up to be an ugly year. And, it was not quite halfway over yet.

Two hours later, the pair of Raiding Forces' twin-engine Avro Anson aircraft appeared. They came in for a landing, one after the other.

Col. Randal said, "Joker, you stay with Captain Merryweather on the return until you can hand him off to one of your counterparts."

"My pleasure, Colonel."

"Sergeant Major," Col. Randal said, gathering his gear, "Keep your eye on the captain for me. He's a warrior. No Charge of the Light Brigade stuff."

"Yes, sir," MSgt. Beckwith said.

"Captain Merryweather," Col. Randal said, "take charge of Raider Patrol. Continue the mission."

He and the dog ran to the first aircraft, while Waldo and King made for the second. The door opened but there were no steps. The German shepherd leaped in. Col. Randal threw his gear aboard, jumped up, and swung in as the plane started to taxi.

Drop-dead gorgeous Lady Jane was sitting in one of the passenger seats. She was laughing, while trying to fight off the excited dog. The animal was doing his dead-level best to lick her to death and not taking no for an answer.

Apparently, the dog liked women—or at least Lady Jane. She clearly liked him. Which was a good thing for him. Lady Jane had been trained by Special Operations Executive to be able to kill an attack dog with her bare hands.

At least that was her story.

The Vargas Girl look-alike pilot, Captain Pamala Plum-Martin, stuck her snow-blonde head out of the door to the cockpit, "Buckle up John, stand by for takeoff—where did you find the puppy?"

"He just showed up."

16
SILK STOCKING BOYS

LIEUTENANT COLONEL SIR TERRY "ZORRO" STONE AND Lieutenant Mandy Paige met the Avro Anson aircraft at the Oasis X airstrip in a pair of jeeps. Colonel John Randal threw his gear in the back of Sir Terry's jeep so Zorro could brief him on developments during the short ride to his quarters at the top of the escarpment. Waldo climbed in the back.

Major the Lady Jane Seaborn and King climbed into Lt. Mandy's jeep. The German shepherd rode with the girls.

Waldo said, "Looks like Lady Jane done stole your hound like she does with everythin' else you got."

Col. Randal said, "I don't think he's a very loyal dog."

He immediately noticed the city of colorful Arab tents that had sprung up at the oasis. A herd of camels was grazing along the banks of the river where there had been none. Oddly, there were no people mingling around the tents or camels.

Lt. Col. Stone said, "The Great Teddy arrived. He set up the tents. We have jeeps parked in some of them. When patrols return, they hide their vehicles inside in the event enemy air ever overflies the oasis. The camels are to make it appear as if a caravan is camped here.

"Lady Jane informed the local sheik he could have the herd after we were through using them as decoys. Major Adair claims it did wonders for civic relations."

"Give me a report, Terry."

"We managed to deploy all of our Raiding Regiment patrols," Lt. Col. Stone said. "A total of six Ranger Force Patrols, four RAF Patrols, four Lancelot Lancer Patrols, and four Desert Patrols, eighteen in all—currently on operations or recently back from a completed patrol. All four patrol commanding officers are in the field riding with one of their elements.

"In addition, Scout Patrols I & II, The Railroad Wrecking Crew II, TNT Patrol, and SOG Patrol are engaged in ongoing independent operations as per your orders. Jack Cool has been on a tear. You shall want to see his patrol reports . . . read like pulp fiction.

"Captain McKoy's White Patrol returned to base last night after an extraordinary string of raids and ambushes; the old cowboy just gets better and better."

"What's the bad news, Terry?" Col. Randal said.

"Airey McKnight has gone dark," Lt. Col. Stone said. "Not a single report in eight days. We listed his patrol presumed lost, killed, or captured."

"He's one of our most experienced patrol leaders," Col. Randal said. "Airey's an excellent officer. If it could happen to him, it could happen to anybody."

"The desert is aflame, John, as you are aware," Lt. Col. Stone said. "Rommel is throwing everything he has into what was initially a local counterattack that morphed into an offensive. Afrika Korps defeated our forces at Gazala, and the Desert Fox has been running wild ever since.

"Almost all our patrols have taken casualties. Seven men KIA, not including Airey's patrol, and we have evacuated over thirty men wounded to date. If this battle keeps going much longer, Raiding Forces shall suffer a greater percentage loss than we did in CRUSADER—by a substantial margin."

Col. Randal said, "That's what I've been worried about."

"The fall of Tobruk had a devastating effect on morale at GHQ," Lt. Col. Stone said. "The fortress surrendered after only one day of fighting. We lost thirty-five thousand men captured in a single stroke—most of them from the South African Division. A national disgrace.

"I was in Cairo yesterday to coordinate with the Operations Division at Grey Pillars. The battle is so confused no one could give me any real indication of what the military situation is. The staff appears to have completely lost control of Eighth Army's maneuver elements. GHQ is rattled.

"Stopped by the Long Bar at Shepard's—Joe, the bartender, knew more about developments than the Operations Division."

Col. Randal said. "Pull everyone still back at RFHQ out to Oasis X immediately, Terry."

"Already done. All female personnel are on site now—to include certain Clipper Girl crew members who cannot be allowed to fall into enemy hands by priority request of MI-6," Lt. Col. Stone said.

"Captain Merritt is leading a jeep convoy transporting the rest of our support troops out here as we speak. I shanghaied beached sailors, 575th troopers who did not make the Blood in the Sand cut. Jack Merritt committed his Sudanese and Sammy Sansom hired every Egyptian driver he could lay hands on to move our excess vehicles—over seven hundred of them—to the oasis. They should arrive in the next couple of days. Each of the vehicles is bringing a tent for concealment.

"Fairly shortly, this place shall look like something out of the Arabian Nights."

Col. Randal said, "Teddy has his work cut out for him."

"Ensign Hamilton is no longer in residence," Lt. Col. Stone said. "The lad flew out to work with Admiral Ransom, Dudley Clarke, and U.S. Navy Lieutenant Douglas Fairbanks, Jr.—the movie star. Some project called 'sonic beach deception.' Major Corrigan and Sea Squadron are actively involved."

Col. Randal said, "Teddy gets around."

"Fine-looking dog," Lt. Col. Stone said. "Present for Jane, old stick?"

VERONICA PAIGE SAID, "THIS IS PROBABLY NOT THE BEST time, Colonel. However, with all the POWs in German hands now, it is imperative we commence our Escape program at the earliest possible opportunity."

Colonel John Randal was sitting out on the deck of the Oasix X apartment he shared with Major the Lady Jane Seaborn. He was freshly showered and in a clean set of faded BDUs. Rita and Lana were playing with the German shepherd. Lady Jane was packing.

"What are your thoughts, Veronica?"

"We have massive numbers of prisoners in Libya, with some being held in Italy, and others expected to be transferred in the near future," Veronica said. "There are two parallel approaches to pursue.

"First, if we can arrange to have our POWs in Libya stage escapes, they should tie down quite a significant number of Rommel's troops trying to recapture them. The Nazis obsess over escaped POWs.

"Second, if we can develop some way to smuggle in the parts to build radios, we can have the prisoners provide vital intelligence information about what they see taking place around the POW camps. Make them into spies for MI-6."

Col. Randal said, "Captain McKoy would call that turning a lemon into lemonade.

"What do you need from me?"

"All I want at this point," Veronica said, "is for you to help me advance the concept from an idea to a workable plan."

Col. Randal said, "Lady Jane, Mandy, and I are flying out to the States. As soon as we return, I'll do it.

"Thank you."

Col. Randal said, "I know MI-9 has been left flapping in the breeze, Veronica. We'll work something out—why don't you get The Great Teddy to start thinking about the idea of smuggling radios in to the prisoners?"

"Wonderful. That is a marvelous idea—it has been frustrating."

CAPTAIN "GERONIMO" JOE MCKOY SAID, "I UNDERSTAND you're headed to Washington to see Bill Donovan, the new honcho of the Office of Strategic Services."

"Roger that," Colonel John Randal said. "Lady Jane, Mandy, and I are flying out of here within the hour."

"Make sure," Capt. McKoy said, "to tell Bill I said howdy."

"You know Wild Bill Donovan?"

"Yep," Capt. McKoy said. "Only he ain't real wild. Bill's a' quiet, reserved individual. We served together in the Punitive Expedition against Pancho Villa. He was commanding an outfit called the Silk Stocking Boys when I was the chief a' scouts for Blackjack Pershing."

"Silk Stocking Boys?"

"Troop I, 1st Cavalry Regiment, New York National Guard—bunch a' rich blue bloods formed 'emselves a' cavalry troop and elected Donovan captain."

"National Guard troops were still electing their officers in those days?" Col. Randal asked. "I thought that went out before the Spanish American War."

"Bill couldn't even ride a' horse," Capt. McKoy said. "Taught hisself. He was born poor, became a' star college football player—went to school with President Roosevelt, married himself a' rich socialite woman, and makes a' lot a' money as a' New York lawyer. Word is he spends it as fast as he makes it—maybe faster.

"Down in McAllen, Texas, for a' man with no formal military background, Donovan was a' real martinet. Had his troops doin' forced marches through those mesquite thickets night and day. The Silk Stocking Boys never made contact with any Mexican bandits, but they turned themselves into real sharp cavalry troopers and were better men for it.

"Then, about a week or so after comin' back home from the border, Bill got mobilized into the Fightin' 69th, New York's finest, and shipped out overseas to France in command of a' battalion. That's where he got the name Wild Bill.

"When the troopship arrived, Donovan paraded his battalion off in a' column a' fours and took 'em on a' high-speed, forced march to 'limber 'em up.' While they was humping along, one a' his boys shouted at him to slow it down because 'we ain't as wild as you, Bill' and the name stuck.

"Brought back a' Medal of Honor."

Col. Randal said, "Sounds like a good man."

"He'll do to ride the river with," Capt. McKoy said. "But to understand Bill Donovan, you need to keep in mind he's mostly a' failed politician. Ran for office, got thumped, never got over it. And he ain't no spymaster or special operations man no matter what job description they give him."

"I'll keep that in mind, Captain," Col. Randal said. "I have no idea why it's so urgent for me to see Donovan with this battle in progress."

"Don't let him rope you into nothin' you can't get out of, John," Capt. McKoy said. "Wild Bill's pretty slick. He's probably got his eye on Raidin' Forces for his new OSS outfit. We got us a sweet deal goin' here—small-scale guerrilla marauders livin' wild and free. Ain't nobody exactly sure who we report to.

"Militarily speaking, it don't get any better than that. Be careful not to do anything to clarify our status."

"Jim will be there," Col. Randal said, "to make sure I don't."

MAJOR THE LADY JANE SEABORN SAID, "BENTLEY, I WANT you to take care of my puppy while John and I are away in America."

Sub-Lieutenant Bentley St. Ledger asked, "What's his name?"

Lady Jane said. "Mandy and I decided to call him Happy."

S/Lt. St. Ledger rubbed the German shepherd between his ears. When she stopped, the animal aggressively nuzzled her, wanting more. "He seems like a very social dog."

"I believe Happy is only about a year old," Lady Jane said. "He may become lonely after having been captured, then abandoned while we travel."

"We cannot allow that to happen," S/Lt. St. Ledger said. "I shall keep Happy company."

"Rita and Lana love him. Make sure you have one of them go along when you take him for walks—that is an order, Bentley."

"I will, Lady Jane."

Colonel John Randal was downstairs in the apartment Rikke Runborg shared with Veronica Paige.

He said, "I received a message from Brigadier Maunsell, instructing me to take extra precautions to make sure you're safe while I'm away in the States."

The sexy Norwegian blonde said, "How thoughtful of R.J.."

"Apparently he has plans for you I'm not authorized to know about," Col. Randal said. "Never leave the complex without Rita or Lana. Is that clear?"

"Perfectly."

"If you go into the village, King tags along. I'm putting him in charge of your personal security," Col. Randal said. "Stay in at night."

"Yes, John," Rocky said. "I made a prudent choice choosing you to be my protector."

Col. Randal said, "Don't get killed on my watch."

Captain Billy Jack Jaxx arrived at Oasis X with SOG Patrol. Col. Randal pulled him aside for a quick conversation before he had to board the Hudson to Cairo.

"Sorry to hear about Jake, Colonel."

"Yeah," Col. Randal said. "That one's on me."

"I doubt it was your fault, sir."

"Give me a report, Jack," Col. Randal said.

"SOG has been working in close proximity to the rear of Rommel front lines west of Tobruk, sir," Capt. Jaxx said. "Targets everywhere— lot of confusion. Hit, run for your life, and try to hide.

"To be honest, Colonel, everything's sort of a blur. The action's been nonstop. British and German units intermingled, artillery firing around the clock—theirs, ours, who knows? Massive dust clouds kicked up by the convoys and maneuver elements, the RAF strafing the Via Balbia during the day. Never knew what was going to happen next, sir."

"How's SOG performing?" Col. Randal asked.

"My boys have been on one mission after another nonstop from the minute the Five-Seven-Five first arrived," Capt. Jaxx said. "Crammed a lot of experience into a short period of time.

"You'll be impressed next time we work together, sir."

Col. Randal asked, "What happened on the RED INDIAN?"

"Dry hole, sir," Capt. Jaxx said. "We jumped in and took down the target. Captured four German weathermen. No intelligence of any significant value."

"Here's what I want you to do, Jack," Col. Randal said. "Stand down, re-arm, re-equip, and get some rest. I need SOG to be on call, ready to respond to a priority mission should one present itself while I'm away. Stay in touch with Brandy. Any alert order will come through her or Commander Fleming."

"Yes, sir."

"Raider Patrol will be returning in the next few days. When they arrive, you take charge and attach 'em to SOG," Col. Randal said. "In the event a SOLID GOLD or RED INDIAN target comes up, feel free to use all or part of the combined patrols for your mission."

"Wilco."

"You can have King, too, in the event SOG is called out. If King leaves the Oasis, Waldo has to fill in as Rocky's bodyguard."

Capt. Jaxx said, "OK with you, Colonel, if I guard Rocky too?"

"She's out of your league, Jack."

"I'd like to take a crack at talking Miss Runborg into posing for a swimsuit photo, sir," Capt. Jaxx said. "The idea is to rotate the pictures in my Plexiglas pistol grip. Rocky would be crazy hot!"

Jack Cool.

"Permission granted—good luck with that, stud."

BRIGADIER RAYMOND J. MAUNSELL, WHO LIKED TO BE called R.J., met Colonel John Randal's party—which consisted of Major the Lady Jane Seaborn and Lieutenant Mandy Paige—at the departure lounge for Pan American Airlines. He was not his normal debonair self.

"Tobruk was an unmitigated disaster," R.J.. said. "Our generals are hopeless. Field Marshal Auchinleck sacked General Ritchie. The Auk assumed command of the Eighth Army—second time he has had to step in and take personal control of a battle gone wrong.

"Afrika Korps is only sixty miles from Alexandria. The town is being evacuated as we speak. The European civilian population panicked and is trying to flee the city. I was there yesterday. It was like the scene in the movie *Gone With the Wind* when the Yankees are about to overrun Atlanta. People fighting to get on the train, driving wildly through the streets, mad with fear.

"The mood among the Egyptian population here in Cairo has turned ugly. Taxi drivers are telling British officers, 'I drive you today. When Rommel comes tomorrow, you drive me.'

"Major Sansom is running around like his hair is on fire, arresting Nazi sympathizers. Internal security is increasingly becoming a problem."

"Maybe I should stay and assist Sammy," Lt. Mandy said.

"Not on your life," Lady Jane said. "You are going shopping with me in Manhattan."

"Only a thought," Lt. Mandy said.

"There seems to be no stopping Rommel this time," R.J.. said. "Nothing our forces have done so far has even slowed him down."

Col. Randal said, "My patrols have not reported any indication Rommel is leap frogging advanced supply bases forward. He's charging straight down the Via Balbia with all guns blazing.

"Simple logistics dictate Rommel has to pause eventually."

"Unhappily," R.J.. said. "Even if you are right—and I have no doubt you are, Colonel—our side has lost so many tanks at this point there is no reserve. If or when Afrika Korps does run out of steam, Eighth Army will not have anything left to counterattack with."

Col. Randal said, "That is a problem."

JAMES "BALDIE" TAYLOR MET THE PAN AMERICAN FLYING Clipper when it arrived in New York. He was in the Plaza Hotel's VIP limousine. Major the Lady Jane Seaborn's Bradford Hotel in London had a reciprocal agreement with the Plaza. Her office had booked a suite of rooms for their stay.

While Col. Randal had orders to travel on to Washington to meet with the Office of Strategic Services, Lady Jane viewed the trip as a shopping safari. And, New York was where MI-6 had its U.S. office. It was run by the Canadian Bill Stephenson—a man called "Intrepid."

She had business with MI-6.

Also in the limo was Commander Ian Fleming, RNVR. He was in the States acting as the naval liaison between British NID, MI-6 and OSS. The suave intelligence officer had played a prominent role in organizing the lobbying effort for Colonel "Wild Bill" Donovan to be named as the head of the Office of Strategic Services.

There had been those in Washington who opposed the appointment.

With Cdr. Fleming and Jim representing all the major British intelligence services, to include Special Operations Executive (Jim represented MI-6 *and* SOE, though the latter mistakenly believing he reported only to them), the future of Raiding Forces was assured. Now it was simply a matter of going through the motions to finalize the details.

Military politics was a dance—or more accurately a knife fight.

Jim said, "OSS is the official foreign intelligence gathering agency for the United States. All military intelligence is to flow through it. Unfortunately, the U.S. Navy, the Army, and the FBI view OSS as a competitor and they refuse to share their intelligence. A major turf war is brewing in the halls of the War Department and on Capitol Hill.

"None of which is of any concern to you, John, except to understand that OSS is not going to hit the ground running. It is in for a protracted political battle and then can be expected to experience serious growing pains once the dust settles.

"What will happen on this trip is you meet with Donovan in his Washington office. He will show you a chart he is quite proud of—his Table of Organization.

"Office of Strategic Services will be at the top of the page, then there will be two legs under the title. On the right, Secret Intelligence—called SI—and on the left side Special Operations, which is called SO.

"Donovan is prepared to offer you the post of Director of Special Operations. However, you are going to turn down that offer, attractive as it might be. Then Wild Bill will ask you where you see yourself fitting in OSS.

"Study the chart, and on the left side under SO, gaze down until you come to the box labeled Special Projects. You say, 'Special Projects.'

"No one has any idea what that means. It is merely a placeholder on the TO&E schematic. Fleming and I will arrange for the Special Projects Branch Officer, meaning you, to report directly to Donovan instead of going up the chain of command through SO. Since I happen to be the liaison between Raiding Forces and OSS—you work through me. Business as usual."

"Raiding Forces continues its current mission?" Col. Randal asked. "Nothing changes?"

"OSS has already decided it will not micromanage guerrilla wars or special operations. The senior commanders of SO field units will run their own compartmentalized independent campaigns, reporting only to the local theatre-level army commander," Cdr. Fleming said, tapping his elegant sterling silver case with one of his custom-blended cigarettes with the three gold rings.

"As Special Projects Officer, you shall have the prerogative to skip army level, which is not an issue because there is not a U.S. Army command as such in Egypt. You report directly to Donovan through Baldie. Once the precedent is established, you will continue that protocol no matter what theatre Raiding Forces happens to be operating in."

Jim said, "The icing on the cake for Donovan is the fact Raiding Forces will be the only element of OSS actually engaged in an active war zone for the foreseeable future."

Cdr. Fleming said, "Starting the minute you sign on, OSS will receive credit for everything Raiding Forces does. Which means the Outfit, as they are calling it, will shower you with personnel, modern equipment, and decorations to motivate your troops.

"Donovan is highly incentivized to see Raiding Forces succeed and he does not care at what."

Jim said, "All Wild Bill wants is for you to kill bad guys so he can brag to the President about it behind closed doors.

"Questions?"

Col. Randal said, "I can do that."

"What say you, Lady Jane?" Cdr. Fleming asked, unable to hide the fact that he was cutting his eyes at the Sheba Diamond sparkling on her left ring finger."

"Marvelous."

Lieutenant Mandy Paige asked, "Who *will* John be working for?"

"Everybody and nobody," Jim said. "Smoke and mirrors.

"Alice through the looking glass."

JAMES "BALDIE" TAYLOR SAID, "DONOVAN WAS unexpectedly called to the White House to confer with the President. Our meeting today has been canceled."

He and Colonel John Randal were sitting with Major the Lady Jane Seaborn and Lieutenant Mandy Paige in the world-famous Palm Court restaurant, in the lobby of the Plaza Hotel, enjoying the hotel's renowned champagne breakfast.

Jim said, "What is going to happen instead is we are to catch a plane to Fort Jackson, South Carolina. There is a battalion of special service troops being raised down there. Wild Bill would like you to evaluate them for possible employment by OSS. The U.S. Army has not shown much interest in the unit."

"I'd like that," Col. Randal said.

"Jimmy Roosevelt elected not to be a part of OSS," Jim said. "He has gone back into the Marines. They raised two battalions based on our British Commandos.

"You will never guess what they call them."

"What might that be?"

"Marine Raiders," Jim said. "Jimmy is going to be the executive officer of the 2nd Raider Battalion."

"No kidding—good for him."

"Think Raiding Forces had any influence on the name?" Jim laughed. "The Marines did not want to form the Raiders—an elite within an elite. The President had to intervene.

"Have to hand it to Jimmy," Col. Randal said. "He used his political influence to get *into* a combat outfit—not to find a safe staff job to ride out the war."

Lady Jane said, "We have tickets for the theatre at 2000 hours. You have John back before curtain time, Jim. Part of the idea behind this trip was for him to have a few days' respite from the war."

"We are hitching a ride on an Air Corps C-47 conducting a training mission," Jim said. "It will have orders to fly us straight back here as soon as we inspect the troops."

Col. Randal asked, "What's the name of the play?"

Lady Jane laughed, "*Billy the Kid.* Mandy and I thought choosing a Western was the only way we could talk you into attending."

Lt. Mandy said, "We really wanted to see *Argentina.*"

Col. Randal said, "Maybe we can go to that one tomorrow night."

JAMES "BALDIE" TAYLOR SAID, "THERE IS ONE OTHER reason Donovan wants to have you on board OSS as soon as possible."

The MI-6 officer and Colonel John Randal were in the back of a Dodge staff car being driven out to one of the remote training areas of Fort Jackson.

"He is a colonel. You are a colonel. Wild Bill wants to be a brigadier general. Get the picture?"

"Got it."

The staff car arrived at a bivouac that consisted of a single general purpose (GP) tent and a series of neatly lined pup tents. A handmade sign from the side of an ammo crate read HHC 10th Ranger Battalion.

When the Dodge stopped, the driver hopped out, came around back, and opened the door for his passengers, then stood at a rigid position of attention. A young captain in fatigues stepped out of the GP tent and saluted.

Col. Randal returned the salute. "I'm Colonel Randal. This is the General."

"Captain Dance, sir," Captain Jack Dance said. "Commanding officer, welcome to the 10th Ranger Battalion, gentlemen."

Captains do not normally command battalions. A sign of how far down on the military totem pole the 10th Ranger Battalion fell. Rock-bottom.

Capt. Dance was curious as to why a paratroop colonel (the only decoration he was wearing was a pair of silver Jump Wings) and a general with no name in a tailored business suit would arrive out of nowhere unannounced. Neither of the two visitors seemed inclined to clarify the situation.

Col. Randal said, "I'd like to review your battalion, Captain. Understand you have been left pretty much to your own devices."

"That would be an understatement, sir," Capt. Dance said. "The army formed this outfit based on the TO&E of the First Ranger Battalion currently being raised in England. Then no one knew what to do with us.

"I'm the fourth battalion commander in five months. No one wants this job, sir—no future in it."

"British Commandos have had a similar experience," Col. Randal said. "Why don't you show us around—brief us at the same time."

"Yes, sir,"

As they headed for the training area, Col. Randal asked, "How did your battalion get the Tenth designator?"

"One story is," Capt. Dance said, "to be safe, when the unit was originally being raised, they simply added a zero to the one of the First Ranger Battalion because no one knew exactly how many battalions were in the process of being organized on different bases, sir. The Ranger program does not seem to be coordinated and it is listed as Provisional.

"Another version," Capt. Dance said, "are there no other Ranger Battalions being formed. However, the powers that be wanted to make it look like there are a lot of them, sir. They gave us a big number."

Col. Randal said, "Typical."

Capt. Dance said, "There are Rangers undergoing training at Fort Sam Houston in Texas. I've heard there is a Ranger school of some type in Hawaii. And the word is at least two other Ranger Battalions are slated to be raised here in the States," Capt. Dance said.

"I can't imagine why. No one seems to have a mission for us. We're a bastard outfit. Don't even have a unit patch, sir.

"Bad career move to command a battalion no one wants, sir. That's why the other commanders transferred out. Well, one was relieved for being an alcoholic—job got to him.

"You're the first senior-grade visitors we've had since I've been in command, sir."

"Orphans," Col. Randal said.

The inspection took two hours. The Rangers were training hard. They were deep in the forest, patrolling against each other. No one in authority may have had an interest in the unit, but that did nothing to curb the intensity of their daily physical fitness routine, weapons training, and tactical exercises.

Col. Randal liked what he saw.

"So what's your plan, Captain?"

"Sir, I don't have a plan."

"If I were you," Col. Randal said, as they returned to the battalion HQ prior to departing, "I'd route march my battalion down to Fort Benning and put my men through Jump School."

"Sir, it's over three-hundred-fifty miles to Columbus, Georgia," Capt. Dance said. "We don't have orders authorizing the Tenth Rangers to become parachute-qualified."

"That's the beauty of it," Col. Randal said.

The C-47 arrived back in time for him to link up with Major the Lady Jane Seaborn and Lieutenant Mandy Paige for the play. It was a surprise. *Billy the Kid* turned out to be good.

Afterward, as they were walking out to the Plaza Hotel limousine waiting under the bright theatre lights at the curb, Lady Jane asked, "Do you believe the Ranger captain you visited today will take your advice, John?"

Col. Randal said, "We'll see."

17
SEX TOY

COLONEL JOHN RANDAL WAS SITTING ON A COUCH IN THE waiting room of Colonel William "Wild Bill" Donovan's Washington Office of Strategic Services. It was raining outside and he still had his raincoat on, which covered up his rank and insignia. He had been sitting there for quite a while.

The plan was to meet Major the Lady Jane Seaborn and James "Baldie" Taylor to be introduced to Col. Donovan.

When Col. Randal had arrived, there was no one at the receptionist desk, but a brunette girl had arrived soon after and taken her place at the desk. She studiously ignored him. He was too young to be anyone important; however, the scar on his tanned left cheek was interesting. Not impressed, she decided her nails needed filing.

Another girl arrived and the two started chatting. They sounded like Ivy League college girls. Col. Randal realized they were talking about Lady Jane.

"Were you able to have a look at the ring?"

"I have seen larger stones."

"As have I, but Lady Jane's is the *Sheba* Diamond."

"Do you believe there actually *was* a Queen of Sheba?"

"She's in a lot of Hollywood movies—they can't all be wrong. Besides, Lady Jane has Sheba's diamond on her finger and it's a firecracker."

"The story is her boyfriend shot the bandit who stole . . ."

A slim girl with the biggest mop of honey-colored hair Col. Randal had ever seen came into the office. She looked vaguely familiar—so pretty it seemed like a light was shining down on her.

The blonde glanced at him, made eye contact, and immediately walked over to the couch. In a soft, smoky Texas accent she asked, "Are you Colonel Randal?"

"That would be me."

"Do you know Billy Jack Jaxx?"

Col. Randal said, "Tri-Delta, I presume."

"I'm Beverly Blackwell. Billy Jack has written me tons of letters with stories about you, Colonel."

"You can't believe what Jack says," Col. Randal said. "Thought I recognized you, Beverly. I've seen your picture."

In the Plexiglas grip of Jack Cool's pistol.

"That boy is pretty wild," Beverly said. "Does Billy do everything you tell him to?"

"Not exactly . . ."

Lady Jane came out the door of Col. Donovan's office. "John, I thought I heard your voice. We have been waiting for you for ages. Where have you been?"

"Right here."

The two Ivy League girls looked horrified.

Col. Randal said, "Jane, let me introduce you to Beverly Blackwell. Good friend of Billy Jack's. Instrumental in his military career."

"How nice to meet you in person, Beverly," Lady Jane said, green eyes sparkling. "I have seen your photograph."

Col. Donovan burst out of the office, rushed over, and put his arm around Col. Randal's shoulder as he ushered him into his office.

"I have been dying for the two of us to get together at last, Colonel. Your reputation has preceded you. It's all good—at least most of it."

Col. Randal liked Wild Bill right from the start.

There was a copy of *Jump on Bela* on his desk. "Would you autograph this for me? I intend to have it reprinted and made mandatory reading for all of my Special Operations personnel." The man was clearly a politician.

He knew how to schmooze. Which put Col. Randal on his guard. Nevertheless, Wild Bill was very personable.

Col. Randal signed the book, then turned to Lady Jane. She produced a wooden presentation box from out of her shoulder bag and handed it to him.

"I brought something you may find of interest," Col. Randal said.

"What is this?"

"High Standard Military Model D .22," Col. Randal said. "The civilian model is called the HD. Captain Joe McKoy designed the silencer. He said to tell you hello."

"*Captain* Joe McKoy?"

"Claimed he knew you from the Punitive Expedition chasing Pancho Villa—Silk Stocking Boys."

"Chief-of-Scouts carried the rank of lieutenant colonel," Col. Donovan said. "*Colonel* McKoy had quite the reputation as a gunfighter in those days—called him Widows and Orphans—W.O. for short. Rumor had it he killed more men than Billy the Kid and Jesse James combined."

"Still running up the score," Col. Randal said. "The captain's my most successful gun jeep patrol leader."

"Is this pistol quiet?" Col. Donovan asked, admiring the handgun.

Jim accidentally knocked the leather pencil holder off the highly-polished desk. When Col. Donovan stooped to pick it up, the MI-6 officer produced his High Standard from inside the jacket of his beautifully tailored suit and fired a single round into a decorative pillow on the couch against the wall in the office. *WHIIICH.*

When the Chief of OSS raised back up with the pencils, he saw Jim holding his pistol in one hand and the pillow bleeding feathers in the other.

"Pretty quiet," Col. Randal said.

"Amazing," Col. Donovan said. "I intend to repeat this performance for the President in the Oval Office this very afternoon."

"We have to secure these for OSS immediately—High Standard Military Model D?"

"You won't be disappointed," Col. Randal said. "Excellent weapons."

The courtesies out of the way, the rest of the meeting went exactly as briefed. A flip chart with TOP SECRET stenciled on the canvas cloth cover sat on a three-legged stand next to the desk. Col. Donovan flipped back the cover.

And there was the TO&E of OSS.

Wild Bill began a hush-hush briefing, using a small collapsible pointer. The performance was very melodramatic, cloak-and-dagger all the way—clandestine. Everything he said was classified but it did not have much depth or substance.

More like show and tell.

Col. Randal played his role of interested observer as instructed, while Jim and Lady Jane looked on. Wild Bill had wrapped up the part where it was mutually agreed Col. Randal would fill the Special Projects Officer slot when there was a knock on the door.

Col. Donovan barked, "What?"

Beverly opened the door. "Sir, an urgent communiqué has been delivered from the Commo Department for Colonel Randal. It's marked TOP SECRET/SOLID GOLD."

"Bring it in."

Beverly handed over the message. After she left, Col. Donovan said, "Daughter of one of my law firm's clients. Big South Texas ranch, been in the family since the Texas Revolution. Raise mostly oil wells.

"I hunt quail there every year."

The message read:

```
SOLID GOLD STOP RETURN CAIRO ASAP STOP
SIGNED BRANDY STOP
```

As Col. Randal passed the flimsy to Jim, he said, "Colonel Donovan, you're about to have your first OSS direct-action mission in Egypt. I'll be flying out as soon as air transport can be arranged."

Glancing up from the telex, Jim said, "Bill, SOLID GOLD is the single most important target in Middle East Command. Field Marshal Auchinleck has confided to me on numerous occasions he considers it an even higher priority for Eighth Army than GOLDEN FLEECE. And, as we both know, *nothing* is higher than that."

"Terrific," Col. Donovan said.

Jim said, "I shall provide you a private, TOP SECRET/Need to Know Only briefing to include means and sources on the mission details later. But first, we have to arrange to fly Colonel Randal back to Cairo immediately."

Wild Bill was ecstatic. Special Operations Executive was up and running—at least the SO branch. Boots on the ground in Middle East Command before the nameplate had even been screwed on the door of his office. He had estimated it might take up to a year to recruit, train, and have an OSS team ready for deployment overseas.

Today's meeting had gone far better than hoped. Col. Randal had signed on with OSS and not asked for one single condition in return. Col. Donovan would have agreed to almost anything to bring Raiding Forces under his umbrella—he was fairly sure that had been obvious. OSS success on the battlefield would be invaluable in the turf war he was waging with the Army and Navy.

"My people will organize your travel," Col. Donovan said. "You're one of us now, Colonel.

"Before you rush off, in addition to 'God Speed', I want to tell you I'm particularly fascinated by the stories Jim and Commander Fleming have been telling me about your Sea Squadron activities. We're in the process of forming something called Operational Groups—four officers, thirty handpicked men we intend to call OGs.

"How would you like it if OSS recruited an OG made up of U.S. Marines and Navy underwater demolition specialists called Scouts and Raiders from Fort Pierce to work with your amphibious squadron?"

"That would be fine," Col. Randal said, "as long as you understand I'll use the men where needed."

"Colonel, it has been chiseled in stone that theatre-level commanders of OSS missions have a free hand to run their own show with no outside interference. That directive is written in our Operational Groups Field Manual. You can read it as soon as we have the handbook printed for distribution.

"Besides, as Director of Special Projects, you report directly to me, through Jim, and I don't care how you choose to manage your troops, organize your command, or anything else, except to read summaries of Raiding Forces' successful operations.

"Send plenty of those."

"I can do that."

"In return, what you can expect from me," Col. Donovan said, "is to provide what it takes to get the job done. All you have to do is ask."

Lady Jane said, "I want Beverly."

THE PAN AMERICAN 314 SPLASHED DOWN IN THE NILE River. Colonel William "Wild Bill" Donovan had demonstrated his political connections by phoning the White House to arrange for one of the President's military aides to personally escort Colonel John Randal's party aboard the Flying Clipper. A very unhappy Air Corps brigadier general and three of his field grade staff officers had to be bumped from the flight to make room.

No one from Raiding Forces was at the Pan American dock to meet their party since all personnel had been relocated to Oasis X. Col. Randal, Major the Lady Jane Seaborn, Lieutenant Mandy Paige, and Beverly Blackwell squeezed into a cab for the ride to the Gezira Club Restaurant. They were to meet Brandy Seaborn and Captain Penelope "Legs" Honeycutt-Parker for lunch and to receive a briefing on the SOLID GOLD target.

When the cab pulled up in front of the restaurant, the women exited as Col. Randal was reaching for his wallet. The Egyptian driver looked over his shoulder to the back seat with an ugly sneer. "I drive you today. Tomorrow when Rommel comes, you drive me."

"Is that right?"

"Maybe I make your lady my sex toy."

"I don't think so," Col. Randal said, laying his .22 High Standard Military Model D over the driver's shoulder, flat against the man's chest. He fired two rounds straight down at the taxi driver's lap. *WHIIICH, WHIIICH.*

No way to tell if he hit anything or not, but the Egyptian began hyperventilating and screaming hysterically at the same time—only not much sound was coming out. Col. Randal stepped out of the cab as the driver floorboarded it.

The taxi peeled out, burning rubber. Possibly the man intended to drive himself to the nearest hospital, or maybe he only wanted to get far away fast. However, he failed to look both directions before entering traffic and nearly had a head-on collision with a bus. Swerving to miss the bus, the taxi ran up on the curb, hit a fireplug that immediately shot a stream of water thirty feet into the air, and then crashed into a metal light pole.

As Col. Randal joined the women in the lobby of the restaurant, Lady Jane said, "Wonder why our taxi driver was in such a hurry all of a sudden?"

Col. Randal said, "He mentioned something about sex toys."

The restaurant was virtually empty. Only a handful of staff officers from General Headquarters Middle East were at the normally crowded bar. They were drinking themselves senseless.

In the back of the room, in a corner behind a drooping palm leaf, Brandy, Capt. Honeycutt-Parker, and Brigadier Raymond J. Maunsell were sitting at a table.

Introductions were made. Brandy said, "I recognize you from your photograph. You are much more beautiful in person, Beverly."

Lady Jane leaned over and whispered in Col. Randal's ear, "You need to message Billy Jack to take that photo out of his pistol grip."

"Affirmative."

R.J. started to begin his briefing as soon as the waiter had taken their order. He hesitated, glancing at Beverly.

Col. Randal said, "No problem—she's OSS." Which, while technically correct, was not completely accurate. Beverly was not an agent. No one had inquired about her security clearance.

Col. Randal wondered what her grandfather—the judge who sentenced Billy Jack Jaxx to either joining the U.S. Marines or Army Paratroopers for leading a panty raid on the Tri-Delta sorority house—was going to say about the two of them serving together.

It may have been Beverly's black panties Jack Cool was waving in the photograph in the Austin newspaper that got him arrested.

R.J. said, "Tobruk had fallen as you were departing for the States. Y-Service intercepts revealed Rommel was ordered by his boss, Smiling Al Kesselring, to pause for a minimum of six weeks at that point to build up his logistical base of supplies. Afrika Korps has shot its bolt. Afrika Korps lost most of its tanks and the ground troops are spent.

"As you are well aware, Rommel has a supply line that runs from Tripoli to Tobruk. His ground convoys have to travel over two thousand miles round-trip down the Via Balbia and back.

"To make matters worse for him, the RAF Desert Air Force—operating in conjunction with the U.S. Air Task Force—finally came to its senses. They started daylight air raids on the Via Balbia. Flew over nine hundred sorties one day. Since the Axis convoys are roadbound, it has been a slaughter and it is not letting up.

"If our generals had been up to the task, we could have put paid to the myth of the Desert Fox, then and there. Unfortunately, they were not. Auchinleck fired Richie and assumed personal command of Eighth Army. He is putting in defensive boxes at a small railroad town near the coast called El Alamein.

"Meanwhile, Rommel went over his boss's head directly to Hitler to protest the order to conduct a logistical pause. He promised he could take Cairo if allowed to make one final push, begged Hitler to cancel the attack on Malta, and to assign him the troops earmarked for the operation.

The Führer succumbed to the argument—always in favor of any plea to be allowed to deliver victory. He interceded, overrode Field Marshal Kesselring, and granted permission for Afrika Korps to continue the attack. Hitler canceled the invasion of Malta and ordered the elite German paratroops stationed on Crete, preparing for the drop on the island, to be flown to Afrika Korps as infantry reinforcements.

"And, he shipped more tanks from Italy.

"After a nine-day lull, Rommel resumed the offensive. Afrika Korps is only sixty miles west of Alexandria, with nothing in the way of significant Allied forces standing between that city and Cairo.

"The staff at Grey Pillars, already in a state of depression over the loss of Tobruk, panicked, and what is known as the Flap commenced. The armchair warriors bravely began burning all their documents. Soon the panic spread and the British Embassy started firing theirs too. Total chaos. So many papers were burned parts of the city were covered in ashes. The wags dubbed it Ash Wednesday.

"GHQ displayed cowardice in the face of the enemy, earning the contempt of almost everyone, including the staff members themselves––bloody disgraceful.

"That brings us to where we are now. Brandy and Parker enter the picture, front and center—ladies."

"When everyone relocated to Oasis X," Capt. Honeycutt-Parker said, "I remained behind in Cairo in hopes of picking up the trail to where the German 621st Radio Intercept Company had displaced.

"Colonel Francis de Guingand, the Eighth Army intelligence officer, and I have been working together with Y-Service. We were able to pinpoint Seebohm's Radio Intercept Company. As incredible as it may sound, the 621st is situated right on the forward edge of the battle area. It is positioned on a small hill called Tell Issa Mount, virtually at the water's edge of the Mediterranean on the front line."

Brandy said, "Hard to believe Rommel can be so inept as to allow the most priceless intelligence asset Afrika Korps possesses to be exposed when the 621st could be as effective five or even ten miles to the rear. But he has. We are delighted."

Col. Randal said, "That's crazy."

Capt. Honeycutt-Parker said, "As it happens, the 48th Infantry Battalion, 9th Australian Division, commanded by a Lieutenant Colonel Hammer, with the colorful nickname 'Hard as Nails', is in a defensive position immediately opposite the 621st. Billy Jack is en route to the Australians' location now with SOG. Captain McKoy—who was back from patrol and wanted in on the action—King, Ferguson, and Fenwick are with his patrol.

"He should arrive sometime later this afternoon. The *King Duck* is steaming up the coast.

Brandy said, "Tonight John, you and I are going to parachute onto a drop zone marked by Billy Jack, link up with Colonel 'Hard as Nails' Hammer, and kill Captain Alfred Seebohm before sunrise."

Beverly gulped—louder than she had intended.

Capt. Honeycutt-Parker said, "I shall be standing by at Eighth Army HQ, monitoring the situation with Colonel de Guingand."

R.J.. said, "Colonel, if you take down the 621st, it will be the single most important coup of the desert war. Since we have already put a stop to Rommel reading Colonel Fellers' daily situation reports, if you knock out Seebohm, the Desert Fox will be left completely blind as far as intelligence is concerned."

"Excellent," Lady Jane said. "We shall see how Rommel likes fighting on even terms."

R.J. asked, "What say you, Colonel?"

"Let's do this."

COLONEL JOHN RANDAL WAS LYING ON A LOUNGE BY THE private pool at the suite Major the Lady Jane Seaborn maintained on a permanent basis at the posh Mena House Hotel near the Great Pyramids. Beverly Blackwell had borrowed a swimsuit from Lieutenant Mandy Paige that would have gotten her arrested in any of the 254 counties in Texas. The girls were swimming laps.

Lady Jane was inside on the phone, ordering room service for an early dinner this evening before Col. Randal and Brandy had to depart on their mission.

Brandy Seaborn was on another phone, making arrangements for the latest aerial photos of the night's target to be delivered to the hotel. An RAF photo reconnaissance pilot had flown down the coast and made a single pass over the 621st, after having completed a wide circuit out to sea to make it appear he was merely returning to base from a mission and not interested in the Radio Intercept Company's encampment.

Captain Pamala Plum-Martin would be using the private stretch of road in front of the hotel as a landing strip tonight. Hotel staff had already been alerted to be available to block it for the short time it would take the Vargas Girl look-alike Royal Marine pilot to land and pick up Col. Randal and Brandy. Flanigan would supervise the operation.

As the girls swam past, Col. Randal said, "Beverly, take a break. Let's talk."

The pretty blonde girl lifted herself out of the pool in a single athletic move and walked over to the lounge next to him. She was very physically fit and about as good-looking as it was possible to be. Texas has a reputation for beautiful women, and at the University of Texas, she was one of the "Ten Most."

Beverly stretched out on the lounge Lady Jane had abandoned to make her phone call. She did not seem to be aware of the effect she had on men. That—combined with a childlike innocence and a Texas-sized sense of humor—made her very, very likeable.

"Those are an impressive collection of scars, John. Mandy told me you were reckless—seems she wasn't exaggerating."

Col. Randal said, "I'd take it as a personal favor, Beverly, if you'd stick close to Lady Jane while I'm gone.

"Love to."

"The Middle East is a dangerous place," Col. Randal. "Ask Mandy — anything can happen at any time without warning. Keep your eyes open. Stay alert. We used to say 'expect the unexpected,' only that never works. But you get the idea."

"I promise—Billy Jack wrote me about Mandy shooting an enemy agent in downtown Cairo. She's something else."

In private, Lt. Mandy had mentioned that Col. Randal was overly protective of the women assigned to Raiding Forces. Beverly could not think of one thing wrong with that. Personally, she liked the idea of him looking out for her.

Col. Randal asked, "Do you know how to handle a pistol?"

"I grew up on a ranch, John," Beverly laughed. "I didn't have a brother."

"Right," Col. Randal said. "I knew that—do you *have* a handgun?"

Beverly flashed a blinding smile, perfect white teeth, "You don't really believe Daddy would allow me to go out half-dressed."

Col. Randal was glad "Daddy" did not know about the French-cut swimsuit.

"Let's take a look at it."

Beverly retrieved her purse from a nearby lounge. She produced a small, flat weapon. A Remington Model 51 in .32 ACP caliber. The pistol was profusely engraved with mother-of-pearl stocks.

Except for being a fancy showpiece, it was a professional's choice. Col. Randal knew the Model 51 to be one of the most ergonomically designed handguns ever made—often described as "self-pointing." Some claimed it was like gripping a bar of soap.

"Daddy gave this to me on my twelfth birthday. He thought I would carry it if the gun was pretty enough," Beverly said, in her soft drawl. "Made me promise to never leave home without it."

Col. Randal said, "Why don't we step out in the desert and see if you can hit anything?"

Beverly responded with another Texas-sized smile that on a scale of one to ten, was at least a twelve.

"Why? Toss that Coke bottle up in the air over the privacy fence— nothing out there but a million miles of desert sand."

Col. Randal did a double-check to see if she was joking—apparently not. He stood up and threw the bottle high in the air over the fence as hard as he could.

The Remington barked. The bottle exploded. Beverly had already slipped the pistol back in her purse by the time Col. Randal turned to say, "Nice shot."

From the pool, Lt. Mandy said, "Annie Oakley!"

Right about then, Col. Randal began to consider the idea that there might be more to this little blond cowgirl than a pretty face.

"Let me restate your orders, Beverly," Col. Randal said. "Starting as of now, you're Jane's bodyguard. Stick to her like glue."

Beverly said, "Lady Jane told me from the moment she met you, John, it was like being swept up by a tornado."

"Jane said that?"

"I know how she feels—things have been moving so fast ever since you walked into Colonel Donovan's office," Beverly said. "It's only fair to tell you . . . I can't type."

Col. Randal said, "Not a problem."

"John," Beverly asked, "do *you* have a weapon?"

"Browning .9mm P-35 in the fold of my spare towel right here," Col. Randal said. "Thirteen rounds quick.

"I'm not your father, Beverly—don't leave home without your *pistola*."

Beverly laughed. "Daddy's going to like you."

Major A. W. "Sammy" Sansom arrived poolside. Beverly was back in the pool, standing in the shallow end talking to Lt. Mandy. The Cairo chief of counterintelligence pulled up a chair next to Col. Randal's lounge.

"Lot of turmoil in the city. The natives are restless. Drums beating in the night."

Col. Randal said, "Egyptians don't beat drums."

"Certain radical elements of the local population are anxious for Rommel to hurry up and take Cairo," Maj. Sansom said. "A high percentage of our GHQ staff are convinced it's only a matter of days before Afrika Korps arrives.

"Apparently, Mussolini believes it. He flew to Tripoli with a white stallion he intends to ride in the Victory Parade."

"Really?"

"Dudley Clarke is also in agreement. He is organizing stay-behind parties to go underground when Afrika Korps arrives. The plan calls for them to form secret resistance cells. Rise up and conduct guerilla attacks—Dudley intends to personally command the operation."

"Good luck with that," Col. Randal said.

"A taxi driver high on 'bango' leaving the Gezira around noon today shot himself in the testicles *twice* before attempting to ram a bus, then crashed into a light pole killing himself," Maj. Sansom said.

"Clearly a deranged individual—most likely a Muslim Brotherhood terrorist bent on jihad. Funny, the illegal handgun found on his person was a .25 but the two expended shell casings in the taxi were from a .22."

Col. Randal said, "Man made a direct threat against Lady Jane."

"Next time make it easy for me," Maj. Sansom said. "Leave your card.

"Have to hand it to you, Colonel, the scenery around the pool keeps improving every time I drop by. Almost certain I have seen the new blond girl somewhere."

Col. Randal said, "That's a possibility."

Jack Cool.

BRANDY SEABORN CAME OUT TO THE POOL IN HER swimsuit carrying a manila folder. She handed it to Colonel John Randal before reclining on the lounge next to him. While he looked at the aerial photos, she oiled her perfect golden legs—the inspiration for the codename of the mission SOLID GOLD.

There was an 8x10 photo of Captain Albert Seebohm in the folder.

Brandy began a crisp, dispassionate briefing. "621st *Fernmeldeaufklärung Kompanie*, commanded by Hauptmann Alfred Seebohm. One hundred men strong, experts in wireless communications, linguistics and cryptology mounted in Sd.kfz.251, Sd.kfz.232 and Sd.kfz.232 Fu vehicles. As previously reported, the company is currently in position on Tell Issa Mount—variously translated as 'Well of Jesus' or 'Jesus Mount.' Do not ask why it is called either of those names. I have no idea.

"By gauging strength, direction, the times of transmission, and call signs—plus the fact our side never rotates radio operators—the instant one of our units transmits, Seebohm's communications specialists know exactly who is sending and where they are located. The 621st is able to provide Rommel a complete picture of the British order of battle on a daily basis."

Brandy said, "If you know who your enemy is, where he has concentrated his artillery, where his tanks and infantry formations are located, and the state of the maintenance on his vehicles the way Rommel does, it makes it difficult to lose a battle."

Col. Randal said, "That is a fact."

"Tonight, handsome," Brandy said, "you and I will link up with Lieutenant Colonel H. H. 'Hard as Nails' Hammer and the men of the Australian 48th Battalion. You brief the officers of the battalion, telling them only the minimum information possible about what is going to take place—specifically—you are going to infiltrate the 621st position with a small team, kill or capture the enemy commander, and withdraw.

"Upon return, on your signal the 48th will launch a battalion attack on the position, supported by SOG gun jeeps, reinforced by Duck Patrol—should you elect to have them landed ashore.

"While the Australian assault goes in, you and I will retire to the beach to be transported by DUKW to the *King Duck* and flown back to Mena House.

"After looking at the photos, do you have an inkling of what you intend tonight, John?"

"I do."

"Questions?"

"What do the initials H. H. stand for?"

"No one seems to have any idea," Brandy laughed. "Rumor has it H. H. stands for 'Hot Headed.' Colonel 'Hot Headed, Hard as Nails' Hammer. Sounds like Mr. Personality."

Col. Randal said, "I like him already."

"One last thing," Brandy said. "Seebohm is a hard-core Nazi. He is never going to cooperate with intelligence. Bring me his body to ID— the sole reason I am going along tonight is to confirm the kill.

"We want him dead."

Vice Admiral Sir Randolph "Razor" Ransom walked out of the suite to the pool area. Brandy stood up and dived into the water. The admiral came over and pulled up a chair next to Col. Randal's lounge.

"I understand you and my daughter are planning to take down the 621st tonight," VAdm. Ransom said. "I have Skipper Finley steaming up the coast. He will be standing by for instructions once you reach 48th Battalion and make your final estimate of the situation.

"He can land Duck Patrol ashore, or simply send in a DUKW to extract you and Brandy from the beach."

"Roger, sir."

"In the desert, the issue is in doubt," VAdm. Ransom said. "Rommel may win this thing if we do not soon knock out his Merlin the Magician and explode his crystal ball."

"Field Marshal Auchinleck whipped the Desert Fox once before, Admiral," Col. Randal said. "He might do it again."

"You and Captain McKoy have never bought into the Rommel myth," VAdm. Ransom said. "But everyone else in the entire British Commonwealth and all the ships at sea have.

"Get Seebohm, kill the bloody Nazi—no telling how many tens of thousands of our lads he is personally responsible for murdering."

Col. Randal said, "Donovan of OSS expressed an interest in Sea Squadron operations, Admiral. I think you should travel to Washington and meet with him at your earliest convenience, sir.

"Strike while the iron's hot."

"I cannot possibly leave with the Flap going full bore," VAdm. Ransom said. "Why not send Randy in my place?"

"Good idea, sir," Col. Randal said. "Wild Bill will like Hornblower."

"I shall order Randy to hand over command to his Number Two," VAdm. Ransom said, "and repair to Cairo for immediate departure to the United States to—as you say—'strike while the iron is hot.'

"Good luck tonight—do the right thing, Colonel."

After VAdm. Ransom departed, Lieutenant Mandy Paige came over and lay down on the lounge. "I shall be retrieving the static lines after you and Brandy jump tonight."

"Negative," Col. Randal said. "Get someone else."

"Lady Jane is the only other person who has ever done it before," Lt. Mandy said. "Everyone with any experience is at Oasis X or out on patrol.

"Can Beverly come along to observe?"

"Are you crazy?"

"Pam says the flight path never crosses enemy territory," Mandy said. "She flies out, drops you and Brandy at 48th Battalion, breaks right, and continues on to the *King Duck.* When you two are extracted after the mission, we all fly back here. Lady Jane is planning a celebration breakfast—do not say I told you that part."

"Clear the idea with Jane first. Just because *you're* a high-risk operator doesn't mean you have to be a bad influence and try to turn Beverly into one too," Col. Randal said.

"She's a beauty queen—wouldn't want her to chip a nail."

"Love you, John."

Lady Jane came out in her swimsuit and took Lt. Mandy's place on the lounge. Tawny gold, drop-dead gorgeous. Col. Randal wondered what his heart rate was right about now.

It could not be good.

"Beverly's a long way from Texas," Col. Randal said. "Keep her close. It wouldn't do for your newest recruit to get homesick."

"How very thoughtful of you, John."

The fact he had told both women a different version of the same story did not bother Col. Randal in the least. He wanted Lady Jane safe.

Beverly could shoot the lights out.

18
REBECCA

THE SUPERMARINE WALRUS WAS FLYING AT CRUISING speed, which was not very fast. Due to the fact that Rommel had driven to within sixty-three miles of Alexandria, the little amphibian did not have to travel very far. The night was pitch-dark. However, there were millions and millions of stars—so many it gave the illusion of lighting up the sky.

All the seats had been removed from the aircraft. Colonel John Randal was laying on his X-type parachute, with his head in Major the Lady Jane Seaborn's lap, asleep. At the last minute, she made the decision to come along rather than be left alone at Mena House.

Brandy Seaborn was sitting up against the bulkhead, leaning back against her parachute. Lieutenant Mandy Paige and Captain Pamala Plum-Martin were sitting with their backs to the cockpit panel.

The two were talking. They had known each other from RAF Habbaniya days. The pitch of the engine changed. Col. Randal's eyes opened. He saw Capt. Plum-Martin.

Col. Randal could transition from sound asleep to wide awake with no in-between, but now he had the wild impression he was hallucinating.

"Who the hell's flying the airplane?"

The Vargas Girl look-alike Royal Marine said, "Beverly."

"Are you serious?"

"Beverly has held a civil aviation license since she was fourteen," Capt. Plum-Martin said. "A list of certifications as long as your arm. Claims to be qualified to fly everything up to a B-17. Her father was a fighter pilot in the last war—owns a crop duster service in South Texas to give himself an excuse to do low-level stunt flying."

"Really."

"The DZ must be coming in sight, John. I need to go up and show Beverly the speed she needs to throttle back to for the drop," the Vargas Girl look-alike Royal Marine said.

"Red light."

Col. Randal asked Lady Jane, "Did you know she was a pilot?"

"Not until tonight."

Lt. Mandy said, "Hook up. Check your equipment."

Col. Randal clamped his snaplink onto the metal D-ring bolted to the steel rim on the side of the door. The Walrus did not have a static line. He and Brandy would be exiting the aircraft from the sitting position. Jumping a Walrus could be a little tricky, as he had learned the hard way during the siege at RAF Habbaniya one dark night.

The pusher-type amphibian aircraft was never intended to drop paratroopers.

Brandy hooked hers on the same metal ring. They ran their hands over their equipment. Col. Randal had his pair of Colt 1911 Model .38 Supers, his .9mm Browning P-35, and the High Standard .22 with silencer. King would have the rest of his gear.

Brandy was wearing her Colt 1911 Model .38 Super on a canvas pistol belt. In her handbag, tucked under the quick release on her parachute harness, she had the profusely engraved M-1935 Beretta .32 that Col. Randal had given her after the jump on Bela Island (of *Jump on Bela* fame). Col. Randal had captured the weapon from the Italian admiral he and Lieutenant Colonel Sir Terry "Zorro" Stone had dropped in to kidnap.

Tonight would be what was referred to as a "Hollywood Jump"— meaning they were not carrying much equipment.

Lt. Mandy went up to the cockpit. The drop zone was in sight. Captain Billy Jack Jaxx was demonstrating his sense of humor, marking it with a giant X made out of glowing red railroad flares.

X marks the spot.

Beverly was in the pilot's seat, the ex-LRDG navigator was sitting next to her, and Capt. Plum-Martin was kneeling between them. The Walrus was flying low and slow, straight at the dead center of the X.

This was the Tri-Delt's first parachute drop.

She could not wait to write her daddy. Tonight, she one-upped him. He had never dropped paratroopers.

"One minute, John," Lt. Mandy said.

Col. Randal slid into the door with his legs dangling outside the aircraft. Brandy scooted up beside him, sitting so close they were touching. The wind was whipping and it was cold. Or, at least it seemed cold.

Lady Jane leaned over his shoulder and whispered, "Be safe."

Leaning around the bulkhead, Col. Randal could see the burning red X coming into sight up ahead. Beverly had the Walrus headed straight and true, though the little plane was jinking back and forth, which was normal.

Brandy gave him a fabulous smile. She was a world-class adventuress, enjoying the moment. Then the X marking the DZ was one point off the toe of his left canvas-topped raiding boot.

Col. Randal said, "Let's go."

He pushed down with both hands and exited the door, the way you would slip into a swimming pool. Brandy came right behind him.

They were dropping from 1,000 feet, and while jumping British X-type parachutes, both were wearing U.S. Army reserve chutes. Col. Randal had mandated reserves on all future Raiding Forces' drops as soon as the 575th Rangers had arrived with a large supply.

There was no sensation of falling, but it seemed to take a long time before the parachute deployed. There was no prop blast from the pusher-type Walrus. Col. Randal was mentally counting, "One thousand, two thousand . . ."

When the chute cracked open, his mind screamed, "CHECK CANOPY!"

This was a command he had learned during his visit to the United States Army Jump School at Ft. Benning, Georgia. The British did not use it. There was no reason to. UK paratroopers did not jump reserves. If a malfunction occurred, there was nothing that could be done about it.

With a reserve, if there were blown panels, a Mae West (meaning a line had gone over the top of the canopy creating a pair of humps), or any of a number of other possible things that could and sometimes did go wrong, the jumper would go back into the tuck position and deploy the reserve.

Having a reserve parachute was very comforting.

Out of his peripheral vision, Col. Randal could see Brandy off to his right, dangling down in a perfect body position. She understood the importance of technique. There was very little breeze. The star-studded sky was fantastic. The night was silent.

Up ahead, the Walrus was making a hard right-hand bank, headed out to sea. The Mediterranean was only 500 yards or so off to the north of the DZ. Somewhere out there, three miles offshore, was the *King Duck.*

Col. Randal clamped his boots together, bent his knees, and wiggled his feet to make sure his knees were not locked. Forearms touching, fists in front of his face with his elbows together resting on the reserve parachute, he was coming in backward. There was a blurring sensation, then he was down—tumbling into a right rear Parachute Landing Fall (PLF).

Capt. Jaxx was recovering his parachute before he could struggle to his feet and hit the quick release.

Captain "Geronimo" Joe McKoy and King were helping Brandy about five yards away.

Capt. Jaxx said, "As soon as you jumped, the Walrus did a wingover like a Spitfire. Never knew amphibians had that kind of move in 'em, sir."

Col. Randal said, "You're not going to believe who's flying it."

COLONEL JOHN RANDAL WAS STANDING AT THE FRONT OF the GP tent 48th Battalion, 9th Australian Division, used as their battalion headquarters. All of the line officers—company commanders and platoon leaders—were seated in folding chairs. The staff stood in the back or lined the walls of the tent.

There was nothing special about 48th Battalion. It was a standard infantry line battalion. Except that the troops had been engaged in almost daily combat at Tobruk for the last eight months. The 9th Australian Division had accumulated more days in direct contact with the enemy than any other unit in the Allied Army.

The Diggers had a reputation for toughness. They liked to fight. If they were not fighting the Germans or Italians, they fought each other. The 9th Australian Division was so rowdy it was banned from Cairo— the way the nonexistent notional US 71st Airborne Division had been— only their banishment was for real.

Australian troops held a reputation for being difficult to command. They hated British officers, whom they called "pommy bastards," almost as much as they did Nazis.

There were no Australians in the Long Range Desert Group, Raiding Forces, or any other Commando unit in Middle East Command. The Australian government refused to allow its troops to be commanded by anyone but their own officers.

For 48th Battalion's commanding officer to be given the nickname "Hard as Nails" by his troops, Lieutenant Colonel H. H. Hammer had to be—hard as nails. He made the introduction.

While Lt. Col. Hammer had most likely never read Raiding Forces' Rules for Raiding, he understood the concept of their rule to Keep it Short and Simple.

He said, "This is Colonel Randal."

The introduction was met with stony silence from the assembled officers. The Australians were big, strapping men. They were not impressed with the young U.S. Army colonel—even if he was wearing three visible pistols and a Fairbairn Commando knife.

On the other hand, Col. Randal was an American, and they did not automatically despise U.S. Army officers, not having had any experience of them. 48th Battalion was willing to give him the benefit of the doubt—for the moment.

Col. Randal studied the Australians, who glared back, trying to stare him down. The "benefit of the doubt" did not include being friendly or even polite. It simply meant listening to what the Yank had to say before they decided to throw him bodily out of the tent.

"This is Mrs. Seaborn," Col. Randal said. "We're all working for her tonight. Treat her with the courtesy you would extend to any major general—is that clear?"

The tent was dead silent.

However, Brandy did merit their attention. Any animosity the Aussies may have felt for British officers did not extend to glamorous English "Sheilas." She was definitely a "ripper."

Unruffled by the audience's lack of response, clearly not intimidated by the hostility—in fact not seeming to notice it, Col. Randal said, "Well, men, I guess you're wondering why I called you here tonight."

The Australians never saw that one coming. There were a couple of snorts and even a chuckle or two. Could the Yank have actually said that?

What a bloody idiot!

In fact, every man in the tent was wondering what the answer was. Why *had* he called them there?

"I'm not here," Col. Randal said. "We're not having this briefing. What's not getting ready to happen never happened."

"However, when it doesn't, you men get to take all the credit. I'm going to make you famous."

The "Rats of Tobruk," as Rommel had scornfully described the Australian 9th Division, were already famous—but not in a good way. However, credit for military exploits is a big-time motivator for hard-fighting military men, though not one man present would have ever admitted it.

The hostility ratcheted down a notch or two.

"Col. Hammer will issue you your Operations Order as soon as I conclude this briefing we're not having. In short, the Nazi 621st Signals Intercept Company—aka The Circus—is located two miles due west of here on the hill to your right front. A regiment of Italian *Bersaglieri* infantry is stationed with it to provide security.

"At zero-two-thirty hours, I intend to infiltrate the 621st position with a small team, carry out a classified task, and return to the 48th Battalion's lines.

"At that point, on Colonel Hammer's signal, 48th Battalion will launch a full-scale assault on the enemy position. Capture as many of the 621st German personnel as possible and move them quickly to the rear.

"Be as gentle as possible. You people have a reputation once your blood is up. We want the Nazis in good enough condition for interrogation.

"I don't care what happens to the Italians."

The officers laughed. It was not a pretty sound.

"This concludes my briefing that never was. Don't ask any questions," Col. Randal said. "Since none of this is taking place, I won't have any answers.

"Mrs. Seaborn, do you have anything you'd like to add?"

Brandy said, "A lucky star has fallen on 48th Battalion. What you do this night may alter the course of the war in Middle East Command—it most probably will."

The Australians were taken off guard. Ground assaults they understood. Patrols they understood. None of them anticipated being told that they could change the war—the cinema was the only place you heard talk like that.

The officers in the tent perked up.

"Every man is expected to do his duty," Brandy said. "Make that clear to your troops, gentlemen."

Someone called, "TEN SHUN!"

Col. Randal and Brandy left the tent. They walked to the location where Captain Billy Jack Jaxx had SOG assembled. Immediately upon arriving, with no fanfare, Col. Randal issued a brief frag order.

"We are currently in the Australian 48th Battalion area. In approximately five minutes, Captain McKoy, Captain Jaxx, King, and I will depart in a single jeep. The idea is to loop around the left flank of the enemy position on the hill two miles to our right front called Tell Issa Mount.

"Upon arriving in the enemy rear, the jeep will drive up the road behind the hill to the CP of the 621st Signals Intercept Company. We will dismount, enter the tent, and shoot everyone inside.

"Immediately upon our return, 48th Battalion will assault up the hill and go in with the bayonet. When the Australians make their attack, SOG, under command of Captain Jaxx, will provide support as requested by Colonel Hammer.

"At that point, Mrs. Seaborn and I will depart the area to rendezvous on the beach with a DUKW from the *King Duck* for extraction by sea.

"SOG will collect all the German prisoners 48th Battalion captured from the 621st Signals Intercept Company. Escort them to Alexandria, with all due speed, for interrogation. Your orders are to drop off the Nazis, then immediately move out for Oasis X.

"Questions? OK—stand by ready."

Col. Randal and Brandy walked back to the 48th battalion CP tent.

"Brandy said, "Carrying the KISS principle to extremes, John?"

"Tonight is pretty straightforward," Col. Randal said. "The Italians' defensive position facing us is an inverted L-shaped line tied into the sea on the open side.

"The bad guys'll think anyone coming in from the west—their rear—is friendly. Either a courier bringing a message or a senior officer stopping by to obtain the latest intelligence—happens all the time.

"Seebohm knows Allied intentions. The 621st will be monitoring the 9th Australian Division's communications. He undoubtedly intercepted the orders placing it in a defensive posture. The Nazi will be paying particular attention to radio traffic from Colonel Hammer's battalion. There's no reason for The Circus to believe it has anything to fear from 48th Battalion in absence of orders to attack."

"You came to that conclusion by the pool this afternoon by the time I asked you if you had a plan?"

"Roger."

"Remarkable."

Lt. Col. Hammer had concluded his Operations Order by the time Col. Randal and Brandy arrived. His plan was simple. The battalion would come on line. At the appointed time, moving as one, it would close up on the foot of Tell Issa Mount and stand by ready. On signal, which would be three red parachute flares, 48th Battalion would fix bayonets and move out up the hill conducting a silent attack.

Lt. Col. Hammer brushed off Col. Randal's suggestion to concentrate all his mortars and fire in one massive barrage before his troops went in. "Hard as Nails" preferred to go in quiet, without giving any advance warning his men were coming.

The Australian also declined the use of SOG gun jeeps to support his attack. However, Lt. Col. Hammer did request SOG be stationed close to his CP so that he could use it as a mobile reserve in the event 48th Battalion hit any determined pockets of resistance.

"Captain Jaxx will stand by here, awaiting your orders," Col. Randal said. "Good luck and good hunting."

Brandy remained in the CP with Lt. Col. Hammer.

Col. Randal walked back to SOG. He climbed in behind the wheel of Capt. Jaxx's command jeep. Jack Cool was riding shotgun. Capt. McKoy and King were sitting in the back.

He glanced at his Rolex, "Lock and load."

Everyone pulled out his .22 High Standard Military Model D, racked the slide partway to make sure there was a round in the chamber, lowered the exposed hammer, and returned the pistols to their holsters.

Col. Randal let out the clutch. The jeep rolled out and headed south, away from the Mediterranean. The team drove two miles inland, then turned west for another mile. There were other German forces in the area, so the important thing was not to accidentally bump into them.

"You're awfully quiet, Jack," Col. Randal said. "What're you thinking about?"

"Blondes, sir."

"Blondes?"

"Yes, sir, Rocky's hair is the color of ice. Pam's is snow," Capt. Jaxx said. "Brandy's looks like wheat, and Beverly, well, hers is pure honey."

Jack Cool.

Col. Randal said, "Glad to see you've got your priorities straight."

At this point the team was behind enemy lines, though Afrika Korps was not on one single solid front. Rommel was concentrating his forces to do battle with Eighth Army at the little railroad town called El Alamein. Large swathes of the desert were not occupied by either side.

The 621st Radio Intercept Company had been parked on the hill next to the sea because the high ground offered the best position to intercept radio traffic. Tell Issa Mount was out of the way, although from a purely military standpoint, it was a criminally stupid location to put the most valuable unit in Afrika Korps—right up on the line.

Bad decision.

Col. Randal turned back east. He came across a dirt track that led up Tell Issa Mount. They drove to the foot of the hill.

"Everybody ready—here we go."

The jeep climbed up the dirt road. It was a rough ride—fairly steep, deeply rutted. The track had not had much traffic over the years.

Security provided by the Italians was not 360 degrees. No one was guarding the back door to the position. Col. Randal had counted on that, though he had a plan if there had been a guard.

When they drove over the military crest, Col. Randal saw a thin line of yellow light, which was a dead giveaway. It was the 621st Command Post/Operations Center. The Circus operated around the clock.

A tent is almost impossible to completely black out at night.

Col. Randal stopped the jeep. He said, "Showtime."

King led out, followed by Col. Randal and Capt. Jaxx, with Captain "Geronimo" Joe McKoy bringing up the rear. The composition of the team was neither random nor arbitrary. Col. Randal had picked the best pistol handlers in Raiding Forces.

The idea was to go in, take down Capt. Seebohm and anyone else in the CP, then return to 48th Battalion with no one the wiser. While that may have sounded simple, it was, in fact, a highly sophisticated special operation—requiring skill, timing, and extraordinary marksmanship. It was not a mission for the faint of heart.

A lot of things could go wrong.

King, as usual in situations like this, was moving like a big hunting cat. Col. Randal was right behind him, clicked on full. Colors seemed brighter, sounds sharper; things appeared to be taking place in slow motion and he had the impression he was looking down from above—watching the events unfold rather than taking part in them. He had experienced the sensation in the past.

It felt comfortable.

Music could be heard coming from inside the tent. It was jazz—Glenn Miller's Big Band playing *In the Mood*. One of the radio operators had apparently dialed in to a station from New York.

As they approached the big tent, they saw no one standing guard outside, or at least performing the duties of a guard. However, there was a German soldier peeking in the crack of the flap covering the entrance. Was he spying on the officers inside? Troops on field maneuvers have been known to do that.

So have sentries bored with their duty.

King shot him twice in the back of his head. *WHIIICH, WHIIICH.* The Nazi went down without a sound. He went from being alive to dead in the time it took to strike a match.

The Merc paused to allow the three Raiders behind him to close up tight. Then, stepping over the body on the ground, he pushed his way inside the tent.

Things happened fast after that. The 621st was a high priority strategic operation and the collection of enemy signals intelligence never stopped. At least ten people inside the tent were on duty, working in the mellow ambience of kerosene lanterns. Cots lined the sides of the room for those people off duty.

The radio intercept operators looked up when the intruders appeared in the tent. They did not immediately realize what was taking place. Italians wore khaki, Germans wore khaki, and the four men who had walked in were wearing khaki. However, the newcomers were pointing strange-looking pistols.

There was a freeze-frame moment—then everything blurred. *WHIIICH, WHIIICH, WHIIICH*—the .22 High Standards were firing fast. From only a few feet away, the only sound to be heard was the slides cycling.

It was a furious fight. The shooting was all one way. The strange thing was, none of the Germans made a noise—no screaming, no shouting, or yelling. Nazis were being knocked down like bowling pins, jumping up, diving to the ground. Some simply sat frozen in place.

Col. Randal was shooting and searching at the same time. He could not find his primary target. Finally, against the wall, he saw a man rise up from his cot with a Luger in his hand—Seebohm.

WHIIICH, WHIIICH, WHIIICH, WHIIICH, WHIIICH.

Col. Randal shot him five times.

Then the whispering of silenced gunfire ceased. From start to finish, the action had lasted less than five seconds. Gunfights in enclosed spaces are fast when everyone knows how to shoot.

Capt. McKoy changed magazines, then walked around and put another .22 round into every Nazi's head. Dead men tell no tales; no one was going to spread the alarm. King and Capt. Jaxx picked up the cot with Capt. Seebohm sprawled on it, carried it out to the jeep, and dumped him in the back.

Col. Randal surveyed the carnage. He was not there to collect intelligence; 48th Battalion could perform that task at their leisure when they arrived.

Something did catch his eye. A tall stack of books was sitting on one of the field desks. The writing on the cover of the top book was in English. Glancing at the spines of the books in the stack, Col. Randal saw they were all the same book—*Rebecca.* Why?

Reloading a third magazine into his pistol, Capt. McKoy said, "Clear."

The two exited the tent immediately and boarded the jeep. With Col. Randal driving, it bounced down the hill and headed back to 48th Battalion at a high rate of speed. Mission accomplished.

Col. Randal pulled up to the battalion CP tent. Lt. Col. Hammer, Brandy, and a crowd of staff officers came outside.

"That was quick, Colonel. Not able to penetrate the perimeter?" Lt. Col. Hammer said. "Hope you did not stir up a bloody hornet's nest for my lads when they go in."

"Seebohm's in the back," Col. Randal said, sticking one of Waldo's thin cigars between his teeth. "I don't think we alerted anyone we were there."

"Bloody amazing," Lt. Col. Hammer said. "You cobbers may actually be as bloody good as they say you are."

Brandy shined a flashlight on the Nazi's face. "Seebohm—still alive."

Lt. Col. Hammer ordered, "Get the bloody medico up here on the double."

Then Lt. Col. Hammer took out a Very pistol and started firing red flares to signal his battalion to commence the attack.

Somewhere out there in the dark, the battle-hardened veterans of 48th Battalion rose up as one—with sword-type bayonets affixed to their .303 Enfield Mark III rifles—advanced up the hill with evil intent, and the wet work began.

Col. Randal said, "Time to go, Brandy."

Capt. Seebohm was lifted out of the back of the jeep. Col. Randal climbed in the driver's side. Brandy rode in the passenger seat, with King and Capt. McKoy in the back.

"Remember," Col. Randal said to Lt. Col. Hammer, "you never saw us."

"How could I bloody forget something that didn't happen, Colonel?"

"That's the spirit."

With Capt. Jaxx following in another jeep, Col. Randal drove the short distance to the beach. A platoon of Australians was providing security for the DUKW parked onshore.

Col. Randal said to the platoon leader, "If you double-time back to your battalion area, you may be able to get in on the action."

"Sir!"

"Take charge of the German prisoners. Escort them back to Alexandria," Col. Randal repeated to Capt. Jaxx. Make it quick."

"Roger," Capt. Jaxx said. "Expect me at RFHQ by nightfall, sir."

Sergeant Major Mike "March or Die" Mikkalis, the acting Duck Patrol leader who had personally brought the single amphibious truck ashore, said, "Ready, Colonel?"

"Let's go, Sergeant Major."

The DUKW putt-putted the three miles out to the *King Duck*. The Lifeboat Serviceman at the helm motored around to the stern where the

Walrus was tied off. Col. Randal, Brandy, Capt. McKoy, and King offloaded to one of the floats and then scrambled directly onto the amphibian. King released the line as the engine to the ugly little aircraft roared to life.

When the Merc swung aboard, Beverly immediately began her take-off run, with Captain Pamala Plum-Martin sitting in the copilot's seat. The ex-LRDG navigator was in the back of the plane, curled up on the floor sound asleep. His services were no longer required tonight.

All Beverly had to do was fly down the coast, staying far enough out to sea not to attract any antiaircraft fire from shore until she came to the Nile River, which was impossible to miss, then turn right. Flanigan would be waiting for them at the Raiding Forces' Headquarters dock.

Beverly lifted off, gained altitude, then threw the Walrus into the hardest banking turn Col. Randal had ever experienced in an amphibian aircraft. Amphibians are not known for having aerobatic capabilities. Since everyone in the back was sitting on the floor because the seats had been removed, they were all thrown across the cabin against the far bulkhead.

Lieutenant Mandy Paige shouted, "Wheeeeee!"

"Beverly believes she is a fighter pilot."

Capt. McKoy said, "A' hotdog, huh!"

King asked, "Who's Beverly?"

Col. Randal said, "The girl in the photo on Jack's pistol."

MAJOR THE LADY JANE SEABORN HAD ARRANGED FOR breakfast to be served at Mena House. It was waiting when Flanigan drove up with half of them in her Rolls Royce and the rest following in the hotel's limousine.

As everyone sat around the table, Colonel John Randal gave a short recital of the night's events from the time his team arrived at Captain Albert Seebohm's 621st Signals Intercept Company's Command Post tent until they returned to 48th Battalion HQ.

Captain "Geronimo" Joe McKoy and King pitched in to describe events from their perspective. It was essential to have a debrief. In a close fast action, not everyone sees things the same way. The information gained from examining every step that took place following a mission falls into the Lessons Learned category.

Professionals conduct extensive debriefings.

Col. Randal said, "There was one thing."

"What, John?" Lady Jane asked.

"A stack of fiction books was sitting on a desk in the tent," Col. Randal said. "About a dozen of 'em. English language—*Rebecca.*"

King said, "Noticed those."

"Jane and I know the author," Brandy said. "Daphne du Maurier."

"Daphne is married to 'Boy' Browning, the commander of the 1st Airborne Division," Lady Jane said. "Remember I told you Boy designed a wine-colored beret for Airborne Forces based on her favorite claret.

Col. Randal said, "Why would Seebohm need a dozen of the same books in English?"

Capt. McKoy said, "Them Nazi boys didn't strike me as the kind to be readin' much English romance."

Lieutenant Mandy Paige said, "The 621st would be the logical unit to receive radio messages from enemy agents operating in Egypt. Seebohm would undoubtedly brief all new agents preparing to cross the line in radio procedure. We need to alert R.J.. immediately."

"Spot on, Mandy," Brandy said, as she stood up from the table. "I shall place the call."

Col. Randal said, "I'm a little lost here."

Lady Jane said, "One of the simplest codes is for the sender, meaning an enemy operative, to transmit a coded message based on a certain page in a certain book. The receiver, who has a copy of the same book, turns to the chosen page and decodes the signal.

"Simple, effective, and secure."

"So now," Capt. McKoy said, "Counterintelligence needs to figure out who's readin' *Rebecca.*"

"Exactly," Lt. Mandy said. "Valuable observation, John. Twelve copies would seem to indicate the 621st, working with the Abwehr, was planning on launching a tidal wave of spies at us."

Col. Randal said, "Books looked out of place."

He made a note to pay closer attention the next time Lt. Mandy was entertaining him with tales about her counterintelligence training. She was the one who had suggested he always keep his eyes open for things that did not quite fit the picture.

Beverly said, "This is like a real-life movie."

Brandy returned, saying, "R.J.. is flying a counterintelligence team to 48th Battalion. He suspects *Rebecca* may be the key to decoding the messages transmitted by the OPERATION KONDOR network Parker and I have been attempting to disrupt.

"R.J.. says the Australians captured the Circus virtually intact. Billy Jack is en route to Alexandria with seventy-two German prisoners.

Beverly asked, "Does anyone around here ever get a chance to catch their breath?"

Lt. Mandy said, "We spent the afternoon around the pool."

19
DEAD MAN

JAMES "BALDIE" TAYLOR ARRIVED BACK FROM THE UNITED States. Colonel John Randal and Major the Lady Jane Seaborn were waiting for him when his plane touched down. They drove to the Gezira Club for lunch.

Jim knew more about the situation in Egypt than the staff officers at Grey Pillars did. Sitting behind a palm in the back of the restaurant, he briefed them on his trip, what he knew about Afrika Korps, and future plans.

"Wild Bill was over the moon when we received word of your success taking out Seebohm and the 621st. Bragging around Washington that OSS had carried out the biggest intelligence coup of the desert war. He is not exaggerating by much. Now Rommel has not only lost his eyes but his ears too.

"Good job, Colonel.

Col. Randal said, "Wasn't a lot to it."

Jim said, "To pull that mission together on short notice was extraordinary. No one else could have done it."

"Brandy and Parker deserve the credit," Col. Randal said. "Once they were on his trail, Seebohm was a dead man."

"I understand he died in hospital," Jim said. "Never gave up a bit of information. Reason we were ambivalent if you captured or killed him, we knew that Nazi was never going to talk."

"Didn't have much chance," Col. Randal said.

Jim said, "Poor Bonner Fellers is back in the U.S. He is going to work for Donovan at the Office of Strategic Services—Propaganda Department—with the famous radio personality, Edward R. Murrow. Through no fault of his own, Colonel Fellers can no longer serve in the European Theatre of Operations, and that is unfortunate.

"Lieutenant Seaborn arrived as I was leaving. OSS is excited about the prospects of having a maritime raiding capability. Good idea sending Hornblower; perfect timing. Something good will come from his trip."

"If OSS listens," Col. Randal said, "Randy knows his stuff. I'm hoping the Razor can get away to go back him up."

"Two local items of interest," Jim said. "First, Auchinleck has checked Rommel at El Alamein. The battle, if you can call it that, was a draw—but enough for us to claim a victory. Truth is, Rommel ran out of steam—ground down by the simple law of logistics. Now he is stalled, with nightmare supply lines extending all the way back to Tripoli under constant unrelenting attack.

"The Desert Fox may not know it yet but he is in trouble. Burned up all the Axis reserves of men and materiel in this part of the world in a failed offensive Afrika Korps was originally ordered not to make. Then he talked Hitler into doubling down with the irresistible promise of taking Cairo, if given just a few more men and tanks.

"Malta is the key to the war in the Mediterranean. The Royal Navy has to have it as a base of operations. Lose the island and we are undone in the Middle East Command, which means the entire Mediterranean.

"Because Rommel convinced Hitler to send him the German paratroops who were marshaling for a drop on the island, the Nazi's OPERATION HERCULES to capture Malta has been canceled indefinitely. The finest airborne soldiers in the world turned out to be virtually worthless in the desert without organic transport. The Desert Fox admitted as much to his boss, Field Marshal Kesselring, in a message we intercepted.

"Smiling Al is furious—wants to fire Rommel. We have Y-service intercepts that indicate even some senior Italian generals have lost confidence in him. While he is a magnificent tactician, Rommel has no grasp of the operational arts, which in the desert are based on logistics, logistics, and logistics.

"Now, Afrika Korps is parked at El Alamein. Time and distance constraints will prevent it from staying there indefinitely. Rommel has to either build up his forces and attack, or else retreat. My guess is he is going to try to patch Afrika Korps back together, regroup, resupply, and attempt to continue the offensive—though that may not be possible.

"The problem is the Nazis are fully committed in Russia. There are no spare tanks, other armored fighting vehicles, troops, or much of anything else for Berlin to send to a theatre the German High Command now considers a backwater. As far as resupply, Afrika Korps is out of luck.

"Hitler has managed to immerse himself in a two-front war without the industrial capacity to support both at the same time."

Lady Jane said, "Over his skis—uh-oh!"

Col. Randal said, "Hate it when that happens."

"Me too," Jim laughed. "Afrika Korps and Eighth Army are like two punch-drunk boxers standing in the middle of the ring, too exhausted for either one to throw a punch. Which is a good thing for our side.

"We have a short supply line and the ability to resupply from the U.S. Rommel has a long, highly vulnerable supply line, with no possibility of more than token resources to replace his losses.

"And that gives Eighth Army the strategic advantage."

Col. Randal said, "General, that's the first positive assessment I've heard since the war started."

"Agreed," Lady Jane said. "Marvelous."

"There is good news and bad news," Jim said. "Your orders are to redouble efforts against the Via Balbia—go after wheeled transport in a big way. Keep hammering Rommel's line of communications."

"We can do that, General," Col. Randal said. "Be advised, we may break Raiding Forces beyond repair if the campaign lasts more than a few weeks."

"If Rommel can be boxed up at El Alamein," Jim said, "Eighth Army can reconstitute itself, replace its tank losses with shipments of M-3 Grants from the U.S., and kill Afrika Korps, or at least drive it all the way back to Tripoli. The potential gain justifies the risk.

"Come up with a plan to siphon off some of your most experienced operators. Hold them in reserve for high-priority missions. Later, they will be available as a core to rebuild around in the event Raiding Forces does, in fact, suffer the kind of losses you anticipate.

"Go for the Via Balbia with everything you have, Colonel."

"Yes, sir."

"Now for the bad news."

"You're kidding," Col. Randal said.

"Afraid not," Jim said. "The Kriegsmarine has a new U-boat signaling system."

The Germans had added a fourth wheel to their Enigma encoding device, making it mathematically undecipherable. However, neither Jim nor Col. Randal were cleared for that piece of information.

"For reasons not completely understood," Jim continued, "the new system is currently only being used on U-boats in the Atlantic. The Royal Navy *and* the U.S. Navy are in a state of near panic. Merchant ship sinkings have skyrocketed to the highest level ever—unsustainable losses.

"Your presence is required in the U.K. to confer with Commander Fleming and his boss at NID—to devise a way for Raiding Forces to station RED INDIAN teams at selected locations bordering the Atlantic to be on standby to carry out pinch missions to capture the new equipment, if and when the opportunity arises. Fleming's GOLDEN FLEECE takes priority over anything else."

"You want me to order a suicidal series of raids on the Via Balbia," Col. Randal said, "then fly off to England?"

"Take a week to get organized," Jim said, "then be on the next airplane."

"Yes, sir."

"Now," Jim said, barely above a whisper, "would you care to hear a piece of gossip that can never, ever leave this table and we all three have to take to our grave—no exceptions on the Need to Know list?"

"Absolutely," Lady Jane said. "Yummy."

"Donovan told me," Jim said, "he and Edward R. Murrow were in the Oval Office late on the afternoon of 7 December 41.

"According to Donovan, the President did not appear surprised the Japs bombed Pearl Harbor. FDR was *only* shocked by how much damage they inflicted on the fleet."

"James," Lady Jane said, "that was more information than I needed to know. The implications are earth-shaking."

Col. Randal said, "Affirmative."

"Yes, they are," Jim said. "Yes, they certainly are."

CAPTAIN BILLY JACK JAXX ARRIVED AT A VIRTUALLY abandoned Raiding Forces' Headquarters with his SOG. He had dropped the prisoners from the 621st off in Alexandria, where they were undergoing interrogation. Colonel John Randal met him outside RFHQ when the patrol drove in.

"Jack," Col. Randal said, "pack your gear. You and your SOG boys are flying out to Achnacarry, Scotland. Take Sergeant Beckwith along with you.

"Time for you to earn your green beret, stud."

"Yes, sir!"

"Get plenty of rest on the trip. You're going to need it. Lady Jane and I will travel up to the Special Warfare Training Center to check on you sometime in the near future. We'll try to smuggle in some extra chow."

"I'll look forward to it, sir," Capt. Jaxx said.

"Coordinate with Parker," Col. Randal said. "She's making your flight arrangements. SOG will be shuttling out on RAF aircraft en route to the U.K. Someone from Seaborn House will meet the flights as they come in.

"You'll continue on to Scotland by rail."

"Roger," Capt. Jaxx said. "Is the battle over, sir?"

"Turned into a stalemate," Col. Randal said. "Now is as good a time as any for you to get away to complete your Commando training. Come in useful for operations we may contemplate for SOG down the road."

That was almost the truth.

"Yes, sir."

Major the Lady Jane Seaborn was in their suite when Col. Randal arrived back on the third floor. Lieutenant Mandy Paige and Beverly Blackwell were with her.

Lady Jane said, "Mandy and Beverly are accompanying us when we fly out. While you are doing whatever it is you are going to be doing, I shall take the girls around to introduce them to the staff at the Secret Intelligence Service, Special Operations Executive, and a few other people who don't officially exist."

"Sounds like a plan," Col. Randal said. "Maybe you ladies can work in some shopping."

Col. Randal was trying to be a good sport, but his heart was not in it. He did not want to go. Leaving Egypt for a conference while his troops were committed to a major offensive against Afrika Korps' supply lines ran contrary to every principle of leadership he believed in.

To his way of thinking, officers led by example—from the front. If not actually on the sharp end, at least they needed to be in the field fighting alongside their troops. Col. Randal was concerned his men would think he was running out on them.

All troops judge their officers all the time. Every combat commander has to live with knowing that a single moment of weakness, real or perceived, can destroy his standing in the eyes of his men in a heartbeat. Being the CO of fighting troops is a test of character—and the test never stops.

The thought occurred that possibly Jim had cooked up this trip to England to keep *him* out of harm's way.

Col. Randal said, "Beverly, you might want to go say hello and good-bye to Billy Jack. He's flying out to the Special Warfare Training Center in Scotland this afternoon."

Beverly laughed. "That boy is always up to something."

THE HUDSON, PILOTED BY CAPTAIN PAMALA PLUM-MARTIN, with Beverly Blackburn in the co-pilot's seat, landed at Oasis X. The normally quiet little green spot the size of the head of a pin on a largely white map had turned into a beehive of activity. Patrols were refitting, pulling maintenance, and repairing battle damage to their jeeps. Some were departing for their AO. Other patrols were returning from operations.

Sub-Lieutenant Bentley St. Ledger picked them up in a jeep. Happy, the German shepherd riding in the seat next to her, seemed glad to see everyone. The dog was so excited that he jumped up, put his paws on Major the Lady Jane Seaborn's shoulders, and tried to lick her face, nearly knocking her down. Lieutenant Mandy Paige gave him a hug. The dog went over to Beverly Blackwell and introduced himself, nuzzling her until she was forced to pet him.

"Happy," Beverly laughed, "what a perfect name."

Lt. Mandy said, "I think he is a people-dog."

Colonel John Randal said, "I don't think he knows he's a dog."

Arriving in their apartment over the Operations Room, Col. Randal and Lieutenant Colonel Sir Terry "Zorro" Stone immediately went into conference.

Col. Randal said, "I've been ordered to England. Depart within the week. You'll assume command of Raiding Forces while I'm away."

"Vacation, old stick?"

"Hardly," Col. Randal said. "The Naval Intelligence Division wants to discuss pre-positioning Raiding Forces' teams at strategic places bordering the Atlantic. The idea is to have qualified troops in place, on call—available to carry out RED INDIAN missions."

"A plan we can ill afford," Lt. Col. Stone said, "that shall draw down our troop strength."

"Your orders are to launch an intensive campaign of gun jeep raids on the Via Balbia in my absence," Col. Randal said. "Maximum effort, Terry. Release Ranger Force from the restriction not to operate in the northern quadrant of their AO. Let them go after the Via Balbia."

"What is this all about, John?"

"Rommel's ground to a halt at some place called El Alamein," Col. Randal said. "Leaves Afrika Korps sitting in the sun with a long logistical tail and no way to resupply by sea. The trucks hauling his supplies have to make round trips of over two thousand miles.

"Destroy as many of 'em as possible, Terry.

"Your secondary target is fuel distribution depots and/or fuel tank storage farms. My guess is you'll want to adjust patrol AOs farther west toward Tripoli. Keep your Raiding Regiments patrols as far away from Afrika Korps' main line of resistance at El Alamein as possible.

"Hit 'em where they ain't, Terry."

"Delighted to, old stick," Lt. Col. Stone said. "Whatever that means."

"Now, here's the tricky part," Col. Randal said. "We need to be looking to the future. If past experience proves anything, Raiding Regiment is going to take heavy casualties through attrition due to the constant patrolling."

"We both know that shall be the case," Lt. Col. Stone said.

"I've been ordered to hold some of our most experienced people back to use as a core to rebuild after this campaign is over," Col. Randal said.

"SOG is flying out to Achnacarry for training. I'm ordering Raider Patrol to RFHQ, with orders to stand by for a potential TOP SECRET Mission—there's not going to be any mission.

"You decide who else you can siphon off and come up with an excuse for limiting their exposure to patrolling."

Lt. Col. Stone said, "You are asking me to choose who lives and who dies?"

"Negative—I'm ordering you to do it."

The handsome Life Guards officer, who bore a striking resemblance to Errol Flynn, only tougher, was the most talented officer Col. Randal had ever served with. He was a stone-cold professional, though he tried not to let it show.

Sir Terry cared deeply for the welfare of the troops under his command.

"It is always darkest before pitch-black," Lt. Col. Stone said. "Worst order you have ever issued to me, old stick."

"Yes, it is," Col. Randal said. "Rommel will be in a static position. We know where he is, where the Via Balbia is, and where all the secondary tracks are located. The convoys will have to come to him—so we know where the trucks will be headed.

"Gives us an edge."

"That is true."

"Lay down strict rules of engagement," Col. Randal said. "No joyriding, shooting up targets of opportunity. Order your patrol leaders to concentrate on ambushes—far ambushes being better than near ambushes. Hit and run," Col. Randal said.

"Pull Mad Dog off patrol. Have him set up a Parachute School. Run anyone who hasn't qualified yet through it. That'll buy you some time.

"This might not turn out as bad as it sounds."

Taking a Player's out of his elegant silver cigarette case, Lt. Col. Stone said, "You think so, old stick?"

"No."

COLONEL JOHN RANDAL WAS SITTING IN THE APARTMENT talking to Captain "Geronimo" Joe McKoy in the living room. Major the Lady Jane Seaborn was out on the deck playing with Happy.

Capt. McKoy said, "You tell Wild Bill I said howdy?"

"Roger that," Col. Randal said. "He informed me you held the rank of Lieutenant Colonel when you were Pershing's Chief of Scouts."

"It was just honorary, John."

"Said you had a reputation as a gunfighter."

"Well, so do you."

The two had Waldo's custom-rolled cigars in their teeth but they were not lit. Lady Jane did not allow cigar smoking indoors. Capt. McKoy had returned from another successful patrol. No one except Captain Roy Kidd came anywhere close to running up the score on thin-skinned vehicles like he did.

The difference was, Capt. Kidd sniped his from long range with scoped Boys .55 caliber antitank rifles. Capt. McKoy killed his up close with the organic machine guns on his jeeps. The old cowboy was deadly on patrol.

He may not have actually fought Geronimo, but growing up in Arizona as a boy, he knew a lot of older men who had. Around a hundred campfires, they had passed along a wealth of invaluable knowledge about how the Apache warrior had carried out his guerrilla raids.

Information Capt. McKoy put to good use the rest of his life in a half dozen wars.

"What'd you want to talk to me about, John?"

"I've been ordered to the U.K.," Col. Randal said. "I don't want to leave, but there it is."

Capt. McKoy said, "Yeah, know how that goes. Duty calls."

"I've sent Billy Jack and SOG to Special Warfare Training Center. This is as good a time as any for them to get their amphibious training out of the way—be gone a month. They're going to skip the first two weeks. Go straight to the tactics work."

"Good idea."

"What I need," Col. Randal said, "is for you to take charge of Raider Patrol while I'm away. Combine it with your White Patrol and stand by ready at RFHQ for a RED INDIAN mission.

"Take Waldo with you."

This was basically a total lie. There was not going to be any RED INDIAN mission for the simple reason that the Nazis had new signals devices that could only be captured from targets in the Atlantic. Pinching devices in the Mediterranean was a waste of time. While Col. Randal did not know anything about the actual signals devices, he did know that much.

Capt. McKoy took his cigar out of his mouth with his finger curled around it, "John, one a' the things I always admired about you the most is, you ain't much of a' hand at pullin' the wool over a' feller's eyes.

"Why don't we back up and try this here fairy tale one more time?"

Col. Randal said, "Rommel's been checked at El Alamein. He can't attack and he's too stubborn to make a strategic withdrawal to shorten his line of communications.

"Raiding Forces has been ordered to launch an all-out attack on Afrika Korps convoys hauling supplies to El Alamein. Odds are we're getting ready to sustain losses on the same scale we did in CRUSADER. I've been ordered to hold some people back to reconstitute Raiding Forces once this campaign plays itself out.

"You're my key man."

"Don't like it much," Capt. McKoy said, studying the tip of his unlit cigar, "but I can do that, John—makes good sense.

"No need to pull White Patrol off operations. You're gonna' need 'em out there doin' their job. My second in command'll be just fine without me. He ain't gonna take a' lot a' casualties.

"My boys'll be around after the dust settles, when you need 'em."

"Thanks, Captain," Col. Randal said. "I can always depend on you."

"Don't go gettin' teary-eyed on me, John," Capt. McKoy said. "No one ever said commandin' a' lot a' men was gonna be easy—it ain't."

"You've pointed that out to me once or twice before," Col. Randal said.

"Talk around town in Cairo," Capt. McKoy said, standing up to leave, "is you shot a' man in the *cojones* for sassing Lady Jane.

"That true, John?"

"Not entirely."

King stuck his head in the door. "You wanted to see me, Chief?"

"I have a mission for you," Col. Randal said. "While Lady Jane and I are away in England, I'm assigning you to be in charge of Rocky's security detail. Waldo's been performing that task, but I'm sending him to RFHQ with Captain McKoy."

"My pleasure, Chief," King said, "provided I don't have to do PT with her ladies every morning."

"You have to accompany the run," Col. Randal said. "Follow 'em in a jeep or on horseback for all I care—tell the women you need to carry a lot of heavy firepower."

"Any special reason?" King asked. "A threat I should know about?"

Col. Randal said. "With Colonel Fellers out of the picture and Rommel no longer able to read his confidential messages, R.J.. and Colonel Clarke have big plans for Rocky—that's classified.

"I have no idea what those plans are."

"Understood," King said, "loud and clear."

Captain "Pyro" Percy Sterling arrived. He and his Railroad Wrecking Crew had been on continuous operations longer than any unit in Raiding Forces—virtually nonstop from Abyssinia to date.

Col. Randal offered him one of Waldo's long, thin cigars. "You can't smoke it in here."

"Wilco."

"Percy, you've been in the field too long," Col. Randal said. "You've lived up to the 'Death or Glory' standards of your regiment and then some.

"Time to take a break, stud."

"Yes, sir."

"Have your patrol report to Capt. McKoy at RFHQ. He'll send 'em on leave. You're headed to Achnacarry. I've arranged for you to spend four months there teaching demolitions."

"Are you quite sure, sir?"

"Absolutely," Col. Randal said. "Butch Hoolihan is at the Special Warfare Training Center now, taking the same rest cure."

Capt. Stirling said, "Shall I be allowed to return to Raiding Forces after my tour as an instructor is over, sir?"

Col. Randal said. "I'm sending you to Scotland to share your special operations experience with the students, chase women, get rested, then come back here ready to start blowing things up again."

"Appreciate that, sir."

"Don't worry, I'm not about to let you be reassigned out of Raiding Forces," Col. Randal said. "When you blow something up, it stays blown up."

As he was standing up to leave, Capt. Stirling asked, "When are *you* planning to take a break, sir?"

"Lady Jane and I are headed to England in a few days. We'll come up to check on you—have dinner at Spean Bridge."

"I would like that, Colonel."

King stuck his head in the door again. "Rocky to see you, Chief."

The ice-blonde Norwegian rippled into the room. Her normal uniform of ballet togs, ballet slippers, and leg warmers did a lot to help remind everyone exactly how physically fit she was. Her trademark ten gold bangles were dangling from her left wrist.

Rocky had a way of sucking the oxygen out of the room.

"You wished to see me, John?"

"Roger," Col. Randal said. "Everything going all right for you, Rocky?"

"I love it here at Oasis X. I may choose to stay on after the war. Only now there are so many people coming and going, it interferes with my yoga meditation classes.

"Wish things were the way they were before all the new patrols arrived—peaceful."

"Afraid the war caught up with Oasis X," Col. Randal said.

"A pity," Rocky said.

"Lady Jane and I have to travel to England."

"How long will you be away?" Rocky asked, with a hint of concern in her sexy Norwegian voice. She was dependent on Col. Randal for protection. It was believed there were bad actors from at least three countries who wanted to do her harm.

"A few weeks at most," Col. Randal said. "I'm assigning King to take over your security detail while we're away.

"Rita and Lana have to guard the WRENS when they go out, but they'll be on call to pull duty as your bodyguards as well. Sir Terry will be checking to make sure you're satisfied with your protection detail. I want you to feel safe while we're gone."

"I shall be fine," Rocky said. "Do not worry about me while you are away."

"Billy Jack try to talk you into posing for a photo to put in his pistol?" Col. Randal asked.

"We decided on a nude."

Jack Cool.

"Red to see you, Chief."

The stunning Clipper Girl walked in. She and six other BOAC stewardesses were staying at Oasis X during Rommel's offensive, at the request of the British Secret Intelligence Service, MI-6.

"Pack your bags, Red," Col. Randal said. "You're flying out to the States."

"My bags are always packed," Red said. "What shall I be doing in America, John?"

"Your presence has been requested by Colonel "Wild Bill" Donovan, Office of Strategic Services," Col. Randal said. "He requires advice on how best to utilize stewardesses as OSS agents.

"Apparently, you're the leading expert."

"Lovely," Red said. "Not all that complicated, actually."

"What do Clipper Girls do for MI-6, exactly?"

"Sometimes we shadow suspected enemy agents or carry out clandestine assassinations," Red said. "Mostly we sleep with persons of interest on layovers to inveigle information from them during pillow talk."

"Really?" Col. Randal said, looking up from the .9mm Browning P-35 he was cleaning.

He knew from past experience that under her ice-cool, Clipper Girl exterior beat the heart of a hell-raiser. Red was responsible for Zorro being banished to Middle East Command for drinking a Black Strap in the Life Guards officers' mess late one night.

Tradition stipulated the regimental drink must be consumed while standing on your head. No one had bothered to inform Red that the rule did not apply to the female guests.

"No, John," Red laughed. "We perform mundane tasks. Flight attendants make superb couriers because we fly all over the world. One of our primary duties is to keep our ears open in airport bars between flights.

"Travelers who interact with flight attendants never expect to ever see them again—works to lower their guard."

"OSS wants you, Red," Col. Randal said. "Have a nice trip."

"You as well, John."

Col. Randal heard men shouting outside. Captain Pamala Plum-Martin and Lieutenant Mandy Paige rushed into the room and ran out on to the deck. Col. Randal followed, to see what was taking place.

One of the IMAM Ro.63 short landing and takeoff liaison airplanes captured from the Regia Aeronautica was directly overhead, flying inverted up the escarpment—screaming past. Col. Randal looked up and could see the upside-down pilots as the airplane blasted past so low that everyone on the deck, including Happy, ducked.

The Ro.63 did a snap roll, righted itself, then zoomed straight up into the sky over the top of a giant loop and came back down, having completed a full circle followed by a barrel roll.

Each maneuver was beautifully executed, razor-sharp.

Col. Randal said, "What's going on, Pam?"

"I told Ronnie about Beverly having a long list of civil aviation certifications," Capt. Plum-Martin said, never taking her eyes off the dancing spirals and loops.

"Ronnie thinks Beverly is red-hot so he offered to give her a check ride—he likes girls."

"Showing off?"

"Not the way you imagine," Capt. Plum-Martin said. "Beverly's at the stick."

Lady Jane said, "*Beverly* is flying that airplane?"

"Ronnie's not capable of aerobatics like that," Capt. Plum-Martin said. "Nobody is. I do not even know the name of most of those stunts."

The Ro.63 finally came down and started to beat up the landing strip, performing a series of low-level victory rolls.

Lady Jane said, "Let's go meet Beverly when she lands."

They went outside, down the stairs, and climbed in a jeep; the dog jumped in with them. All around the oasis, men were cheering and throwing their hats in the air. None of them had ever seen flying to equal the air show.

Col. Randal parked on the side of the strip as the Ro.63 was coming in for a landing. He was standing, leaning against the hood of the jeep, smoking one of Waldo's cigars when Wing Commander Ronnie Gordon aka "Flash Bang" came past with his parachute slung over his shoulder.

W/Cdr. Gordon was exhibiting symptoms of the "thousand-yard stare." He walked straight by the jeep in a daze, realized what had he had done, stopped, and made a U-turn. "Will someone pray tell me what in the name of the Great Horned Serpent a 'crop duster' is?"

"So, Ronnie," Col. Randal said, "you'd rate Beverly a competent pilot?"

W/Cdr. Gordon looked at him with glazed eyes. "I had the Regia Aeronautica flight manual for your Ro.63s translated. The book specifically states that those stunts cannot be performed in that aircraft. You will never see them again.

"Not with me in the copilot's seat."

Beverly strolled up with her chute slung over one shoulder, wearing a black baseball cap with her long, honey-colored ponytail hanging out the back. There was a University of Texas Longhorn logo and three triangles embroidered on the front of the cap—Delta, Delta, Delta.

Beverly said, "Hi, y'all."

COLONEL JOHN RANDAL WAS IN THE TOC AT OASIS X. HE had all the Patrol Commanders, Patrol Leaders, and their NCOs assembled who were in from patrol. The huge wall map of Libya and Egypt was behind him.

Col. Randal said, "Raiding Forces has been ordered to launch a raiding campaign designed to interdict Afrika Korps supply lines.

"Rommel has stalled right about here," Col. Randal tapped El Alamein with a pointer. "Every stick of his supplies has to be shipped from Italy to Tripoli by sea, under threat of attack the whole way. Then hauled by truck transport all the way down the coastline to the Axis fighting troops. It's over two thousand miles round-trip.

"According to intelligence, Afrika Korps only has something like ten thousand two-ton trucks. I'm not a logistician, but I'm told the math says Rommel can't do it.

"Some estimates indicate over a third of the Axis trucks will be sidelined for maintenance at all times due to normal wear and tear from the driving. More if they continue to use the secondary tracks. With British and U.S. fighter bombers operating against the Via Balbia by day, and Raiding Forces shooting up his convoys and mining the roads by night, Rommel is in for some serious hard times.

"Remember—we're guerrillas. Do not fight pitched battles. Do not attack fortified positions, except to harass them. Do not go joyriding down the Via Balbia or the secondary tracks, looking for targets of opportunity, and do not take unnecessary risks.

"Strike from long range. Use your mortars lavishly. Call for airstrikes on large concentrations of trucks or any tank formations laagered for the night. Be bold but think out your moves in advance.

"Hit and run.

"It's your mission to inflict maximum damage on Rommel's supply system, but I want you to keep in mind it is important to live to fight another day. Future missions for Raiding Forces are being planned as we speak.

"Think of this campaign as a marathon—not a sprint. Take care of your troops. Take care of yourselves. You are no good to me dead.

"Is that clear?"

"CLEAR, SIR!"

"Rangers, stand fast. Everyone else, dismissed," Col. Randal said.

After the rest of the Raiding Regiment people departed, Col. Randal said to the Rangers, "Lady Seaborn would now like to explain the system of awards and decorations she has worked out for the 575th.

"Lady Jane. . . ."

VICE ADMIRAL SIR RANDOLPH "RAZOR" RANSOM AND Major Taylor Corrigan were sitting in the British Overseas Airways Corporation's (BOAC) departure lounge with Colonel John Randal, Major the Lady Jane Seaborn, Lieutenant Mandy Paige, and Beverly Blackwell.

The girls were excited about the trip.

Col. Randal said, "Admiral, I know you have a worldwide commitment as Director of Operations Irregular. And you have other things going on all over the Mediterranean. But would you consider taking command of Sea Squadron while we're away so Major Corrigan can concentrate on attacking the Via Balbia?"

"Hoping you would ask," VAdm. Ransom said. "I shall oversee administration, victualing, and dock yard support, leaving Major Corrigan to focus on tactical command. Need you to return my WRENS to RFHQ to staff the Operations Section."

"You OK with that, Taylor?" Col. Randal asked.

"Yes, sir," Maj. Corrigan said. "A huge weight off my shoulders, actually. We shall try to be out every night somewhere on the Via Balbia striking from the sea—doing bad things to bad people."

"Good," Col. Randal said. "Here's what I want. No attacking fixed installations like roadhouses. Carry out the smallest raids possible—true pinpricks. Land a few Raiders ashore, mine the road, return to the *King Duck,* go somewhere else and do it again.

"Guerrilla war and plenty of it—bring it hard. Same thing for the MAS boat teams operating up west."

"Understood, sir."

"What I want to hear from you when I get back is we carried out fifty road mining raids and never heard a shot fired in anger," Col. Randal said. "You make that happen, I'll give you an OBE."

"Rest assured, Colonel," Maj. Corrigan said. "I shall take great care handling Sea Squadron troops in your absence."

Col. Randal knew he was not fooling anyone. Leaving for the U.K. was a bad idea. And everyone knew it.

"You do that."

20
BAD FEELING

COMMANDER IAN FLEMING, RNVR, WAS WAITING WHEN
Colonel John Randal, Major the Lady Jane Seaborn, Lieutenant Mandy
Paige, and Beverly Blackwell's BOAC flight landed on the Thames
River. The limousine from the exclusive Bradford Hotel was also
dockside. The debonair naval intelligence officer had met Beverly in
Washington, D.C. at the Office of Strategic Services. However, he was
surprised to learn she was now a member of Lady Jane's entourage.

Cdr. Fleming said, "You ladies ride to the hotel in the limousine
while Col. Randal and I follow in my staff car. That way, we shall not
bore you with shop talk."

When Cdr. Fleming climbed in behind the wheel, Col. Randal said,
"No driver, Commander? I would have expected you to have the best-
looking WREN in the navy."

"I do, and she gives a rather decent massage as well," Cdr. Fleming
said. "Unfortunately, it is actually true, 'loose lips sink ships.' What we
shall be discussing, no driver is cleared to hear—even mine. In fact,
Colonel, neither are you for the most part."

"Fine," Col. Randal said. "We can just ride along and listen to the
radio."

"Here is what you need to know for the moment," Cdr. Fleming said,
ignoring the comment.

"An operation we thought canceled has resurfaced and unexpectedly gone live. It requires my immediate attention. I shall give you a quick and dirty version of the arrangement Naval Intelligence Division desires to work out with Raiding Forces so you can be thinking about it while I am tied up for the next couple of weeks.

"Then the two of us shall have the luxury of spending as much time as we feel necessary sorting out the details."

Col. Randal said, "You expect me to sit around for two weeks in a five-star hotel waiting for you to have some spare time while my troops are fighting in the desert?"

"Calm down, Colonel," Cdr. Fleming said. "We have worked together far too long by now for you to believe I would intentionally waste your time. What I am involved with is a true unforeseen intelligence bonanza, with far-reaching national implications for both of our countries.

"Go to Seaborn House. Inspect Raiding Forces Europe. Then travel up to Achnacarry to visit your men. Captain Jaxx and his SOG people have all arrived. C/575 Rangers are wrapping up their course. Colonel Vaughn reports they performed extremely well during the training.

"When you return, I should be free to devote the time and attention we need to craft a project I can assure you is of vital importance."

Col. Randal said, "Keeping an eye on my people, Fleming?"

"That I am, Colonel," Cdr. Fleming said. "We have plans for your lads in the future.

"As you are well aware, Raiding Forces conducts RED INDIAN pinches from time to time. You are not the only Commando officer involved in the project on the military side. However, your ability to make complex tasks simple, not fight the problem, and simply go accomplish the mission—that's why you were called away from your command at a critical juncture to meet with NID," Cdr. Fleming said.

"The Kriegsmarine has a new communications device for its U-boats that is mathematically unbreakable. Since we have no way to crack the machine, our only option is to pinch it or its codebook from the Nazis. But we can never let the other side know we did.

"In naval warfare, more than any other form of military enterprise, the element of surprise is what determines victory. Without being able to penetrate the U-boat's signals system, we have no way to locate enemy submarines, reroute our convoys around them, or sink the blighters. Which means we concede to the German Navy the element of surprise for all of our surface shipping.

"We, meaning the U.S. and Great Britain, have to keep the sea lanes open or lose the war. To accomplish that objective, we have to stop the U-boats from sinking our merchant fleet faster than we can build new ships to replace our losses.

"Are you following me, Colonel?"

"So far."

"We have no other option except to conduct pinch raids to collect the intelligence we require," Cdr. Fleming said, "However, we are restricted by the absolute ironclad requirement that no RED INDIAN can ever be carried out simply to make a pinch.

"Maybe," Col. Randal said, "you better run through that part again, Fleming."

"RED INDIAN raids were born out of desperation and necessity," Cdr. Fleming said. "You are not cleared and never will be cleared to know the details behind the missions. You probably have figured out the what, but you have not the faintest idea as to the why or how of our intentions—nor the results the pinches produce."

"That is a fact," Col. Randal said.

"NID is after something called SPECIAL INTELLIGENCE," Cdr. Fleming said. "I realize that tells you absolutely nothing but it is all you are ever going to be told. I am bending the rules telling you even that much.

"The purpose of the exercise is to outfox the Nazis in the pursuit of what we are after. That means Raiding Forces' RED INDIAN raids have to be handled with a velvet touch and a great deal of finesse. Any pinch has to be covered by some other operation.

"The pinch has to appear to be a byproduct of the covering mission—something that simply occurred in the course of the military action.

"I see," Col. Randal said, which meant he did not.

"In short, Colonel, the other side can never know what it is you are doing or why you are doing it," Cdr. Fleming said.

"And they can *NEVER* know you conducted a pinch *intentionally.* RED INDIAN raids have to appear incidental to another combat endeavor that may be so massive the other side would never in its wildest imagination guess it was planned to cover a pinch.

"There are three types of pinches: chance, opportunity, and by design. They all have to appear to be unintentional—fortunes of war."

Col. Randal said, "Got it."

"Keep this in mind, Colonel," Cdr. Fleming said. "RED INDIAN missions will be an ongoing joint NID/OSS operation for the remainder of the war.

"You are our go-to pincher."

Col. Randal said, "How will that work?"

"Jim is the Special Operations liaison officer between OSS, MI-6, and SOE. I perform the same function for NID.

"Donovan has agreed OSS / Raiding Forces will be available on call to MI-6 and NID for special tasks. No one is willing to risk your people running hare-brained missions for SOE—those people are not even cleared to know RED INDIAN/GOLDEN FLEECE exists.

"So, never discuss anything with SOE you have not cleared with Baldie first."

"Understood," Col. Randal said.

"You and I operate as we have in the past," Cdr. Fleming said. "You work through Jim. Expect me to show up from time to time when things are particularly urgent.

"Besides, I may make a point of spending more time in Egypt to get to know that smashing Texas girl better. Do you think Beverly ever grows tired of laughing?"

"Not that I've noticed," Col. Randal said.

"Lady Jane must certainly be confident in your relationship to keep bringing knockouts like her around."

What Cdr. Fleming did not tell Col. Randal—because he did not have a Need to Know—was the decision had been made by OSS, U.S. Navy, the Admiralty, NID, and the Naval Section at Bletchley Park, in Huts 3 and 8, to implement a uniform and systematic worldwide program of pinching. Upgrading the missions to top priority: ULTRA SECRET.

The President of the United States and the Prime Minister of Great Britain had signed off on the project.

Cdr. Fleming also failed to mention he had formed his own RED INDIAN outfit—30 Commando aka 30 Assault Unit—to make pinches. It had not created a stellar record to date, which was another reason Raiding Forces was being tapped to have primary responsibility for RED INDIAN/GOLDEN FLEECE.

Forming an elite raiding team had turned out to be a considerably more difficult proposition than NID imagined.

Col. Randal said, "Next time you make it out to Egypt, ask Beverly to take you for a hop in one of our Italian Ro.63s."

"She a pilot?"

"Oh, yeah."

COLONEL JOHN RANDAL INFORMED MAJOR THE LADY JANE Seaborn of the change in plans, to include most of the details he probably was not supposed to tell her. They were in her private suite on the private floor in the exclusive Bradford Hotel, which she owned. The last time he had stayed in the hotel he had been assigned her husband's suite, complete with a butler—the commander having been thought to be KIA.

That seemed like a lifetime ago.

Lady Jane said, "Fabulous."

"Well," Col. Randal said, "I wasn't too happy about it."

Ignoring him, Lady Jane said, "First, we shall take you and Beverly to Chatterley's. He has new U.S. Army uniforms ready for your final fitting. I ordered them ages ago, hoping we would eventually get back to the city.

"Beverly wants to wear a uniform since all the other girls have them."

"Well, she's not in the military."

Lady Jane laughed, "When has a minor detail like that ever bothered you, John?

"We shall do for her what you did for Mr. Treywick. No rank, U.S. insignia on both collars and on the lapels of her jackets. Beverly will look smashing in jodhpurs and riding boots."

Col. Randal said, "I'm sure she will."

"Then," Lady Jane said, "while you go to Seaborn House to see Lionel, I shall take the girls around to the intelligence agencies and introduce them to the right people. We may even spend a day at the Beaufort Hunt.

"When you return, you and I board the train for Achnacarry. We shall be in my private car, alone for the entire twelve-hour trip."

"Sounds good to me," Col. Randal said. Meaning the alone part. The two of them had very little time without other people around. He valued it.

"Ian can make arrangements with Admiral Godfrey for Mandy to spend at least a week in Room 39 observing the workings of the Naval Intelligence Division. Beverly will go to Ringway, take the short course, and earn her parachute wings."

"You're a fast planner," Col. Randal said.

Lady Jane zapped him with one of her patented, heart-attack smiles. "Learned it from you, John."

She was clearly having fun. There was no reason for him to rain on her parade. Col. Randal started to relax. Lady Jane had that effect on him, no matter how stressful a situation might be.

Lady Jane said, "Airborne Forces have adopted the wine-colored beret Daphne du Maurier's husband, Boy Browning, designed for his 1st Airborne Division. Since all of my Royal Marines are parachute-qualified, I have been considering it for their wear.

"What is your opinion, John?"

"Get one of the Airborne Forces' berets. We'll have a style show," Col. Randal said, not quite believing he was hearing himself say something like that. "Compare it to my green beret. See which one you like best.

"Your Marines can wear a Commando beret if you want—First Rule is 'There Ain't No Rules.'"

"Excellent!"

"Personally," Col. Randal said, "I'd go with green—look great with your eyes."

Another heart-attack smile, which was pretty close to the lethal limit. "Fun!"

Maybe the down time was not a bad idea. Lady Jane was enjoying herself. And, he was almost not preoccupied thinking about his troops.

The operative word being *almost*.

COLONEL JOHN RANDAL AND BEVERLY WERE IN THE SMALL bar off the lobby of the plush Bradford Hotel. They were waiting for Major the Lady Jane Seaborn and Lieutenant Mandy Paige, who had disappeared to who knew where.

Beverly said, "Lady Jane must be big rich."

"That is a fact," Col. Randal said.

"Ever bother you, John?"

"No," Col. Randal said. "Why do you ask?"

"Daddy's big rich," Beverly said. "Intimidates a lot of the boys I meet."

"Don't believe it's the family money that intimidates the boys," Col. Randal said.

Beverly laughed, "Are you paying me a compliment?"

"Yes, I am."

"I heard Lady Jane had a lot of men chasing her, including a major movie star, when y'all met—she picked you, right?"

Col. Randal said, "You know girls always pick."

"I do," Beverly laughed. "Wondered if you did?"

Never comfortable talking about his relationship with Lady Jane, Col. Randal said, "I guess you'll be spending most of your time flying with Pam once we get back to RFHQ?"

"Flying is something I grew up doing," Beverly said. "I can drive a big rig hauling cattle too, but that doesn't mean I want to be a truck driver.

"Lady Jane recruited me to be her token OSS representative. Like a pop-up cardboard person—be seen and not heard.

"I'm good at that," Beverly said. "I'd like to work with her."

Col. Randal asked, "How did you manage to get involved with OSS?"

"Daddy wanted me to experience Washington, D.C. and New York City on my own while I was single," Beverly said. "He got me a summer job.

"The plan was to finish college next year. Raise hell in Austin with wild boys like Billy Jack until I graduate. Then come home. Daddy'll tear down the fence to the adjoining ranch, which is about fifteen miles away, and I'll marry the boy next door.

Col. Randal said, "What's the boy next door been doing with himself while you're away?"

"Joined the Marines." Beverly laughed. "He's an Aggie. Graduated from Texas A&M."

"That what you're going to do," Col. Randal asked, "marry the neighbor?"

"Not even a chance, John," Beverly laughed. "Daddy's going to be soooo disappointed in me. Our neighbor's ranch is about twenty thousand acres—sitting on top of the Pettus Oil Field—and they own one hundred percent of the minerals.

"Sorry, Daddy."

Col. Randal asked, "How's your mother going to take the news?"

"Momma ran off with a roughneck when I was three years old," Beverly said. "Daddy always did have a roving eye and Momma never liked living in South Texas—she was from Connecticut."

"So, Beverly," Col. Randal said, "what's your opinion of the OSS?"

"I don't think Colonel Donovan has it all together yet," Beverly said. "The Outfit is sort of like a club. Most of the people are his cronies, former law firm associates, Wall Street types, real estate developers, politicians—even a few B-list movie actors from Hollywood.

"The joke is OSS stands for 'Oh So Social.'"

"Really?"

"Colonel Donovan is setting up a training facility on the grounds of the Congressional Country Club—you can't make something like that up."

"No," Col. Randal said, "you can't."

"Those snobs in the office the day you were there," Beverly said, "Ivy League girls. They treated me like a hayseed. Subtracted ten points from my IQ as soon as they heard my accent."

Col. Randal said, "I like hayseeds."

Beverly rewarded him with a Texas-sized, Ten Most-quality, beauty-queen smile. It was hard to imagine her as a tomboy, growing up on a working ranch.

"Lady Jane is letting me start parachute training tomorrow. Mandy says jumping out of airplanes is better than sex. Is that true, John?"

Col. Randal said, "Why don't you get back to me on that one?"

MAJOR LIONEL HONEYCUTT-PARKER PICKED COLONEL John Randal up at the train station in the tiny village a few miles from Seaborn House in the Restricted Zone. First thing, Col. Randal reached in his pocket and produced lieutenant colonel's insignia.

"Long overdue, Lionel."

"Thank you, sir," brand-new Lt. Col. Honeycutt-Parker said. Staying in Raiding Forces after the Abyssinia campaign had meant sacrificing the opportunity for rapid advancement.

Lt. Col. Honeycutt-Parker could have been commanding a regiment had he chosen to go back into the regular army. And that said everything about the man anyone needed to know.

On the drive, Col. Randal noticed that security along the single lane leading to Seaborn House had been increased since the last time he had been there. He was surprised at how glad he was to be back. This was where Raiding Forces had been formed. Off in the distance was the Blind Eye Inn where he had first met Lady Jane.

As he drove, Lt. Col. Honeycutt-Parker briefed him on Raiding Forces Europe's ongoing operations.

"We have one MOST SECRET—or TOP SECRET, as we call it now that the U.S. has come in the war—long-term commitment. I can brief you on the general outline of the mission; however, the operation itself is classified above TOP SECRET.

"You shall not be allowed detailed knowledge of the exact nature of the operation, even though you command Raiding Forces. In fact, *I* do not know the purpose of the exercise exactly, and neither do our Raiders who carry it out."

"I see," Col. Randal said, which meant he did not. The mysterious mission had been made reference to several times. He wondered what it was.

"That particular operation is being conducted by the detachment of Lovat Scouts we recruited before the regiment refused to allow us to pilfer any more of their men, currently under the command of Captain Dick Courtney. What I am at liberty to tell you—Raiding Forces is conducting long-range strategic reconnaissance somewhere in France for the Naval Intelligence Division in conjunction with the Secret Intelligence Service, sir.

"Dick was an excellent choice of officers for you to send us, sir. He and his two strikers, X-Ray and Vanish, are simply without peer at deep penetration reconnaissance. They mesh extremely well with the Lovat Scouts."

"Outstanding," Col. Randal said, "I was concerned Dick might not be a good fit, having spent most of his life in Africa.

"What else do you have going on?"

"Our other operation consists of running agents across to the other side in our motorized fishing vessel or the HMY *Arrow* for MI-6, sir," Lt. Col. Honeycutt-Parker said.

"Major Lawrence Grand, the chief of Section D for Destruction, either left SOE to return to the Royal Engineers or was fired for looking after MI-6's best interests instead of their own—depending on whose story you choose to believe. When he departed, our contact with Special Operations Executive came to a screeching halt."

"Really?"

"A mysterious and somewhat depressing story, sir," Lt. Col. Honeycutt-Parker said. "SOE is charged with forming guerrilla cells to 'set Europe ablaze.' A fantastic mission—one I know you would love to be actively involved with.

"To date, SOE has not managed to establish one single clandestine arms dump in enemy-occupied France. There are no Resistance units being controlled by Special Operations Executive agents, sir. SOE is a total bust at running guns or forming a guerrilla army on the Continent.

"Some say MI-6 plays a role in sabotaging their attempts."

"Inter- service rivalry," Col. Randal said, "never lets up."

"Not to worry, Colonel—at least as far as Raiding Forces is concerned," Lt. Col. Honeycutt-Parker said. "MI-6 turned up straightaway. Ordered me to cease any contact with SOE at this juncture and to stand by to transport their 'Joes' to France.

"And that is what we have been doing, Colonel. The motorized French fishing vessel and/or the HMY *Arrow* ferry MI-6 agents across almost on a nightly basis."

"Outstanding," Col. Randal said. "Had any problems?"

"Had to remove the torpedo tubes from the *Arrow,* sir," Lt. Col. Honeycutt-Parker said. "What sounded like a good idea on paper did not work out in practice. The torpedoes made the yacht virtually unmanageable in almost any sea. "

"So you have two high-intensity operations going," Col. Randal said. "Do you have adequate men and equipment to sustain the mission?"

"Yes, sir. The platoon of the 575th Rangers you assigned us completely resolved all our personnel needs since small-scale raiding is no longer in vogue. The Admiralty has ordered a raiding freeze temporarily. Seems there is a turf war between the Vice Admiral in Charge of Channel Operations and Combined Operations over who has final authority on approving pinprick raids. Spurred on by the Prime Minister, who appears to have grown disenchanted with small-scale raiding. COHQ is only interested in large raids.

"SOE has responsibility for raids of less than fifty men, but they are not running any."

Col. Randal said, "I'm pretty sure the Prime Minister got fed up with pinprick raids after the first one."

"Fine by me, sir," Lt. Col. Honeycutt-Parker said. "Leaves Raiding Forces free to concentrate on our long-range strategic reconnaissance mission and landing agents for MI-6. We are very busy."

"Any other problems?"

"None to speak of, Colonel," Lt. Col. Honeycutt-Parker said. "A few of the Sea Rover Scouts Randy recruited have reached draft age. MI-6 is in the process of working out exemptions to keep the boys from being called up.

"Squadron Leader Wilcox set up a small Special Operations flight of Walruses manned by some of the Canadian bush pilots who flew for Force N out of Lake Turkana. He also arranged for civilian ground crew to service them. The air section runs like a Swiss watch, sir.

"Admiral Ransom drops in every time he is in the U.K. He personally conducts a detailed inspection of the French fishing vessel, the *Arrow,* their crews, and the retirees who service the boats, sir. God help anyone or anything not measuring up to his standards—the Razor is a holy terror."

"He can be," Col. Randal said.

"Terrifies me, sir."

They drove past Seaborn House, down to the dock. Col. Randal went aboard both boats and talked to the officers and men. They seemed glad to see him and he was definitely enjoying being back where Raiding Forces had its very shaky start. It seemed like a long time ago.

Everything seemed smaller than he remembered.

What struck him most were the crews. When he deployed to Africa, they had been made up of enthusiastic amateurs, volunteers to a man, or in a lot of cases, teenage boys. Every one of them had to learn the tricky business of clandestine small-scale naval operations by on-the-job training in dangerous waters. Now, the seagoing element of Raiding Forces Europe were all seasoned professionals—Special Operations sailors.

Col. Randal was favorably impressed.

When they drove back to Seaborn House, a message was waiting.

RETURN LONDON ASAP STOP
SIGNED J. STOP

MAJOR THE LADY JANE SEABORN WAS WAITING IN ONE OF
the Bradford Hotel limousines when the Supermarine Walrus carrying
Colonel John Randal landed at Great West Aerodrome, near the small
village of Heathrow outside of London. Royal Engineers were rapidly
expanding the airfield. The Royal Air Force had plans to turn it into a
major base of flight operations.

"Thanks for the lift," Col. Randal said to the Canadian bush pilot,
as he deplaned the small amphibian.

"Nice to see you again, Colonel. I laugh every time I think about
you shooting that giant crocodile 'Tyrannosaurus Croc' with your
pistol."

"Lucky shot," Col. Randal said.

Lady Jane was standing outside the limousine. "Your bags are
packed, John. We are on the way to the railway station. Plans have
changed."

"What's up, Jane?"

"The 1st U.S. Ranger Battalion—made up of volunteers from the 34th
Red Bull Infantry Division and the 1st Armored Division—have arrived
at the Commando Depot for training. The graduation ceremony for our
troops has been moved up because Colonel Vaughn needs the space,"
Lady Jane said.

"We are to proceed to Achnacarry to pick up the C/575 Rangers.

"Let's enjoy our train trip."

COLONEL JOHN RANDAL AND MAJOR THE LADY JANE
Seaborn were sitting in lawn chairs, out in front of Achnacarry Castle,
aka Castle Commando. Seated with them were Lord Cameron of
Lochiel, the owner of the estate who had loaned it to the army for the
duration; Lt. Col. Charles Vaughn, the commanding officer of the
Commando Training Depot; and Major William O. Darby, commanding
the U.S. 1st Ranger Battalion.

Lord Lochiel was on site inspecting the property and observing
training, as he did from time to time. He had noticed that a stag headed

beech tree planted in 1745 had developed root rot. It stood in a glen, in full view of the stately baronial style castle 300 yards away.

"Could Lt. Col. Vaughn's sappers remove the eyesore?"

"Certainly, we have a highly-decorated demolitions officer recently arrived. Right Man, Right Job," Lt. Col. Vaughn said, quoting from Raiding Forces' Rules for Raiding.

Down in the dale, calculations were made on how much "gelly" to use to topple the ancient timber. Captain "Pyro" Percy Stirling decided to err on the generous side—why take a chance? It was a big tree.

No one thought to open the castle's windows.

Col. Randal leaned over and whispered to Lady Jane, "I have a bad feeling about this."

KAAAAABOOOOM!

The tree disintegrated into a puff of 200-year-old dust. However, the deafening blast was accompanied by the tinkle of breaking glass. Every window in the castle was shattered—blown out by the shock wave.

Lord Lochiel was not pleased.

21
REGARDLESS

THE BRADFORD HOTEL LIMOUSINE WAS WAITING WHEN the train pulled in. Colonel John Randal and Major the Lady Jane Seaborn stepped off. The C/575 Rangers and Captain "Pyro" Percy Stirling, who had been banned from the Commando Special Warfare Training Center for life, stayed on board. Their cars would be shuttled to a new set of rails that would carry them to the village outside of Seaborn House.

A message had arrived for Col. Randal to report to Combined Operations Headquarters (COHQ).

Lady Jane instructed the Bradford Hotel's driver to take them to Richmond Terrace. On the ride, she briefed Col. Randal about Vice Admiral Louis "Dickie" Mountbatten, DSO, RN, the relatively new Chief of Combined Operations. He had held the job for approximately six months.

"Dickie Mountbatten is the great-grandson of Queen Victoria and the second cousin once removed to Princess Elizabeth. Went into the navy when he was thirteen years old. Now he is in his early forties.

"His destroyer, the *Kelly,* was sunk by a Stuka dive bomber while he was on the bridge reading a C. S. Forester novel. Dickie was set to take command of the aircraft carrier *Illustrious* when the Prime Minister unexpectedly appointed him Chief of Combined Operations, causing a gnashing of teeth in certain quarters.

"Dickie has a palace playboy image, matinee idol looks, royal bloodline, and a reputation as quite the charmer. Churchill took the extraordinary step of making him an Air Marshal in the RAF and a Lieutenant General in the Army. He and the King are the only two men in the U.K. to hold rank in all three services.

"After a successful Commando raid on Saint Nazaire, COHQ is basking in glory. Dickie sent the obsolete destroyer *Campbletown* packed with explosives to ram the dry dock at Normandy—the largest in western France and the only one capable of housing the German battleship *Tirpitz*.

"Some are calling it 'The Greatest Raid of All.' Unfortunately, 2 Commando supplied the ground troops and was virtually wiped out—its commander captured."

"Mountbatten," Col. Randal said, "sounds like a hard charger."

"The admiral has almost as many detractors as he does supporters," Lady Jane said. "Some say he was only appointed because of his Royal Family connections. Others claim it was because the Prime Minister sacked his father as First Sea Lord in the last war for having a Germanic-sounding name and is trying to make up for it now. More than a few are simply jealous."

"What do you think, Jane?"

"All three are true," Lady Jane said. "Some of the things said about Dickie behind his back are quite wicked and do not bear repeating. His house-partying, socialite wife, Edwina, vowed to give up chocolate until after the war. Scandalously promiscuous—loves men in uniform.

"You stay away from Edwina."

"Gave up chocolate," Col. Randal said, "for men in uniform?"

"No, John."

Lady Jane was a good storyteller. Nearly all of her stories had twists and turns he never saw coming. And they were invariably true, which is what made them so interesting.

Col. Randal liked to tease her from time to time when she told them.

"Ian Fleming claims Dickie was selected because of his background in signals intelligence. He is a school-trained Signals Officer," Lady Jane said.

"'C' of MI-6 put his name forward for the post."

Col. Randal asked, "Why would signals intelligence be a qualification to command Combined Operations—the Commandos?"

"GOLDEN FLEECE/RED INDIAN," Lady Jane whispered so softly the driver could not hear. "Ian believes the entire war effort centers around pinches."

Col. Randal said, "He is fixated on 'em."

"Obsessed," Lady Jane said.

Col. Randal asked, "You know Admiral Mountbatten?"

"Mallory served as his Number 2 on HMS *Daring* before the war."

"What did he have to say?"

"The two did *not* get along."

"Why?"

"Possibly Edwina."

JAMES "BALDIE" TAYLOR WAS WAITING WHEN THE Bradford Hotel's limousine arrived at COHQ. He looked a little worse for wear, but was dressed in a beautifully tailored suit, which was a recent affectation. Major the Lady Jane Seaborn had introduced him to a tailor in Cairo who had a relationship with Pembrooks Military Tailors in London.

When Jim caught wind of what was being proposed for Colonel John Randal, he had hopped the first flight out to the U.K. The first available aircraft was an unpressurized Lancaster bomber. It had been a miserable trip.

The three were immediately whisked in to Vice Admiral Louis "Dickie" Mountbatten's spacious office. Lady Jane made the introductions.

The admiral was everything he was advertised to be. He looked like a sailor out of central casting. Big, handsome, magnificently tailored uniform with gold braid up both sleeves almost to his elbows, composed, exuding self-confidence, and oozing charm.

VAdm. Mountbatten said, "I followed your exploits even before assuming command of Combined Operations. Read the book *Jump on Bela.* When Admiral Ransom is in London, he keeps me briefed on

Raiding Forces' operations in Middle East Command. Complimentary of you, which is a fine rare thing coming from the Razor.

"Anyone capable of winning the hand of Lady Jane, what does one say?"

Col. Randal said, "You know the admiral, sir?"

"Served under him in destroyers," VAdm. Mountbatten said. "In my opinion, the finest fighting sailor of our time."

"Why are we here?" Jim asked, testy from his long, uncomfortable travel experience.

Col. Randal clicked on. Jim was clearly not a member of the Dickie Mountbatten fan club. That was worth noting.

"Follow me," VAdm. Mountbatten said, unruffled. He led the three into a small chart room next to his office. There was a large map on one wall. Immediately noticeable—there were no place names visible.

VAdm. Mountbatten said, "OPERATION RUTTER, a large raid originally planned by General Bernard Montgomery, a horrid little ferret-faced popinjay with a high opinion of himself. The largest combined operation of the war to date, consisting of the Second Canadian Division under Major General Roberts reinforced by fifty-eight Churchill tanks, two parachute battalions, supported by Air Vice Marshal Leigh-Mallory's No. 11 Group Fighter Command and the Royal Navy.

The idea was to make a full-on frontal assault of an enemy port. The purpose of the exercise is to discover how difficult it will be to land ashore and capture a port city. We shall need to know once the big day comes when we invade the continent of Europe for real.

"RUTTER was intended to be a live-fire training exercise. By definition, a raid with a planned withdrawal—no intention to stay.

"The lessons to be learned from such an operation were thought to be invaluable and could save thousands of lives when we eventually invade France in a big way.

"RUTTER was canceled. Montgomery departed for Egypt. Life went on.

"Suddenly out of the blue, with no advance warning, the raid was back on—this time styled OPERATION JUBILEE. As originally planned, it was a true air, sea, and land combined operation to include, as I mentioned, two battalions of parachutists.

"The Airborne task was to eliminate the German coastal artillery batteries positioned on both flanks of the main objective. The guns threaten the two hundred fifty Royal Navy ships that will be transporting and providing fire support for the Canadian 2nd Division.

"Regrettably, this time around, Airborne Forces opted out. Claim more time was required to stage for the jump. Time is the one element we do not have.

"The plan was modified.

"Now, 3 Commando under Durnford-Slater will land on the left flank, and 4 Commando under Lord Lovat will land on the right to take out those artillery positions. The Commando battalions will be augmented by small elements of U.S. Rangers from the 1st Ranger Battalion—a symbolic gesture from our new allies. The first American ground troops of the war to attack the continent of Europe.

"The batteries are typical commando targets—the kind they have trained for. We substituted our two best commando units under our two most talented and experienced amphibious raiding commanders for the parachutists.

"All was well.

"Until, that is, RAF photo-reconnaissance took this series of photographs of the area where 4 Commando under Lord Lovat is slated to go in."

VAdm. Mountbatten handed Col. Randal a stack of 8x10 glossy photos. The pictures clearly showed a three-gun battery of large caliber coastal guns. The cannon could be seen protruding from their heavy concrete bunkers. The big guns were impressive.

The barrels looked the size of telephone poles.

"Two-hundred-forty millimeter, with the range to cover the entire invasion area. Reach more than halfway across the channel," VAdm. Mountbatten said. "The guns are located too far inland for 4 Commando to land, take its primary objective, then reach in time before the main force goes in."

Col. Randal said, "That is a problem."

Lady Jane was no longer smiling.

Jim looked stone-faced.

"JUBILEE is scheduled to land ashore in forty-eight hours," VAdm. Mountbatten said. "What can you do for me, Colonel?"

"Contingent on you being able to provide C-47 Dakotas, sir," Col. Randal said, "I can drop with ninety-five U.S. Paratroopers under cover of darkness to take out your 240mm gun battery in advance of 4 Commando's attack."

"Bloody marvelous," VAdm. Mountbatten said. "Extraordinary."

Col. Randal said, "You have to fly twenty of my Raiders from Achnacarry to my headquarters at Seaborn House, to arrive no later than this afternoon, sir."

"The 12th Troop Carrier Squadron, 60th Transport Group of the United States Army Air Corps has recently arrived at Chelveston," VAdm. Mountbatten said. "They have a liaison officer here at COHQ. I am confident the squadron would be delighted to have the opportunity to participate in a combat mission. We should be able to arrange for your Raiders to arrive at your headquarters this afternoon."

"In that case, sir," Col. Randal said, "Raiding Forces will silence those Long Toms."

AT THIS POINT, SEVERAL THINGS BEGAN TAKING PLACE more or less simultaneously. Colonel John Randal, Major the Lady Jane Seaborn, and James "Baldie" Taylor departed COHQ in Lady Jane's white Rolls Royce en route to Seaborn House. Lady Jane dispatched the Bradford Hotel's limousine to the NID offices to pick up Lieutenant Mandy Paige, take her back to the hotel to collect their luggage, then drive her to Seaborn House.

"I called Lionel," Lady Jane said. "He is sending a Walrus to retrieve Beverly from No. 1 Parachute School. She was making her final jump this morning."

Neither one would have any active role in the raid, but Lady Jane wanted her girls around her. She was not happy. This was supposed to have been a pleasure trip.

JUBILEE sounded dangerous.

In Scotland, Captain Billy Jack Jaxx was halfway up Ben Nevis, eighteen miles from the Commando Castle, on a forced march that was actually more of a run. Two Bedford trucks rolled up alongside the fast-marching column.

Captain Butch "Headhunter" Hoolihan leaned out the window and shouted, "Quick time, *MARCH,* Jack!"

"What's going on, Butch?"

"Have your boys hop on the trucks," Capt. Hoolihan said. "We are headed back to the castle to pick up your gear. Raiding Forces has been alerted for a mission. As soon as you pack up, we will be trucked fifty-five miles to RAF Longman. SOG, augmented by a party of five 1st Battalion Rangers provided by Major Darby, will board C-47 aircraft from the 12th Troop Carrier Squadron to be flown to Seaborn House.

"I shall be coming with you."

"Any idea about the mission?"

"Negative."

At the Commando Castle, Major William O. Darby was talking to Lieutenant Marvin Johnson and four handpicked Rangers in front of the operations Quonset hut when the two Bedford trucks carrying SOG arrived.

"You men have been selected to represent the 1st Ranger Battalion on a combined operations commando raid, making you among the first U.S. troops to see ground combat in the European theatre of operations.

"You men will be attached to Raiding Forces, commanded by the legendary Colonel John Randal we have all heard so much about. There are other 1st Battalion Rangers going on the raid, assigned to 4 Commando and 3 Commando.

"Keep in mind at all times, you represent the United States of America, the 1st Ranger Battalion, and *me.* Do your duty."

At 4 Commando Headquarters, Lieutenant Colonel Lord Simon "Shimi" Lovat, DSO, was enjoying a cup of tea with his staff when the orders arrived for him to fly to Seaborn House. The 15th Lord Lovat and the 25th Chief of the Clan Fraser of Lovat was a law unto himself. He did not give a fig about military rank, protocol, or etiquette. No matter the reason, the last thing Lord Lovat wanted to do was be called away from 4 Commando only hours before OPERATION JUBILEE.

He threw the mother of all temper tantrums, cursing in three languages. Then Lt. Col. Lord Lovat ordered up his car. His driver drove him to catch his flight.

Lieutenant Colonel Ralph Livesay, commander of 12th Troop Carrier Squadron, 60th Transport Group, was in the officers' mess when one of his staff rushed up breathlessly and informed him the squadron had been alerted for a night parachute drop.

"Training exercise?"

"No, sir!"

Lt. Col. Livesay jumped up, knocking over his chair. The pilot took off at a dead run to his squadron CP. Upon arrival, he was handed the orders.

Twelfth Squadron was to dispatch two C-47s to RAF Longman to pick up a team of U.S. Army Rangers from the 575th Ranger Force and the 1st Ranger Battalion. They were to be flown to a clandestine airfield in the Restricted Zone south of England described as a "black site." Lt. Col. Livesay had never heard of it.

He and his operations officer were ordered to immediately proceed with all due haste to Seaborn House, also in the Restricted Zone—another place he had never heard of. Upon arrival, Lt. Col. Livesay was to coordinate with a Colonel John Randal, an officer he had never heard of, to conduct a combat parachute drop to take place within the next forty-eight hours, on an undisclosed DZ somewhere in France.

There had to be a record-breaking number of unknowns in the short set of orders which took up less than half a page. No problem. Lt. Col. Livesay was a "can do" squadron leader.

He ordered his staff, "Make it happen."

In his battalion CP, Lieutenant Colonel Edison Raff, the commanding officer of the 2/503rd Parachute Infantry Regiment, was sitting at his desk reading a set of orders marked SECRET. His battalion had recently arrived in Scotland attached to the British 1st Airborne Division for training. The cocky, bantam-sized paratrooper, known to his troops as "Little Caesar," was itching to get in the war.

Lt. Col. Raff was attempting to make sense of the orders.

```
DELIVER 100 RESERVE PARACHUTES
TO RAF LONGMAN STOP EXPEDITE,
EXPEDITE, EXPEDITE STOP
```

SEABORN HOUSE WAS BUZZING WITH ACTIVITY. SHORTLY after Colonel John Randal, Major the Lady Jane Seaborn, and James "Baldie" Taylor arrived, COHQ liaison officer Lieutenant Delbert McNamara, RN, drove up. The naval officer was shown into the operations room. He immediately began to post a mosaic of aerial photos of Raiding Forces' objective area on one wall.

Beverly Blackwell arrived, having been flown to Seaborn House in one of Raiding Forces' Walruses. The UT beauty queen had completed No.1 Parachute School's "short course." She was now an official, school-trained paratrooper.

"Beverly asked for you to pin on her jump wings, John," Lady Jane said. "There was no time for a ceremony at the school."

"Really?" Col. Randal said. "I'd have thought you'd be the one to do that."

"As would I, actually," Lady Jane said. "I believe Beverly likes you. She is wary of most men."

Col. Randal said, "That's probably smart—the cautious part."

"We are from two entirely different worlds," Lady Jane said. "Still, the two of us have quite a lot in common. Billy Jack says Beverly is 'Texas royalty.' I love her."

"I'll do the wings," Col. Randal said. "You figure out how to make it happen without me getting slapped."

Lady Jane laughed. "Maybe you could wear gloves."

Lieutenant Colonel Ralph Livesay and his operations officer, Major Jeff Landers, touched down on the Raiding Forces' airstrip in a USAAF L-4 Grasshopper. The two officers were ushered into the map room, where Lt. McNamara filled them in on the mission. Col. Randal stood listening, with one of Waldo's custom-rolled cigars in his teeth, studying the map with no names. He was not impressed with the lieutenant's briefing.

Col. Randal asked, "Have you ever dropped paratroops before?"

"Yes, sir," Lt. Col. Livesay said. "My squadron supported the Jump School at Ft. Benning for six months before shipping out to England. We have a lot of experience."

"How good are your navigators?"

"Why do you ask, sir?"

"You have to drop us on a target the size of a pinhead, with absolute precision, on a hostile shore, during the hours of darkness," Col. Randal said. "Zero margin of error—and you may have to do it under fire."

"We knew where the drop zones were at Benning," Lt. Col. Livesay said. "My boys flew the routes several times a day, like I said, for six months—find 'em in our sleep."

"That's what I thought," Col. Randal said. "I'm going to recommend one of my special operations pilots ride in the cockpit of your lead aircraft. My people have a lot of experience performing pinpoint navigation under cover of darkness."

"You won't get an argument from me, sir," Lt. Col. Livesay said. "I'll be the command pilot on the lead ship—take all the help I can get."

"Then I'll be jumping your airplane," Col. Randal said. "You drop my Rangers on time, on target, Ralph, and I'll see you get the Distinguished Flying Cross.

"You ever drop at three-hundred-fifty feet?"

"Negative."

"Well, that's our jump altitude."

Lt. Col. Livesay turned pale. A lot could go wrong at such a low level. Five-hundred feet was the lowest the squadron had ever dropped.

Lieutenant Mandy Paige arrived. She was in the Operations Room with Lady Jane, Jim, and Beverly, studying the diagram map of the objective and the mosaic of aerial photos of the German coastal battery that Lt. McNamara had pinned to the wall.

Col. Randal, Lt. Col. Livesay, and Maj. Landers walked over.

Lt. Mandy said, "Wrong aerial photos, John."

"How would you possibly know?" Lt. McNamara said. "The location of the target is classified. No one will be provided that detail until unit commanders open sealed orders after the fleet sails—or in Raiding Forces' case, after the planes are airborne.

"You have no idea what you are talking about."

"I recognize the place," Mandy said. "The terrain on the schematic map where you mark the gun battery is open pasture land.

"Your photos show hills."

"Exactly," Lady Jane said. "Before the war, Brandy, Penelope, and I used to sail over to the casino located in the port, now designated as JUBILEE, for a night of gambling.

Beverly said, "Awkward."

"Get on the horn to COHQ," Col. Randal said. "Straighten this out, McNamara, or Raiding Forces will stand down *now*."

"Sir!"

Lt. McNamara scurried off to call his office.

"Don't let the Hollywood looks of the female component of Raiding Forces fool you," Col. Randal said to Lt. Col. Livesay. "These women are dangerous—watch yourself at all times, Colonel."

"SNAFU," Lt. Col. Livesay said. "Doesn't do much to improve the old pucker factor."

"Too much publicity after the Saint Nazaire raid," Jim said. "Never pays to believe one's own press. Not when sending other people on high-risk missions. The staff at COHQ struck me as under-prepared, over-confident—almost giddy."

"Agreed," Lady Jane said. "I had the same impression, Jim."

Lt. Col. Livesay said, "Poor prior planning produces poor results—got their stack of aerial photos mixed up."

Col. Randal said, "We only have to worry about our part of the operation—drop in, take out the battery, withdraw by sea. Hit and run.

"We're good at that."

One of Lady Jane's Royal Marines appeared. "Captain McKoy phoned from the railroad station. He requests transportation."

Col. Randal said, "Captain McKoy?"

"He and King found out I was flying to the U.K. because Raiding Forces Europe had been alerted for a mission," Jim said. "No way to keep those two from coming, provided they could hitch rides from the RAF."

"Good for them," Col. Randal said. "You too, General—glad you're here."

Lt. Col. Livesay cocked an eyebrow when he heard Col. Randal address the bald man as General. No one had bothered to introduce him. A general in civilian clothes who did not seem to be taking charge? Not something he encountered every day.

The Royal Marine returned, "A Lysander with Lord Lovat of 4 Commando is inbound for landing, Colonel."

Lieutenant Colonel the Lord Simon "Shimi" Lovat arrived, wearing a green Commando beret with a Lovat Scout regimental badge pinned to it, even though he had been serving in the Scots Guards before joining 4 Commando. He could wear whatever badge he chose—his grandfather formed the Scouts during the Boer War.

Lady Jane said, "Hello, Shimi."

"Jane," Lt. Col. Lord Lovat said, "fancy meeting you here."

"This *is* Seaborn House," Jane said.

"True," Lt. Col. Lord Lovat said. "I thought the place had been taken over by some hush-hush outfit for the duration."

"True," Lady Jane laughed. "I was part of the package. Let me introduce you to Colonel Randal."

Lt. Col. Lord Lovat possessed a cool brain, cunning, a love of natural beauty, and movie-star good looks. His family's ancestral estate stretched from coast to coast and covered over 250,000 acres. Before the war, he and Lady Jane traveled in the same social circles. He realized there was more to the introduction than met the eye.

"Time is short," Col. Randal said. "You need to get back to your command, Colonel. I'll give you a quick rundown on a new JUBILEE target you most likely do not know about.

"Then you and I need to work out coordination between Raiding Forces and 4 Commando. Our units will both be exfiltrating from the same beach.

"In that case," Lt. Col. Lord Lovat ordered, "everyone out."

Col. Randal waited until the room cleared. Lt. Col. Lord Lovat took operational security seriously—point in his favor.

"Lady Jane and I were in England to discuss another project when Admiral Mountbatten called me away to COHQ," Col. Randal said.

"Photoreconnaissance recently discovered a previously unknown battery of three 240mm guns a mile inland from your objective. Mountbatten said 4 Commando can't reach them in time to prevent the guns from firing on the invasion fleet, nor do you have enough troops to take on an additional target.

"At zero-three-thirty hours the day after tomorrow, ninety-five men of the 575th Rangers from Raiding Forces under my command will drop by parachute a half-mile inland from the three-gun coastal battery located here," Col. Randal tapped the map.

"We will attack the battery from the rear, then make a fighting withdrawal through 4 Commando's position to Orange beach."

Lt. Col. Lord Lovat stepped up to the map. "Why are so many of the aerial photos missing?" he asked, staring at what looked like an unfinished puzzle pinned to the wall.

"COHQ sent the wrong photographs," Col. Randal said. "The correct shots are on the way, but you'll be long gone before they arrive.

"Chair-borne commandos," Lt. Col. Lord Lovat said. "Pays to keep a canny eye on those who plan daring missions for others to carry out."

"Yes, it does."

"My plan, Colonel, is to split my assault force of four-hundred-thirty-five officers and men into two elements," Lt. Col. Lord Lovat said. "One third of my troops will land here on Orange Beach Able, six miles west of the port city currently being described as JUBILEE, under Mills-Roberts, my number two. They will set up a base of fire.

"I will land on the other side of this split on Orange Beach Baker with the main body of my Commandos, attack up these two ravines to assault German Battery Hess containing six 150mm guns located here," Lt. Col. Lord Lovat tapped the diagram map.

"Both parties will then withdraw to their respective beaches and sail away home while the Canadians go in for the kill at the port."

"Three motor launches will accompany your assault element to Orange Beach Baker to extract my paratroopers," Col. Randal said. "One of my officers—Captain Hoolihan—and a small team, will accompany you to coordinate the link-up between our people on your objective.

"Hopefully, you'll have knocked the battery out by the time we arrive. If not, my men will lend a hand."

"Hoolihan," Lord Lovat said, "is he any good?"

"Oh, yeah," Col. Randal said. "Royal Marine, DSO, MC with bar, MM. They call Butch the 'Headhunter.'"

"With a moniker such as that," Lord Lovat said, "he should fit right in with my band of cutthroats."

"If Captain Hoolihan does not work for you," Col. Randal said, "we have another officer, Captain Percy Stirling, you may know."

"My cousin, actually," Lt. Col. Lord Lovat said. "Heard about the lighthouse Percy blew up. So you are the man who has been purloining the Lovat Scouts."

"I'll take all I can get," Col. Randal said.

"So would I, actually," Lt. Col. Lord Lovat laughed. "Banned me from recruiting any more of the lads."

"Well," Col. Randal said, "I have a way around that if you find one or two you really need.

"Questions?"

"Send me the Headhunter fellow," Lt. Col. Lord Lovat said. "I may take you up on the offer of the Scouts one day."

"You do that."

"Good hunting, old boy," Lt. Col. Lord Lovat said, sticking out his hand. "See you on Battery Hess day after tomorrow before first light. Never fear—the position shall be secure by the time you and your Rangers arrive."

Col. Randal shook his hand. Both men knew Raiding Forces and 4 Commando would be fighting a vicious private war when the balloon went up on JUBILEE. The units would be dependent on one another. It was not a bad thing their two commanding officers liked each other from the start.

Captain Billy Jack Jaxx and Captain Butch "Headhunter" Hoolihan arrived, with a small convoy of "deuce and a half" trucks transporting C/575th Rangers and the five-man team from 1st Ranger Battalion.

Col. Randal took Captain "Geronimo" Joe McKoy and Capt. Hoolihan into the map room for a private briefing.

"Day after tomorrow you two will land on Orange Beach Baker from three motor launches with Lt. Col. Lord Lovat's 4 Commando. Captain McKoy, you will secure the beach. Get with Lionel Honeycutt-Parker. He'll have to scrape up Raiders or Lifeboat Servicemen for your party."

"We brought five 1st Battalion Rangers," Capt. Hoolihan said. "Major Darby sent them to be attached to Raiding Forces."

"They're not jump qualified," Col. Randal said. "Use 'em for your team, Butch. Your assignment is to travel with Colonel Lovat to coordinate the linkup between Raiding Forces and 4 Commando.

"We'll be jumping into a pasture right about here," Col. Randal pointed to the proposed drop zone. "Attack the three-gun battery located here, then withdraw through Lord Lovat's position to Orange Beach Baker.

"Questions?"

"Why're we knockin' out those Nazi cannons, John?" Capt. McKoy asked, studying the map. "Somethin' else goin' on you failed to mention?"

"The 2nd Canadian Division is making an amphibious assault, landing at the unnamed port city six miles east of our objective."

Capt. McKoy said, "Just gonna sail in, get out on the beach like a' bunch a' tourists?"

"That's the plan."

"What does the educated idiot who dreamed this one up think the Germans will have to say about it?"

"You just worry about having those three motor launches ready to bring us home when we show up on Orange Beach Baker," Col. Randal said. "I'll be wanting to get the hell out of Dodge—fast."

"The boats'll be there, John," Capt. McKoy said. "I'll have a' man stationed on board each one to put a' pistol in the ear of any skipper who gets antsy while we're hangin' around waitin' for you."

"In that case, Captain, I won't give the motor launches another thought."

Col. Randal saved Capt. Jaxx for last. He showed him the map. He explained the operation. He pointed out the fact the 12th Troop Carrier Squadron had never flown a combat mission.

Capt. Jaxx said, "Drop in a team of five SOG pathfinders under my command thirty minutes prior to the jump, sir. We'll mark the DZ. Can't risk green pilots overflying it in all the excitement."

Col. Randal produced a cigarette and lit it with his old battered U.S. 26th Cavalry Regiment Zippo, "May be the most dangerous assignment I've ever asked an officer to carry out, Jack."

"If it were easy, sir, anybody could do it."

Jack Cool.

When he had a chance, Col. Randal pulled Jim aside, "What do you have against Mountbatten?"

"Simply this," Jim said. "Behind his back some of his staff—men whose judgment I value—privately call him 'Regardless.'"

"What's that supposed to mean?"

"Regardless of effort, regardless of risk, regardless of cost."

AT TWENTY HUNDRED HOURS, COLONEL JOHN RANDAL issued a Warning Order to Raiding Forces' officers and NCOs, the COHQ liaison officer and the liaison officers recently arrived from the 15th Motor Gunboat Flotilla, 12th Troop Carrier Squadron, and 4 Commando. He said, "Situation: The Germans are over there. We're over here . . ."

Later that night, as he and Major the Lady Jane Seaborn were having dinner alone by candlelight in the private dining room, Col. Randal said, "OK, not that it matters, Jane—where are we raiding?"

"Dieppe."

—————

TO BE CONTINUED IN

~ *STRATEGIC SERVICES* ~

BOOK XII IN THE RAIDING FORCES SERIES

THE RAIDING FORCES SERIES CONTINUES . . . ALL THE WAY TO VE DAY.

—————

To be on our notification list for the next book, contact
phil@philward.com

ABBREVIATIONS
ORDERS & AWARDS

Bt	Baronet
CB	Companion of the Bath
CMG	Companion of the Order of St. Michael & St. George
DCM	Distinguished Conduct Medal
DFC	Distinguished Flying Cross (Royal Air Force)
DSC	Distinguished Service Cross (Royal Navy)
DSO	Distinguished Service Order
GC	George Cross
GCB	Grand Cross in the Order of the Bath
GM	George Medal
KBE	Knight Commander of the British Empire
KCVO	Knight Commander of the Royal Victorian Order
LG	Lady Companion of the Order of the Garter
MC	Military Cross
MM	Military Medal
MVO	Member of the Royal Victorian Order
OBE	Order of the Empire
VC	Victoria Cross

RAIDING ROMMEL
ACRONYMS

AO—Area of Operation
APL—Assistant Patrol Leader
ASDIC—Anti-Submarine Detection Investigation
        Committee (device)
AVG—American Volunteer Group
BAR—Browning Automatic Rifle
BDU—Battle Dress Uniform
BOAC—British Overseas Airways Corporation
CIE—Vichy Colonial Secret Police
CO—Commanding Officer
COHQ—Combined Operations Headquarters
COW—Coventry Ordnance Works
CP—Command Post
DE—Destroyer Escorts
DZ—Drop Zone
FUBAR—Fouled up Beyond All Recognition
GERD 97—97th Foreign Legion Divisional
        Reconnaissance Group
GHQME—General Headquarters Middle East
GP—General Purpose
HE—High Explosive
I&R—Intelligence & Reconnaissance (platoon)
IOC—Officer in Charge
ISSB—Inner Services Security Board
LCT—Landing Craft Tank
LMG—Light Machine Gun
LUP—Laying Up Position
MEHQ—Middle East Command Headquarters
NCO—Noncommissioned Officer
NID—Naval Intelligence Division
OG—Operational Group
ORP—Objective Rally Point
OSS—Office of Strategic Services, previously Office of
        Coordinator of Information
PIR—Parachute Infantry Regiment
PLF—Parachute Landing Fall

ACRONYMS

PWE—Political Warfare Executive
RAF—Royal Air Force
RFHQ—Raiding Forces headquarters
SAS—Special Air Service
SI—Secret Intelligence
SIM—*Servizio Informazioni Militare*, Military Intelligence
       Service (Italian)
SIME—Security Intelligence Middle East
SIS—Secret Intelligence Service
SNAFU—Situation Normal All Fouled Up
SO—Special Operations
SOE—Special Operations Executive
SOG—Small Operations Group
SOP—Standard Operating Procedure
TOC—Tactical Operations Center
TO&E—Table of Organization and Equipment
WRENS—Women's Royal Navy Service

RAIDING ROMMEL
LIST OF CHARACTERS

Acting Provisional Sub-Lt.
    Skipper Warthog Finley,
    OBE, DSO, RNPS
Beverly Blackwell
Brandy Seaborn, GC
Brig. Raymond J. "R.J.."
    Maunsell
Capt. "Geronimo" Joe McKoy,
    OBE
Capt. "Pyro" Percy Stirling, DSO,
    MC, 17/21 Lancers
Capt. Airey McKnight
Capt. Billy Jack Jaxx, MC, SSM
Capt. Butch "Headhunter"
    Hoolihan, DSO, MC, MM,
    RM
Capt. Cord Granger
Capt. Duke Slater
Capt. Earl Longstreet
Capt. Hawthorne Merryweather
Capt. Jack Dance
Capt. Jack Masters
Capt. Pamala Plum-Martin, DSO,
    OBE, DFC, RM
Capt. Penelope "Legs" Honeycutt-
    Parker, OBE, GM RM
Capt. Roy Kidd, MC
Capt. Roy "Mad Dog" Reupart,
    MC
Cdr. Ian Fleming, RNVR
Col. Bonner Fellers
Col. Dudley Clarke
Col. John Randal, DSO, OBE,
    DSC, MC
Col. William "Wild Bill"
    Donovan
CWO Hank W. Rawlston
Flanigan
FM Claude Auchinleck
Frank Polanski
Guido "GG" Grazinni, MC
Guns
Joker
King
Lana Turner

Lovat Scout Lionel Fenwick
Lovat Scout Munro Ferguson
Lt. "Dynamite" Dick Coogan
Lt. Mandy Paige, OBE, RM
Lt. Charles Duffield

Lt. Clint Hays
Lt. Dan Morgan
Lt. David Granbury
Lt. Delbert McNamara, RN
Lt. Eddy Ryder
Lt. Jake Hannity
Lt. Marvin Johnson
Lt. Preston Butterfield III
Lt. Stephanie Fawcett-Tatum, RM
Lt. Tom Green
Lt. Col. Charles Vaughn
Lt. Col. Edison "Little Caesar"
    Raff
Lt. Col. H. H. "Hard as Nails"
    Hammer
Lt. Col. Lionel Honeycutt-Parker
Lt. Col. Lord Simon "Shimi"
    Lovat, DSO
Lt. Col. Ralph Livesay
Lt. Col. Sir Terry "Zorro" Stone,
    KBE, DSO, MC
Maj. A. W. "Sammy" Sansom
Maj. Baltimore "Mongo"
    Farquhar, MC
Maj. Clive Adair
Maj. Everard Beauchamp
Maj. Jane Seaborn, LG, OBE, RM
Maj. Jeb Pelham-Davies, DSO,
    MC
Maj. Jeff Landers
Maj. Taylor Corrigan, DSO, MC
Maj. Travis McCloud
Maj. William O. Darby
Maj. Gen. James "Baldie" Taylor,
    OBE
Maj. Gen. Philippe Francois
    Marie Leclerc de
    Hauteclocque
Mr. Heart
Mr. Zargo

LIST OF CHARACTERS

MSgt. Mack Beckwith
Percy Mather
Rikke "Rocky" Runborg
Rita Hayworth
S/Lt. Bentley St. Ledger
S/Lt. Pippa Duncan-Sackville
S/Lt. Tabitha Walpole
Sgt. Ned Pompedous
Sgt. Rex Blackburn
Sgt. Maj. Mike "March or Die"
    Mikkalis, DSM, MM
S/LdR.J.ohnny Page
VAdm. Louis "Dickie"
    Mountbatten, DSO, RN
VAdm. Sir Randolph "Razor"
    Ransom, VC, KCB, DSO,
    OBE, DSC
Veronica Paige, OBE
Waldo Treywick, OBE
W/Cdr. Ronald "Flash Bang"
    Gordon

ABOUT THE AUTHOR

Phil Ward is a decorated combat veteran commissioned at age nineteen. A former instructor at the Army Ranger School, he has had a lifelong interest in small-unit tactics and special operations. He lives in Texas, on a mountain overlooking Lake Austin.

~ ~

OTHER BOOKS IN THE RAIDING FORCES SERIES:

Those Who Dare

Dead Eagles

Blood Wings

Roman Candle

Guerrilla Command

Necessary Force

Desert Patrol

Private Army

Africa 1941

The Sharp End